THIRD EDITION

WORKBOOK
of CURRENT
ENGLISH

THIRD EDITION

WORKBOOK *of* CURRENT ENGLISH

William E. Mahaney
Salem State College

Scott, Foresman and Company
Glenview, Illinois   London, England

An *Answer Key with Teaching Suggestions to accompany Workbook of Current English,* Third Edition, is available. It may be obtained through a Scott, Foresman representative or by writing to English Editor, College Division, Scott, Foresman and Company, 1900 East Lake Avenue, Glenview, Illinois 60025.

ISBN: 0–673–15959–0

PREFACE

The *Workbook of Current English* is a comprehensive text that may be adapted to the individual interests and needs of both students and instructors. Although it is a companion volume to the *Handbook of Current English,* seventh edition, it is also an independent text that may be used with any handbook or by itself in developmental or regular composition sections, in writing laboratories, or in independent student work. The *Workbook* is comprehensive both because of its breadth of coverage of writing problems and because of the number and variety of its exercises. This breadth allows instructors to select materials according to their own philosophies of writing and the level and needs of their students.

The arrangement of material in the *Workbook* increases its adaptability. The text is divided into four units: Grammar and Usage, Punctuation and Other Conventions, Composition, and Words. Within each unit are several chapters, each of which contains a number of sections. (Chapter 4, Common Sentence Errors, for example, contains sections on Sentence Fragments, Comma Splices, Run-on Sentences, and Mixed Constructions.) At the beginning of each chapter appears explanatory material for all of its sections. The chapters, sections, and exercises are numbered to correspond to Chapters 1 through 30 of the *Handbook of Current English.* (Chapters 24, 31, 32, and 33 of the *Handbook* do not lend themselves to further exercise practice and so are not included in the *Workbook.*)

The materials in the *Workbook* may be employed in the order in which they appear, or they may be used in whatever order an instructor chooses. Parts of speech, for instance, could be approached before the grammar of sentences, or paragraphs could be studied before sentences.

The *Workbook* is also organized so that the material generally increases in difficulty and sophistication. The exercises for most sections move students from identifying structures and problems, to correcting errors, to writing their own sentences and paragraphs. All chapters have a Review Exercise which helps students review the sections and work with several related writing problems at the same time. These Review Exercises may also be used as quizzes. Each unit concludes with a Further Practice Exercise which may be used either as a test or as an exercise to help students review the unit and combine various writing skills covered in the unit.

To assist students, the *Workbook* also contains a number of problem solvers (labeled HINT) which help students avoid situations that often lead to errors. A Correction Chart appears inside the front cover, referring students to specific sections in the *Workbook* where the problems are discussed. A Checklist for Revising and Correcting a Paper appears inside the back cover. (A more detailed checklist in Chapter 23 refers students to particular sections of the *Workbook* for solving particular problems.) And cross-references throughout the book help students tie the units of writing together.

In the third edition of the *Workbook*, the chapters dealing with sentence structure have been expanded, and opportunities for students to practice their writing skills have been increased. The *Workbook* is not merely a collection of short-answer exercises. Rather, the text attempts to provide students with the explanatory material they need and to involve them actively in the writing process from the beginning. Students have the opportunity to write imaginatively and correctly on a number of topics and, by doing so, to develop an awareness and appreciation of the variety of ways in which they can express themselves. The *Workbook*, then, is one in which students work at writing *by* writing.

For their suggestions on this third edition, I wish to thank Richard H. Bogue, Northern Illinois University; Milton Hawkins, Del Mar College; Stanley J. Kozikowski, Bryant College; Patricia M. Licklider, John Jay College of Criminal Justice; Robert Merkel, Monroe County Community College; Mary Sue Ply, Pan American University; and John W. Presley, Augusta College. For their continued support, I am grateful to Amanda Clark, Kathy Lorden, and Ginny Guerrant of Scott, Foresman, to the Salem State College Bureau of Faculty Research, and to Kim and Carol.

William E. Mahaney

CONTENTS

1
GRAMMAR OF SENTENCES

The *sentence* is the basic grammatical and thought unit in English. It contains both a subject and a predicate. The *subject* consists of a noun or noun equivalent and all of its modifiers. The *predicate* consists of the verb and all of the words related to it, such as objects, complements, and modifiers.

1.1 Main Sentence Elements

The main elements of the sentence are the subject, verb or linking verb, direct object, indirect object, and complement. Not all of these, however, will appear in every sentence. Only the subject and verb are essential.

The Subject (S). The *subject* of the sentence is a noun or a noun equivalent (a pronoun, noun clause, gerund, or infinitive):

> The **bridge** was covered with ice. [noun]
> **He** arrived at the airport. [pronoun]
> **What he did** was wrong. [noun clause]
> **Walking** is good exercise. [gerund]
> **To think** is to exist. [infinitive]

The Verb (V) or Linking Verb (LV). The *verb* in a sentence describes an action or process, or expresses a condition. When the verb expresses a condition, it is a *linking verb;* that is, it *links* a word in the predicate to the subject (see Complement):

>   S   V
> Edna **jumped** into the pool. [describes action]

>   S   LV
> She **was** happy. [expresses condition]

The Direct Object (DO). When a verb describes an action, it is often followed by a *direct object*—a noun or noun equivalent that completes the statement begun by the subject and verb. A direct object answers the question asked by adding "what?" or "whom?" after the verb. (He dislikes *whom?* He dislikes *me.*)

> S   V   DO
> The farmer raised **corn.** [noun]
>
> S   V DO
> She shot **him.** [pronoun]
>
> S   DO   V
> He realized **what he had done.** [noun clause]
>
> S   V   DO
> Ralph enjoys **reading.** [gerund]
>
> S   V   DO
> They attempted **to go.** [infinitive]

The Indirect Object (IO). An *indirect object* (used with verbs of giving, receiving, asking, telling, sending, and the like) names the receiver of the direct object. The indirect object precedes the direct object and answers the question "to whom or to what?" or "for whom or for what?" or "of whom or of what?" (The dean sent a letter *to whom?* The dean sent *Scott* a letter.)

> S   V   IO   DO
> Gwen gave **Herman** a ride.
>
> S   V   IO   DO
> The reporter asked the **senator** a leading question.

The Complement (C). When a verb expresses a condition (a linking verb), it is usually followed by a *complement*—a noun or an adjective that is related to the subject by the linking verb. When the complement is a noun (or noun equivalent), it is called a *predicate noun;* when the complement is an adjective, it is called a *predicate adjective:*

> S   LV   C
> Robert Duvall is a talented **actor.** [predicate noun]
>
> S   LV   C
> The pie looked **delicious.** [predicate adjective]

The Expletive (EX). In sentences where *there* or *it* is used with a form of the verb *to be,* the actual subject appears after the verb. In such cases *there* or *it* is an *expletive* or *anticipating subject* which "anticipates" the actual subject that appears after the verb:

> EX   LV   S
> **There** are several reasons for denying your request.
>
> EX LV   S
> **It** is a dark night.

Word Order. Main sentence elements are usually identified by their positions in a sentence. In statements, the main sentence elements usually follow one of three *typical word order* patterns.

1. Subject – Verb – Direct object:

    We   ate   fish.

2. Subject – Verb – Indirect object – Direct object:

    She   told   him   a lie.

3. Subject – Linking verb – Complement:

    The drill   is   noisy.

Inverted word order occurs in questions, exclamations, and emphatic statements, and with expletives:

> V   S   DO
> Have you a hammer? [question]

> C   S LV
> How crowded the store is! [exclamation]

> DO S   V
> A worse storm I never saw. [emphatic statement]

> LV C   S
> There are good reasons for buying a small car. [expletive]

1.2 Secondary Sentence Elements

Besides the main sentence elements, most sentences contain secondary elements. These elements are typically used as *modifiers* to describe, limit, or make more exact the meaning of the main elements. The secondary sentence elements are adjectives, adverbs, nouns used as modifiers, prepositional phrases, verbal phrases, subordinate clauses, appositives, and modifiers of modifiers.

Adjectives (ADJ). *Adjectives* modify nouns and noun equivalents (see 9, Adjectives and Adverbs):

> A **green** rug covered the floor. [modifies the noun *rug*]
> They were **suspicious.** [modifies the pronoun *they*]
> We are in for some **strenuous** hiking. [modifies the gerund *hiking*]

Adverbs (ADV). *Adverbs* may modify verbs, adjectives, or other adverbs (see 9, Adjectives and Adverbs):

> He **certainly** expected better results. [modifies the verb *expected*]
> The sky was **quite** dark. [modifies the adjective *dark*]
> It moved **very** quietly. [modifies the adverb *quietly*]

Nouns (N) as Modifiers. *Nouns* sometimes modify other nouns (see 7.4, Noun Modifiers):

The **bedroom** window was broken. (modifies the noun *window*]

Prepositional Phrases (PP). *Prepositional phrases* can modify any of the main sentence elements (see 1.3, Phrases and Clauses):

The pianist **in the concert** was excellent. [modifies the subject *pianist*]
She gazed **out the window.** [modifies the verb *gazed*]

Verbal Phrases (VP). *Verbal phrases* can also modify main sentence elements (see 1.3, Phrases and Clauses):

Looking out the porthole, he saw a whale. [modifies the subject *he*]
They gathered **to mourn their martyred leader.** [modifies the verb *gathered*]

Subordinate Clauses (SC). *Subordinate clauses* (or dependent clauses) can serve as modifiers (see 1.3 Phrases and Clauses):

An actor **who wants to succeed** must be able to portray many emotions. [modifies the subject *actor*]
He enjoys collecting coins **that are old.** [modifies the object *coins*]

Appositives (AP). An *appositive* is a noun or noun equivalent placed next to another noun and set off from it by commas. The appositive is used to further identify the noun, or to clarify or supplement its meaning:

The orchestra leader, **Zubin Mehta,** raised his baton. [identifies the noun *leader*]
Zubin Mehta, **the orchestra leader,** raised his baton. [identifies the noun *Mehta*]
Banquo is a character in *Macbeth*, **a play by William Shakespeare.** [identifies the noun *Macbeth*]

Modifiers of Modifiers (MM). Secondary sentence elements that modify main sentence elements may themselves by modified by expressions which are termed *modifiers of modifiers*:

The **regional** office manager retired after forty-three years of service. [modifies *office* which modifies *manager*]
The traffic was **quite** heavy. [modifies *heavy* which modifies *traffic*]

1.3 Phrases and Clauses

Sentences are built of single words, phrases, and clauses. Phrases and clauses may function as main sentence elements (S, V, DO, IO, or C) or as secondary sentence elements (modifiers).

Phrases. A phrase is a group of words connected to a main or secondary sentence element by a preposition or a verbal. Because a phrase has neither a subject nor a predicate, it cannot stand alone.

Prepositional phrases (PP). A *prepositional phrase* consists of a preposition *(in, on, over, at, by, of)*, a noun or noun equivalent, and any modifiers of the noun. A prepositional phrase can function as an adjective or an adverb:

> He returned **from the lake.** [modifies the verb *returned*]
> The chair **in the corner** is comfortable. [modifies the noun *chair*]

Verbal phrases (VP). A verbal phrase consists of a verbal (a participle, gerund, or infinitive) plus its object or complement and modifiers. There are three types of verbal phrases.

1. A *participial phrase* functions as an adjective:

> Alligators **hiding in the weeds** make swimming dangerous. [modifies *alligators*]

2. A *gerund phrase* functions as a noun:

> **Discussing the works of Plato and Aristotle** with Professor Armenne helped me understand ancient philosophy. [serves as the subject]

3. An *infinitive phrase* may function as either a noun, an adjective, or an adverb:

> The surest way **to pass this course** [adjective, modifies *way*] is **to work hard.** [noun, serves as a complement]

Clauses. A clause contains a subject and a predicate. Two types of clauses exist: *main* (or independent) and *subordinate* (or dependent).

Main clauses (MC). A *main clause* can stand alone because it is a complete expression. A main clause may be introduced—

1. By the subject itself:

> **The village** prepared for the attack.

2. By a coordinating conjunction *(and, but, or, for, nor, so, yet):*

> **But** the enemy arrived early.

3. By a conjunctive adverb *(however, therefore, nevertheless,* and so on):

> **Therefore,** the village was captured.

Subordinate clauses (SC). A subordinate clause cannot stand alone because it is not a complete expression. A subordinate clause functions as a noun, adjective, or adverb within a sentence. A subordinate clause may be introduced—

1. By a subordinating conjunction (*because, although, when, after, while,* and so on):

    She missed the meeting **because her car would not start.**

2. By a relative pronoun (*who, which, that,* and so on):

    The house **that you hoped to buy** was sold yesterday.

1.4 Sentences Classified by Clause Structure

Depending upon the type and number of clauses they contain, sentences may be classified as *simple, compound, complex,* or *compound-complex.*

Simple Sentences. A *simple sentence* contains one main clause and no subordinate clauses:

> The orchestra played until midnight.

Compound Sentences. A *compound sentence* contains two or more main clauses and no subordinate clauses. The main clauses may be linked—

1. By a semicolon:

    The batter swung at the ball**;** he missed.

2. By a coordinating conjunction (*and, but, or, for, nor, so, yet*):

    The batter swung at the ball, **but** he missed.

3. By a conjunctive adverb (*accordingly, therefore, then, consequently,* and so on):

    The batter swung at the ball; **however,** he missed.

4. By correlative conjunctions (*either . . . or, neither . . . nor, both . . . and, not only . . . but also*):

    Either he took his eye off the ball **or** the pitch fooled him.

Complex Sentences. A *complex sentence* consists of one main clause and one or more subordinate clauses:

> While you were watching the baboon [subordinate], he was watching you [main].
> When I was young [subordinate], I enjoyed the circus [main] because the clowns made me laugh [subordinate].

Compound-Complex Sentences. A *compound-complex sentence* consists of two or more main clauses and one or more subordinate clauses:

> When the police arrived [subordinate], he attempted to escape [main], but he was captured [main] as he tried to jump the fence [subordinate].

1.5 Sentences Classified by Purpose

Depending upon their purposes, sentences may be classified as—

1. Statements:

   The roof leaks.
   Superman wears pantyhose.

2. Questions:

   What is the capital of Guatemala?
   At what time does the train leave?

3. Commands:

   Take your feet off the table.
   Place Tab B into Slot A.

4. Exclamations:

   You ought to be ashamed!
   How polite she is!

Exercise *1.1*   Main Sentence Elements

A. Indicate whether each italicized item is a subject (S), verb (V), linking verb (LV), direct object (DO), indirect object (IO), or complement (C) by writing S, V, LV, DO, IO, or C in the space at the right.

Example (a) *Ice* (b) *covered* the (c) *bridge*

    a.   **S**

    b.   **V**

    c.   **DO**

1. The (1) *shark* (2) *is* a feared (3) *predator*.

2. (4) *Ann* (5) *gave* (6) *John* sound (7) *advice*.

3. After haunting all night the (8) *phantom* (9) *appeared* (10) *fatigued*.

4. (11) *Should* we *give* the (12) *winner* the (13) *trophy* now?

5. (14) *What the law means* (15) *is* (16) *obscure*.

6. (17) *Igor* (18) *remembered* (19) *to lock the torture chamber*.

7. (20) *Beethoven* (21) *was* a musical (22) *genius*.

8. On election day, he (23) *told* his (24) *friends* (25) *to vote early and often*.

1. _____
2. _____
3. _____
4. _____
5. _____
6. _____
7. _____
8. _____
9. _____
10. _____
11. _____
12. _____
13. _____
14. _____
15. _____
16. _____
17. _____
18. _____
19. _____
20. _____
21. _____
22. _____
23. _____
24. _____
25. _____

B. For each sentence below, supply the missing subject (S), verb (V), linking verb (LV), direct object (DO), indirect object (IO), or complement (C) by writing an appropriate word (or words) in the space at the right.

Example The vampire __V__ his __DO__ on the neck.
       V   _bit_
       DO _victim_

1. Television __V__ the values of society.
  1. V _____

2. __S__ sent __IO__ a shrunken head.
  2. S _____
     IO _____

3. At the beach we __V__ in the surf and played __DO__ on the sand.
  3. V _____
     DO _____

4. Fishing in a peaceful stream __LV__ __C__ .
  4. LV _____
     C _____

5. __S__ improves __DO__ .
  5. S _____
     DO _____

6. The __S__ in my hair __LV__ terrifying.
  6. S _____
     LV _____

7. The judge __V__ __IO__ __DO__ .
  7. V _____
     IO _____
     DO _____

8. __S__ can cause __DO__ .
  8. S _____
     DO _____

9. King Kong __LV__ only a __C__ with a glandular problem.
  9. LV _____
     C _____

10. The happy __S__ __V__ __DO__ .
  10. S _____
      V _____
      DO _____

11. The __S__ gave __IO__ its Humanitarian Award; she __LV__ __C__ .
  11. S _____
      IO _____
      LV _____
      C _____

C. For each of the items below write a complete sentence using the words given as the subject (S), verb (V), linking verb (LV), direct object (DO), indirect object (IO), complement (C), or expletive (EX). Be sure that each sentence you write has a subject and predicate.

Example ran (V) *The joggers ran through the park.*

1. Alfredo (S)

2. were (LV)

3. weeds (DO)

4. there (EX)

5. to the rhinoceros (IO)

6. terrified (V)

7. beautiful (C)

8. might have been (LV)

9. the arcade (S)

10. where they came from (DO)

Exercise 1.2   Secondary Sentence Elements

A. Indicate whether each italicized modifier is an adjective (ADJ), adverb (ADV), noun (N), prepositional phrase (PP), verbal phrase (VP), subordinate clause (SC), or appositive (AP) by writing ADJ, ADV, N, PP, VP, SC, or AP in the space at the right.

Example The (a) *timid* rabbit hopped (b) *quickly* (c) *across the field.*

a. _*ADJ*_
b. _*ADV*_
c. _*PP*_

1. Leonardo da Vinci, (1) *Renaissance artist and inventor,* was (2) *left-handed.*

2. (3) *Flying over the Rocky Mountains,* the plane began (4) *to shake violently.*

3. Advertisers (5) *who deceive the public* should be (6) *heavily* fined (7) *by the government.*

4. He worked in a (8) *dance* hall (9) *across the street.*

5. Our (10) *national* bird, (11) *the bald eagle,* is an (12) *endangered* species.

6. (13) *Drawing his gun,* the (14) *tall* sheriff stepped (15) *cautiously* (16) *into the street.*

7. The (17) *glass* dome shone (18) *brilliantly* (19) *in the sunlight.*

8. The cottonmouth, (20) *a poisonous snake,* strikes (21) *quickly* and (22) *silently.*

9. (23) *Water* fowl (24) *that migrate seasonally* may fly (25) *great* distances.

1. _____
2. _____
3. _____
4. _____
5. _____
6. _____
7. _____
8. _____
9. _____
10. _____
11. _____
12. _____
13. _____
14. _____
15. _____
16. _____
17. _____
18. _____
19. _____
20. _____
21. _____
22. _____
23. _____
24. _____
25. _____

B. For each sentence below, supply the missing adjective (ADJ), noun (N), prepositional phrase (PP), verbal phrase (VP), subordinate clause (SC), or appositive (AP) by writing an appropriate word (or words) in the space at the right.

Example Because of its _ADJ_ legs, the ostrich,

_AP_ , can attain great speeds _PP_ .

ADJ *powerful*
AP *a flightless bird*
PP *on the ground*

NAME . . . .   SCORE . . . .

1.   The _ADJ_ woman yelled _ADV_ _PP_ .   1. ADJ _____
                                                               ADV _____
                                                               PP _____

2.   _VP_ , the couple enjoyed the   2. VP _____
     ADJ rain.   ADJ _____

3.   The _N_ salesperson spoke _ADV_   3. N   _____
     _PP_ .   ADV _____
                                                               PP _____

4.   The car _SC_ was already beginning   4. SC _____
     _VP_ .   VP _____

5.   John, _AP_ , tried to explain his   5. AP _____
     actions _PP_ .   PP _____
                                                               _____

6.   The _ADJ_ fox _ADV_ approached the   6. ADJ _____
     ADJ chicken.   ADV _____
                                                               ADJ _____

7.   _VP_ , the boxer began _VP_ .   7. VP _____
                                                               VP _____

8.   The _N_ antenna improved recep-   8. N   _____
     tion as soon as it was placed _PP_ .   PP _____

9.   All those _SC_ will be unable to see   V   _____
     the game.

10. The task _SC_ should be completed   10. SC _____
     first.

11. Mr. Stingley, _AP_ , kept his _ADJ_   11. AP _____
     coins in a _N_ box _PP_ .   ADJ _____
                                                               N   _____
                                                               PP _____

© 1985 Scott, Foresman and Company. All Rights Reserved.

C. Build sentences from the base given by adding the modifying elements called for—adjective (ADJ), adverb (ADV), noun (N), prepositional phrase (PP), verbal phrase (VP), subordinate clause (SC), appositive (AP), or modifier (MM).

Example The door opened
> (ADJ describing *door*)
>
> *The heavy door opened.*
>
> (PP indicating where the door is)
>
> *The heavy door on the vault opened.*
>
> (ADV modifying *opened*)
>
> *The heavy door on the vault opened slowly.*

1. The stove exploded.
   (N modifying *stove*)

   (SC modifying *exploded*)

2. All may enter.
   (SC modifying *all*)

   (PP modifying *enter*)

3. The car stopped.
   (VP modifying *car*)

   (AP modifying *car*)

   (ADV modifying *stopped*)

4. The telephone rang.
   (PP modifying *telephone*)

   (ADV modifying *rang*)

   (VP modifying *telephone*)

5. The stations plays music.
   (N modifying *station*)

   (ADJ modifying *music*)

   (MM *modifying ADJ*)

D.   Add two or three modifiers, including the type given, to each of the
following sentences.

Example The duck quacked. (ADV)

The wounded duck quacked almost inaudibly.

1.   The window closed. (SC)

2.   The music began. (MM)

3.   The ghost appeared. (VP)

4.   The surgeon tried. (N)

5.   The stranger visited the town. (AP)

6.   The lights blinked. (ADV)

7.   The salesperson smiled. (ADJ)

8.   The zebra ran. (PP)

9.   The crowd cheered. (SC)

10.   The snow fell. (VP)

Exercise 1.3   Phrases and Clauses

A. Indicate whether each italicized item is a prepositional phrase (PP), a verbal phrase (VP), a main clause (MC), or a subordinate clause (SC) by writing PP, VP, MC, or SC in the space at the right.

Examples *on the train* _____PP_____

He left *because the party was dull.* _____SC_____

1. *to build an ark* 1. _____
2. *although the alarm went off at daybreak* 2. _____
3. *bounding through the woods* 3. _____
4. *but the lock would not open* 4. _____
5. *in the cabinet* 5. _____
6. *before you hang the wallpaper* 6. _____
7. *however, the hotel had no vacancy* 7. _____
8. *the picture is crooked* 8. _____
9. *with many friends* 9. _____
10. *if it rains all day* 10. _____
11. The wet papers were spread *over the table.* 11. _____
12. Before his guest arrived, *he cleaned the apartment.* 12. _____
13. *Performing before an audience for the first time,* he was nervous. 13. _____
14. She showed early promise *as a composer.* 14. _____
15. *When the rhino charged,* the hunter climbed a tree. 15. _____
16. *60 Minutes* manages *to appeal to many television viewers.* 16. _____
17. The taxi threaded its way *through the traffic.* 17. _____
18. *Waving a stuffed parrot,* the photographer tried to get the baby to smile. 18. _____
19. Tragedy was avoided *because the police arrived.* 19. _____
20. She hiked ten miles *through dense jungle* to seek help. 20. _____

B. Write the missing prepositional phrase (PP), verbal phrase (VP), main clause (MC), or subordinate clause (SC) in the space beneath each sentence.

Examples Count Dracula managed _VP_ .

to escape the trap.

_SC_ the bus finally arrived.

after he waited three hours,

1. In Italy _MC_ .

16

2. She walked him home _PP_ .

3. _VP_ she applied a tourniquet.

4. He placed the pistol _PP_ before he was seen.

5. The startled dog jumped over the table, and _MC_ .

6. Herb could not join the expedition _SC_ .

7. When he was very young, _MC_ .

8. The grandfather clock _SC_ keeps time accurately.

9. He hoped _VP_ early the next morning.

10. Singing _PP_ is enjoyable.

11. _VP_ , he carefully pulled to the curb.

12. The countess _SC_ married for the fifth time.

13. She was taught to play bridge _PP_ .

14. _SC_ , we need to develop new energy sources.

15. Although she was eighty-two, Grandmother wanted _VP_ .

Exercise *1.4* Sentences Classified by Clause Structure

A. Identify each sentence as *simple, compound, complex,* or *compound-complex* by writing the appropriate term in the space at the right.

Example While you are mowing the lawn,
I will repair the roof.

complex

1. James Earl Jones was nominated for an Academy Award for his part in *The Great White Hope;* however, George C. Scott won for his role in *Patton.*

    1. _____

2. Upon reaching the field, the team warmed up thoroughly to avoid injuries during the game.

    2. _____

3. When he died, William Shakespeare willed to his wife his second-best bed.

    3. _____

4. In 1831 Michael Faraday of Great Britain invented the electric generator and Cyrus McCormick of the United States invented the reaper.

    4. _____

5. After a long journey across the continent, the first wagon train arrived in California in 1841.

    5. _____

6. Although the soldiers are ill-fed, they will fight as if their bellies were full; although their uniforms are tattered, they are dressed to kill.

    6. _____

7. The grand tortoises which inhabit the Galapagos Islands can weigh over 400 pounds.

    7. _____

8. Throughout the long afternoon I saw vultures circling high above me.

    8. _____

B. Add one or more subordinate clauses (SC) or main clauses (MC) to the clause or clauses given to create the type of sentence indicated.

Example because her bow was broken (complex)

Because her bow was broken, she could not compete in the archery contest.

1. but also he lost his suitcase (compound)

18

2.   After I got to the attic (complex)

3.   When I first met Fred
        but since I have come to know him (compound-complex)

4.   we traveled by canoe (complex)

5.   Gina took violin lessons (compound)

6.   If automobiles had not been invented (compound-complex)

C.   For each compound sentence, identify the link between the clauses. If
        the clauses are joined by a semicolon only (no linking word), put a **;**
        under **Link** and write **Semi** under **Type.** If the clauses are joined by a
        coordinating conjunction (CC), a conjunctive adverb (CA), or correlative
        conjunctions (COR), write the linking word or words under LINK and
        write CC, CA, or COR under TYPE. (Remember that a semicolon may be
        used along with a linking word.)

	Link	Type
Example Craig was elected president of the club, but I did not vote for him.	*but*	*cc*

1.   Modern society produces tension;   1.   _____   _____
        therefore, it is important to learn to
        relax.

2.   He only had time for a nap; before   2.   _____   _____
        dawn he had to leave.

3.   She wanted to purchase the old   3.   _____   _____
        farm, for she had spent many years
        there as a child.

4.   Not only will you conquer your   4.   _____   _____
        enemy, but also you will conquer
        your fear.

5. The miners were trapped in total   5.   _____ _____
darkness for sixteen days; however,
on the seventeenth day they were
finally rescued.

D. Link each group of simple sentences together into a compound
sentence by using the type of link indicated—semicolon (SEMI),
coordinating conjunction (CC), conjunctive adverb (CA), correlative conjunctions (COR). Be sure that your punctuation is appropriate to the type
of link used.

Example Mavis tried to lift the rock. It was too heavy. (CC)

*Mavis tried to lift the rock, but it was
too heavy.*

1. Property values have increased rapidly. Property taxes have risen more
rapidly. (CC)

2. You complete your assignment. You fail the course. (COR)

3. The journey may seem long. It must be made. (CA)

4. Switzerland is a European country of about 16,000 square miles. It is
surrounded by Austria, West Germany, France, Italy, and Liechtenstein.
(SEMI)

5. You must study both science and the humanities. You cannot call
yourself educated. (CC)

E. Change each simple sentence into the type indicated by adding either a
main clause, a subordinate clause, or both.

Example (simple) The moon shone brightly.

(complex) *As we stepped outside, the moon shone
brightly.*

1. (simple) We crossed the street.

(compound)

2.   (simple) Not a word was spoken.

(complex)

3.   (simple) The rafters creaked.

(complex)

4.   (simple) We visited the Statue of Liberty in New York.

(compound-complex)

5.   (simple) The mayor rose to speak.

(compound)

6.   (simple) The temperature reached ninety-four.

(compound-complex)

7.   (simple) A news bulletin interrupted the program.

(compound)

8.   (simple) The helicopter appeared.

(complex)

F.   For each item, choose one of the topics given; write each type of sentence on that topic.

Example *clothing* or *ships*

(simple) *He wore a tattered hat.*

(compound) *He wore a tattered hat, but his suit was clean.*

(complex) *Although he wore a tattered hat, his suit was clean.*

(compound-complex) *Although he wore a tattered hat, his suit was clean and his shoes were shined.*

1. *bowling* or *football*

   (simple)

   (compound)

   (complex)

   (compound-complex)

2. *a lake* or *food*

   (simple)

   (compound)

   (complex)

   (compound-complex)

3. *politics* or *a gas station*

   (simple)

   (compound)

   (complex)

   (compound-complex)

NAME .... SCORE ....

Review Exercise 1 Grammar of Sentences

A. In the space at the right, indicate whether each numbered clause in the paragraph is a main clause (MC) or a subordinate clause (SC).

Example (a) The army lost the battle (b) because it was
outnumbered.

a. ___*MC*___

b. ___*SC*___

As the twenty-first century neared, conditions on the planet Earth had become critical,
(2) for the number of people was rapidly out-
stripping the ability of Earth to support them.
(3) Advances in medicine had significantly increased the human life span, (4) global government had eliminated international warfare,
(5) and agrichemistry had eradicated hunger.
(6) Because the population was continually increasing, (7) the natural resources of the planet
were nearly depleted. (8) It became necessary
for humans to explore other solar systems and
colonize planets (9) which could provide the ad-
ditional resources (10) that were desperately
needed on Earth.

1. _____

2. _____

3. _____

4. _____

5. _____

6. _____

7. _____

8. _____

9. _____

10. _____

B. For each italicized main sentence element in the following paragraph, indicate in the space at the right whether it is a subject (S), verb (V), direct
object (DO), indirect object (IO), linking verb (LV), complement (C), or expletive (EX).

Example (a) *Fred* gave (b) *Sue* a friendship (c) *ring*.

a. ___*S*___

b. ___*IO*___

c. ___*O*___

When Captain (1) *Astra* (2) *landed* on Helion
to colonize the planet, she (3) *brought* with her
over 20,000 construction (4) *workers* and support
staff. Faced with harsh extremes of temperature
on the planet's (5) *surface*, (6) *she* gave the
(7) *crew* (8) *orders* (9) *to build* a vast underground
city. Although (10) *there* (11) *were* infinite
hardships which (13) *had* (14) *to be overcome*, the
workers (15) *labored* valiantly to achieve their
goal. (16) *It* (17) *was* three years later that
(18) *Astra* showed the (19) *visitors* from Earth the
completed subterranean (20) *complex*.

1. _____

2. _____

3. _____

4. _____

5. _____

6. _____

7. _____

8. _____

9. _____

10. _____

11. _____

12. _____

13. _____

14. _____

15. _____

16. _____

17. _____

18. _____

19. _____

20. _____

C. For each italicized modifier in the following paragraph, indicate in the
first space the type of modifier it is—adjective (ADJ), adverb (ADV), noun
(N), prepositional phrase (PP), verbal phrase (VP), subordinate clause
(SC), or appositive (AP). In the second space, write the word or words it
modifies.

NAME . . . .   SCORE . . . .

	Type	Modifies
Example The **(a)** *gray* elephant charged	a. _ADJ_	_elephant_
(b) *at the lion.*	b. _PP_	_charged_

On a **(1)** *Saturday* morning **(2)** *last*   1. _____ _____

July, Mary and I decided to visit the   2. _____ _____

(3) *local* **(4)** *wildlife* refuge, **(5)** *Wilderness*   3. _____ _____

Valley, **(6)** *which was only three blocks from*   4. _____ _____

our home. **(7)** *Starting along the trail,* we   5. _____ _____

anticipated a **(8)** *most* **(9)** *pleasant* walk   6. _____ _____

(10) *through the woods.* We saw a   7. _____ _____

(11) *great* **(12)** *many* varieties **(13)** *of trees,*   8. _____ _____

shrubs, and flowers **(14)** *which lined the*   9. _____ _____

path. **(15)** *Stopping by a quiet stream,* we   10. _____ _____

spread a blanket **(16)** *on the ground* and   11. _____ _____

ate our **(17)** *picnic* lunch. **(18)** *After lunch,*   12. _____ _____

13. _____ _____

14. _____ _____

15. _____ _____

16. _____ _____

17. _____ _____

18. _____ _____

we followed the stream to Kingley Falls,

19. _____ _____

(19) *a small waterfall deep in the woods.*

20. _____ _____

(20) *Near the waterfall* we heard the song

21. _____ _____

of a **(21)** *small* bird **(22)** *that was singing*

22. _____ _____

(23) *very* **(24)** *happily* **(25)** *in an oak tree.*

23. _____ _____

24. _____ _____

25. _____ _____

D. Rewrite the following paragraph. Turn most of the simple sentences into compound, complex, and compound-complex sentences by combining main clauses and by making some main clauses into subordinate ones. Also, add whatever modifying material you believe is necessary to describe the incident more fully.

(1) The ship was three days from port. (2) The barometer began to fall. (3) The storm struck. (4) The wind was fierce. (5) The rain drenched the crew. (6) The waves tossed the ship. (7) The situation became critical. (8) The ship was taking on water. (9) The captain sent the Coast Guard a message. (10) He told his crew the situation. (11) He ordered them to abandon ship. (12) They launched the lifeboats. (13) A huge wave turned the ship over.

E. Write a paragraph of four to eight sentences, selecting your topic from the list below. Your paragraph should include at least *three* types of sentences (simple, compound, complex, and compound-complex), each clause should have a subject and predicate, and both *main sentence elements* (subject, verb, linking verb, direct object, indirect object, complement, and expletive) and *secondary sentence elements* (adjective, adverb, prepositional phrase, verbal phrase, subordinate clause, and appositive) should be used appropriately.

Topics   computers
          sports
          transportation
          motion pictures

2

SUBORDINATE CLAUSES AND CONNECTIVES

A *subordinate clause* (or dependent clause) has a subject and a predicate, but it cannot stand alone because it is an incomplete statement. Subordinate clauses function as modifiers, subjects, objects, and complements. They may be classified as adjective clauses, adverb clauses, or noun clauses, depending upon their grammatical functions.

2.1 Adjective Clauses (ADJ C)

A subordinate clause that modifies a noun or noun equivalent is called an *adjective clause*. Adjective clauses are usually introduced by *relative pronouns* (*who, which, that,* and so on), which also function as subjects or objects within the clause:

> All customers **who pay cash** will receive a discount. [The clause modifies the noun *customers; who* is the subject of the clause.]
> I admire writing **that is clear and logical.** [The clause modifies the gerund *writing; that* is the subject of the clause.]
> She was betrayed by one **in whom she placed great trust.** [The clause modifies the pronoun *one; whom* is the object of *in.*]

Adjective clauses may also be introduced by *relative adverbs* (*when, where, why,* for example):

> I hurried back to the club **where I left my jacket.** [The clause modifies the noun *club; where* is a relative adverb.]

Clauses Without Relative Words. When an adjective clause is a restrictive modifier (a modifier that is essential to the meaning of the sentence), the relative word is often omitted:

> The only law **[that] I follow** is the law of survival.
> The circus is one thing **[which] everyone enjoys.**

2.2 Adverb Clauses (ADV C)

A subordinate clause that modifies a verb, adjective, adverb, or main clause is called an *adverb clause*. Adverb clauses are introduced by *subordinate conjunctions* (such as *after, before, because, since, although*):

> We left the party **before the trouble began.** [modifies the verb *left*]
> A baboon is dangerous **when it is provoked.** [modifies the predicate adjective *dangerous*]
> Some people work best **when they are under pressure.** [modifies the adverb *best*]
> **Although the clock was old,** it kept time perfectly. [modifies the main clause *it kept time perfectly*]

The words that introduce adverb clauses usually express a relationship of time, place, direction, cause, effect, condition, manner, or concession:

> **After** he opened the damper, he lit the fire [*After* expresses a temporal relationship between the two clauses.]
> She will spend the weekend skiing **if** the weather remains clear. [*If* expresses a conditional relationship between the two clauses.]

2.3 Noun Clauses (NC)

A subordinate clause that serves as a subject, object, complement, or appositive is called a *noun clause*. Most noun clauses are introduced by *that*, but words such as *whatever, whoever, who, what, why, when, where,* and *whether* may also introduce noun clauses.

Noun Clauses as Objects:

> He suggested **that we invest in International Buggy Whip stock.** [direct object of the verb *suggested*]
> I will learn from **whomever I can.** [object of the preposition *from*]

Noun Clauses as Appositives:

> The realization **that they were lost** struck them. [identifies the noun *realization*]

Noun Clauses as Subjects:

> **Whoever came in last** forgot to close the door. [subject of *forgot*]
> **What you are asking** is simply impossible. [subject of *is*]

HINT: Sentences that begin with a noun clause introduced by *that* or *whether* may seem stilted. Such clauses can usually be placed after the verb:

Stilted	**That he would lose the election** did not seem likely.
Revised	It did not seem likely **that he would lose the election.**

Stilted	**Whether we could reach the shelter before the storm began** was our problem.	
Revised	Our problem was **whether we could reach the shelter before the storm began.**	

	Subordinate clauses	
Type	**Use**	**Usually introduced by**
Adjective clause	modifies noun or noun equivalent	*who, whose, whom, which, that, where, when, why*
Adverb clause	modifies verb, adjective, adverb, or main clause	*after, although, as, as if, as long as, as though, because, before, if, in order that, provided that, since, so, so that, that, though, unless, until, when, whenever, where, wherever, while*
Noun clause	serves as subject, object, complement, or appositive	*that* (sometimes by: *what, whatever, when, where, whether, who, whoever, why*)

Noun Clauses as Complements:

His greatest fear was **that he would die at an early age.** [predicate noun]

HINT: Noun clauses used as complements are often awkward. When such awkwardness occurs, reword the sentence to eliminate the noun clause:

Awkward	The amount of violence shown is why some people criticize television programming.
Revised	Some people criticize television programming because of the amount of violence shown.
	Some people criticize the amount of violence shown on television.

Exercise 2.1   Adjective Clauses

A.   Underline each adjective clause in the sentences below. Then identify the noun or pronoun modified by each clause and write it in the space at the right. Some sentences have more than one adjective clause. Remember that in some adjective clauses the relative word is omitted.

Example Any runner who leaves the track will   *runner*
be disqualified.

1.   The police officer who apprehended the suspect should be commended for her bravery.
1. _____
_____

2.   At the Gettysburg battleground we visited the spot where Pickett led his famous charge.
2. _____
_____

3.   Business Law is a course in which you have to work hard but one in which you learn a lot.
3. _____
_____

4.   When we chose our new rug, we tried to select a color which would match our draperies.
4. _____
_____

5.   Egypt is one country I hope to visit.
5. _____
_____

6.   The alligators that are found in the Everglades are descendants of the reptiles which flourished in prehistoric times.
6. _____
_____
_____

7.   The tomatoes we are having in our salad came from the garden we planted last spring.
7. _____
_____

8.   The film suggested some reasons that modern Americans feel alienated.
8. _____
_____

B.   Write each adjective clause into a sentence by adding a main clause and any other necessary words.

Example where we first met

The restaurant where we first met has been demolished.

1. who believes that whales must be protected

2. where the tribal elders were holding a conference

3. why you were unable to find a store open

4. from whom we obtained directions

5. that television creates in young people

C. Rewrite each sentence, adding one or more adjective clauses. Then circle the noun or pronoun modified by each adjective clause.

Example My aunt took us to see a film. *My (aunt) who was visiting from New Jersey took us to see a (film) that won four academy awards.*

1. Alex Haley's novel *Roots* traces his African and Afro-American heritage.

2. A press conference was called to explain the reason.

3. We discovered some old bones.

4. The advertisement persuaded Walter to buy a machine.

5. At the exhibit, Randy saw paintings and statues.

D. Combine the main clauses in each of the following passages into one sentence by making one clause an adjective clause.

Example Joan scored the winning goal. She was playing in her first varsity game.

Joan, who was playing in her first varsity game, scored the winning goal.

1. Chuck Mangione is a popular recording artist. He plays the flügelhorn.

2. Roy and Mary Lou bought a silver Corvette. They drove it from Bangor, Maine, to Ogden, Utah.

3. Diners have made the Casa de Burro the most popular restaurant in town. The owner also runs the chic Maison de Mole.

4. Death lurks in the depths of the lagoon. It strikes swiftly and silently.

5. The taxi rushed to the airport. The charter flight was waiting.

6. Norma's cousin owns a nightclub in New York City. She also owns a resort in Miami.

Exercise 2.2   Adverb Clauses

A.   Underline each adverb clause in the sentences below. If the adverb clause modifies a verb, adjective, or adverb, write that word in the space at the right. If it modifies the entire main clause, write MC in the space. Some sentences have more than one adverb clause; others have none.

Examples We arrived at the post office after it closed.   *arrived*

If I can save enough money, I'll go to Spain.   *MC*

1.   Albert Einstein published his "Special Theory of Relativity" when he was twenty-six years old.   1. _____

2.   If you are domineering and regal, you were probably born under the sign of Leo.   2. _____

3.   He rigged the camera so that it would photograph anyone who opened the door.   3. _____

4.   As long as you are going out, you might as well stop at the post office because we need stamps.   4. _____

5.   After they spotted me hiding behind a large leaf, they acted as if they had never seen an elf before.   5. _____

6.   You may have until the end of the week to complete your assignment.   6. _____

7.   The strike will last longer if both sides refuse to negotiate.   7. _____

8.   Old Bozo is content when he has a bone to gnaw.   8. _____

B. Complete each sentence by adding an adverb clause after the italicized word(s). The italicized word(s) will connect the adverb clause to the main clause.

Example *After*   *the painting dried,*

we placed it in a frame of dark wood.

1. *Provided that*

 we will have enough food in the future.

2. Three crewmen were able to survive in a lifeboat *until*

3. A chameleon changes color *when*

4. Mr. Devlin bought eight tickets *so that*

5. *Unless*

 you will be unhappy.

C. Rewrite each sentence, adding one or more adverb clauses. After each sentence, indicate the type of relationship between each adverb clause and what it modifies (*time, place, direction, cause, effect, condition, manner,* or *concession*).

Example The librarian told us to be quiet.
When we started laughing, the librarian told us to be quiet because we were disturbing people.
    [time; cause]

1. We were able to survive on the island.

2. To most children, cough medicine tastes better.

3. We toured the ancient ruins.

4. She attended Harvard Law School.

5. The nation was threatened.

D. Combine the main clauses in each of the following passages into one sentence by changing one main clause into an adverb clause.

Example We can escape from the tiger. Our situation is critical.

Although we can escape from the tiger, our situation is critical.
        OR:
Although our situation is critical, we can escape from the tiger.

1. We arrived after the game had started. We still saw the first touchdown.

2. Gina, Jody, and Susan gathered in front of the television set. They enjoyed watching *The A-Team*.

3. The lights flashed green. The two vehicles roared down the drag strip.

4. We put the food on the table. We sat down to eat.

5. I lost sight of the elf. He ran into a flower garden.

Exercise 2.3   Noun Clauses

A.   Underline each noun clause in the sentences below. In the space at the right, indicate whether the noun clause is used as a subject (S), object (O), complement (C), or appositive (AP).

Example Ed saw <u>that many people had already left</u>.   *O*

1.   Whoever reads the novels of Faulkner and Heming-   1. _____
     way will have a better understanding of people.
2.   When he was trying to break into the movies,   2. _____
     Marion Morrison decided that he would change his
     name to John Wayne.
3.   We will sell our house to whomever you suggest.   3. _____
4.   Their complaint that there was no heat was ig-   4. _____
     nored.
5.   At the end of the evening, he asked when they   5. _____
     might go out again.
6.   When he released the ball, he knew that he had   6. _____
     thrown a strike.
7.   In writing your term paper, you may draw material   7. _____
     from whatever has been written on the subject.
8.   When we leave is important.   8. _____
9.   His problem is that he is lazy.   9. _____
10. The ancient Egyptians believed that the pharaoh   10. _____
     was immortal.

B.   Complete each sentence by adding a noun clause (NC) where indicated.

Example (NC) should plan to eat dinner early.
*Whoever has a ticket to the concert should plan
to eat dinner early.*
1.   The awareness (NC) comforted him.

2.   Phil said (NC).

3.   (NC) should be ready to defend his or her actions.

4. To control the waiting crowd, the security officer ordered (NC).

5. The subject of Dr. Broyles' lecture was (NC).

C. In the following sentences, the noun clauses used as subjects and complements could be considered stilted or awkward. Revise the sentences to eliminate this possibility.

Examples Bedtime is when I enjoy reading.

I enjoy reading at bedtime.

That the building would collapse was certain.

It was certain that the building would collapse.

1. Whether or not the college should regulate dormitory hours was the issue.

2. A free and open society is what I believe in.

3. Unfortunately, in our society the successful individual usually is considered to be whoever makes the most money.

4. Failure to understand another person's point of view is why many arguments occur.

5. If they were able to make all of the arrangements, that they would call and report to us before we had to leave was understood.

D. Combine each of the following passages into one sentence by using noun clauses.

Example Everyone should drink a cup of hot tea before going to bed. Hot tea helps induce sleep.

Whoever drinks a cup of hot tea before going to bed will fall asleep easily.

1. Rafael will bring charcoal for the fire. He said so.

2. She hoped that his team would win. Her hope was realized.

3. Some of you want to increase the club dues. You should be ready to explain why the increase is necessary.

4. He has a major weakness. He is irresponsible.

5. He knew the kick would be good. He knew it as soon as his foot hit the ball.

6. People should exercise regularly. Regular exercise helps maintain a healthy body.

Review Exercise 2 **Subordinate Clauses and Connectives**

A. Develop each sentence below by adding the clauses indicated—adjective clause (ADJ C), adverb clause (ADV C), noun clause (NC)—to the main clauses (MC) given.

Example The heat was unbearable.
> Add: (ADJ C modifying *heat*) + (ADV C modifying MC)

Even though we were all strong and healthy, the heat in which we had to work was unbearable.

1. Brad returned from the bakery.
   Add: (ADJ C modifying *Brad*) + (ADV C modifying *returned*)

2. Her realization caused her to accept the job.
   Add: (NC as appositive of *realization*) + (ADJ C modifying *job*)

3. Bertha thought.
   Add: (NC as direct object of *thought*) + (ADV C modifying MC)

4. A hot dog tastes best.
   Add: (ADV C modifying *best*) + (ADJ C modifying *hot dog*)

5. The street was narrow.
   Add: (ADJ C modifying *street*) + (ADV C modifying *narrow*)

6. must remember
   Add: (NC as subject) + (NC as direct object of *remember*)

7. The creature was content.
   Add: (ADV C modifying *content*) + (ADV C modifying MC)

8.   Serve your guests mustangburgers.
Add: (ADV C modifying MC) + (ADJ C modifying *mustangburgers*)

B.   Write short, simple, complete sentences about the subjects indicated. Then combine the sentences together into one sentence
by changing one of them into an adjective or adverb clause.

Example a. a relative

My grandfather was a professional wrestler.

b. a hobby of the relative

He enjoyed doing needlepoint.

c. [Combine, using ADJ C]

My grandfather, who was a professional wrestler, enjoyed doing needlepoint.
    OR:

My grandfather, who enjoyed doing needlepoint, was a professional wrestler.

1.   a. something you like to eat

b. when you like to eat it

c. [Combine, using ADV C]

2.   a. a television program

b. the night the program is on

c. [Combine, using ADJ C]

3. a. a school

    b. the location of the school

    c. [Combine, using ADJ C]

4. a. something you dislike

    b. why you dislike it

    c. [Combine, using ADV C]

5. a. a person

    b. a characteristic of the person

    c. [Combine, using ADJ C]

6. a. a movie you enjoyed

    b. a movie you did not enjoy

    c. [Combine, using ADV C]

7. a. a city or town

    b. a trait of the city or town

    c. [Combine, using ADJ C]

8. a. a book you have read

   b. your opinion of the book

   c. [Combine, using ADV C]

9. a. an animal

   b. something good about the animal

   c. [Combine, using ADJ C]

10. a. an embarrassing moment

   b. when the moment occurred

   c. [Combine, using ADV C]

3

VERBALS

Verbals are verb forms that function as nouns or modifiers. Although verbals have many qualities of verbs (they can show tense, have voice, and take objects, for example), they cannot function as verbs in sentences and clauses. (See 6, Verbs.)

3.1 Using Verbal Phrases

The three types of verbals are *infinitives*, *participles*, and *gerunds*. When an object, complement, or modifier is added to a verbal, the result is a verbal phrase *(infinitive phrase, participial phrase,* or *gerund phrase)*.

Infinitives. An *infinitive* is the base form of the verb plus (usually) *to:*

Verb	Present infinitive	Past infinitive
run	(to) run	(to) have run
think	(to) think	(to) have thought
publish	(to) publish	(to) have published
talk	(to) talk	(to) have talked

An *infinitive phrase* consists of an infinitive plus an object, complement, or modifier:

> **to state his case** [infinitive *to state* plus object *his case*]

Infinitives and infinitive phrases can function as nouns, adjectives, and adverbs:

> **To run from danger** is cowardly. [noun, subject]
> I hope **to run in the marathon.** [noun, object]
> She did not have time **to think.** [adjective, modifies *time*]
> **To avoid the long lines,** we shopped early. [adverb modifies *early*]

Participles. A participle is a verb form, typically ending in *-ing* or *-ed*, which functions as an adjective.

44

Verb	Present participle	Past participle
run	running	having run
think	thinking	having thought
publish	publishing	having published
talk	talking	having talked

(NOTE: For irregular verbs such as *run* and *think*, past participle forms must be learned; see 6.2, Irregular Verbs and Auxiliaries.)

A *participial phrase* consists of a participle plus an object, complement, or modifier:

talking rapidly [participle *talking* plus adverbial modifier *rapidly*]

Participles and participial phrases are used as adjectives:

This one volume contains all of her **published** poems. [modifies *poems*]
Running for the train, she fell. [modifies *she*]

Gerunds.
A *gerund* is a verb form, usually ending in *-ing*, which functions as a noun.

Verb	Present gerund	Past gerund
run	running	having run
think	thinking	having thought
publish	publishing	having published
talk	talking	having talked

(NOTE: For irregular verbs such as run and think, the gerund form must be learned; see p. 98.)

A *gerund phrase* consists of a gerund plus an object, complement, or modifier:

talking rapidly [gerund *talking* plus adverbial modifier *rapidly*]

Gerunds and gerund phrases are used as nouns:

Running is good exercise. [subject]
I enjoy **thinking about the future.** [direct object]
She won a medal for **saving the child's life.** object of preposition]
My hobby is **running.** [complement]
She had only one form of exercise, **running.** [appositive]

HINT: Participles and gerunds are often identical in form; they can be distinguished by their functions. A participle or participial phrase functions as an adjective; a gerund or gerund phrase functions as a noun.

She liked the sound of **running** water. [participle, modifies *water*]
Running is excellent exercise. [gerund, serves as subject]
Hiking in the woods is exhilarating. [gerund phrase, serves as subject]
Hiking in the woods, we saw a bear. [participial phrase, modifies *we*]

3.2 Idiomatic Use Of Infinitives and Gerunds

An *idiom* is a customary way of speaking that has been used for a long time. Some idiomatic expressions are completed by infinitives *(honored to speak)*, others by gerunds *(the honor of speaking)*. In idiomatic expressions, one form cannot be substituted for the other *(honored of speaking* and *the honor to speak* are unidiomatic constructions). The following are some common idiomatic expressions; some require a gerund and some an infinitive.

Gerund	Infinitive
cannot help going	ready to go
capable of working	able to work
skilled in writing	the desire to write
the habit of giving	the tendency to give
successful in getting	manage to get
my object in paying	my obligation to pay

In some expressions either a gerund or an infinitive is idiomatic.

a way of wording it   a way to word it

Using *the* and *of* in Gerund Phrases.

Gerunds are awkward when they are preceded by *the* and followed by an *of* phrase. Eliminating *the* and *of* usually improves the sentence:

Awkward	In **the** painting **of** a picture, artists choose their colors with care.
Improved	In painting a picture, artists choose their colors with care.

To with Infinitives.

Most infinitive constructions are introduced by *to:*

They tried **to reach** town before evening.

With a small number of verbs *(do, dare, help, need,* and others) the use of *to* is optional:

Would you dare **visit** the haunted house?
Would you dare **to visit** the haunted house?

Split Infinitives.

Avoid placing an adverb between *to* and an infinitive if the result is awkward:

Awkward	He rose and began **to hesitantly speak.**
Improved	He rose and began **to speak hesitantly.**

In some instances, however, a split infinitive is the more natural form of expression. Attempting to avoid the split infinitive may be more awkward.

Unnatural	Only now am I beginning **really to understand** myself.
Better	Only now am I beginning **to really understand** myself.

HINT: Although whether to retain a split infinitive is often a judgmental matter, it may be helpful to say the sentence aloud twice, once with the infinitive split and once with it not split. If the split infinitive seems awkward or unnatural in speech it should be removed. Try saying aloud, for example, these sentences:

    a. I hope fully to appreciate you.
    b. I hope to appreciate fully you.
    c. I hope to fully appreciate you.
    d. I hope to appreciate you fully.

In *a, fully* seems to modify *hope* when it is supposed to be modifying *appreciate.* In *b,* the placement of *fully* makes the sentence awkward, although it is clear that *fully* modifies *appreciate.* In both *c* and *d,* the modification is clear and the awkwardness has disappeared; there is, however, a subtle difference in emphasis. In *c,* the placement of *fully* gives greater emphasis to *you* (that is, "I hope to fully appreciate *you* rather than anyone else"); in *d, fully* receives greater emphasis (that is, "I hope to appreciate you *fully* and completely and not just in part").

3.3 Misplaced Modifiers (MM)

A misplaced modifier occurs—

1.   When a modifier seems to refer to a word that it cannot sensibly modify, or
2.   When a modifier could refer to either of two elements in a sentence (this type is sometimes called a *squinting modifier*).

Misplaced modifiers can be corrected by placing the modifier immediately before or after the word it is supposed to modify or by rewriting the sentence completely (see also 9.5, Position of Adverbs):

Misplaced	**Nailed to the fence,** we saw several posters. [seems to modify *we*]
Revised	We saw several posters **nailed to the fence.**
Misplaced (squinting)	They saw **coming around the corner** a yellow Mercedes. [could modify *They* or *Mercedes*]
Revised	They saw a yellow Mercedes **coming around the corner.** **As they came around the corner,** they saw a yellow Mercedes
Misplaced	**Sitting on the hill,** they saw several lions. [seems to modify *they*]
Misplaced (squinting)	They saw **sitting on the hill** several lions. [could modify *they* or *lions*]
Revised	They saw several lions **sitting on the hill.** **While they were sitting on the hill,** they saw several lions.

3.4 Dangling Modifiers (DM)

A *dangling modifier* occurs when a modifier refers to a word that is implied but not actually stated in the sentence. To correct a dangling modifier, either supply the word modified or revise the sentence completely. (In revising sentences, it is often helpful to change a verbal phrase into a subordinate clause.)

Dangling	**After learning to dance,** my shyness disappeared.
Revised	**After learning to dance,** I lost my shyness
	After I learned to dance, I became less shy.

HINT: Dangling modifiers and misplaced modifiers often occur when a passive rather than an active verb is used. If the subject of a verb is performing the action, the verb is *active;* if the subject is being acted upon, the verb is *passive* (see also 6.3, Active and Passive Voice):

Dangling modifier	**Working quickly,** the tent was erected. [The verb is passive because the subject *tent* was being acted upon; *working quickly* is dangling because the actor is missing from the sentence—there is no indication of *who* was working quickly.]
Misplaced modifier	**Working quickly,** the tent was erected by Fred. [The verb is still passive. Note that merely including the actor, *Fred,* in the sentence does not make the sentence correct. *Working quickly* is misplaced because it seems to modify *tent.*]

To eliminate these problems, change the passive construction to active:

> Working quickly, Fred erected the tent. [The verb is active because the subject *Fred* is doing the action; there is no problem with the modifier because *working quickly* clearly modifies *Fred.*]

3.5 Absolute Modifiers

A distinction must be made between dangling modifiers and absolute modifiers. *Absolute modifiers* are verbal phrases that modify the statement as a whole. Because such modifiers are complete and independent (or *absolute*), they need not modify any particular word in the sentence:

> **Considering all possibilities,** it would be best to build a brick house.
> **To make a long story short,** I ended up with a broken leg.

Exercise 3.1   Using Verbal Phrases

A.   Underline each verbal and verbal phrase in the following sentences. Then indicate in the space at the right whether each one is an infinitive (INF), participle (PART), or gerund (GER).

Example <u>Taking</u> examinations has always been difficult for me.

GER

1.   In high school and college I enjoyed debating.   1. _____

2.   At a medieval carnival, one could be entertained by dancing bears and jugglers.   2. _____

3.   In the wild a male lion is able to eat up to seventy-five pounds of meat at one meal.   3. _____

4.   To know Charlie is to love him.   4. _____

5.   Jogging is more than walking at a fast pace.   5. _____

6.   They were surprised to see a duck crossing the street.   6. _____

7.   Dr. Saunders attempted to discover the relationship between environment and social behavior.   7. _____

8.   When I first started working at the hardware store, I was given a huge box of assorted screws to sort into piles.   8. _____

B.   Add the verbals and verbal phrases indicated in the following sentences—gerund (GER), gerund phrase (GER P), infinitive (INF), infinitive phrase (INF P), participle (PART), or participial phrase (PART P).

Example Helen hoped (INF P).

Helen hoped to return before morning.

(GER) is one of my favorite activities.

Jogging is one of my favorite activities.

1. (INF) is (INF).

2. The (PART) villain tried (INF P).

3. (GER) made her angry.

4. (PART P), the balloon suddenly began (INF P).

5. (GER P) changed my life because I learned (INF P).

6. (PART P) and (PART P), we soon were able (INF P).

7. (PART P), the salesclerk asked Dave (INF P).

C. In each of the following items, combine the two sentences together into one sentence which begins with an infinitive, a participle, or a gerund.

Example I like to swim. It is one of my real pleasures.

To swim is one of my real pleasures.

The plumber cleaned the clogged drain. He worked all morhing.

Working all morning, the plumber cleaned the clogged drain.

1. Phideaux, my foxhound, has only one fault. He likes to chew on slippers.

2. Carl loves to eat. It is one of his weaknesses.

3. I spent three years in jail. It was the most beneficial thing that ever happened to me.

4. Maria ran from bedroom to bedroom. She was looking for a place to hide.

5. People should follow their dreams. It will help them fulfill their destiny.

6. The birthrate has been declining steadily for the past eight years. That supports my argument.

7. He turned the crank vigorously. He managed to start the engine.

8. Manuel was selected the most fashionable man on campus. He celebrated by purchasing a new suede jacket.

Exercise 3.2 Idiomatic Use of Infinitives and Gerunds

A. In each sentence indicate the proper idiomatic expression by crossing out the unidiomatic expression.

Example Because of his great strength, he is (capable to work, capable of working) long hours in the fields.

1. In Dickens' *A Christmas Carol,* Scrooge develops (the habit of giving, the habit to give) both money and affection to others.

2. Ever since she worked on the school newspaper, Shirley has had (the desire of writing, the desire to write).

3. If you can give me a little more time, I will fulfill (my obligation of paying, my obligation to pay) back every cent I borrowed.

4. Although few people will recognize your contribution, you will at least have the (satisfaction of doing, satisfaction to do) a job that is vitally important.

5. When you see your sister, please do not (neglect saying, neglect to say) that I send her my warmest regards.

6. Professor Sweeney has (the tendency to give, the tendency of giving) surprise quizzes.

B. Rewrite each sentence, replacing unidiomatic expressions with idiomatic ones, eliminating *the* and *of* in gerund phrases, and correcting awkward split infinitives.

Example In the developing of a plan of action, we must first consider the end we hope of achieving.

In developing a plan of action, we must first consider the end we hope to achieve.

1. The chairperson announced that she would not attempt to unilaterally make the decision.

2. The reversing of the decision took great courage.

52

3. The credit for the initiating of the petition must go to Helen who was the first in recognizing the problem.

4. Because I was skilled to operate a computer, I had several job opportunities when I graduated from college.

5. He will need help in the creating of an atmosphere conducive to learning.

6. The obtaining of a second chance persuaded me to really try to succeed.

7. The personnel officer told him that with his education and experience in the repairing of engines, he ought to quickly be promoted.

8. Because of the need to decisively act, she was persuaded in saying that the breaking of the rules would result in immediate suspension.

Exercise 3.3 Misplaced Modifiers

A. In the space at the right, indicate whether each sentence is correct (C) or contains a misplaced modifier (MM). Then revise each incorrect sentence to eliminate the misplaced modifier.

Example Flashing in the dark sky, we saw the lightning.　　　*MM*

We saw the lightning flashing in the dark sky.

1. A woman should have a career while married for several reasons.　　1. _____

2. She attacked the spider taking the feather duster hanging from the ceiling.　　2. _____

3. Passing through town, Ralph stopped to check the oil.　　3. _____

4. The painting was admired by my uncle hanging in the den.　　4. _____

5. We saw strolling in the park a couple obviously in love.　　5. _____

6. We discovered lying in the corner a pile of old letters at the bottom of a trunk.　　6. _____

7. We tried to keep the boat from sinking because of the circling shark bailing frantically.　　7. _____

54

8. They saw observing closely a small chipmunk.   8. _____

9. To find the lost explorers, the dense jungle was   9. _____
searched by the relief party.

10. The dog disturbed the baby barking in the night.   10. _____

B. Add a main clause to each of the following modifiers; be sure that the
resulting sentences contain no misplaced modifiers.

Example standing at the top of the hill
*standing at the top of the hill we could see smoke
rising in the distance.*

1. hopping on one foot

2. to excel in the field of nuclear physics

3. circling slowly

4. spilling oil all over the pavement

5. turning quickly

C. Provide the type of modifier indicated for each sentence; be sure to
avoid misplaced modifiers.

Example The tiger jumped from the rock.
(Add VERBAL PHRASE modifying *tiger*)

*Hearing the shot, the tiger jumped from
the rock.*

1. The boss gave Wilma a raise.
   (Add VERBAL PHRASE modifying *boss*)

2. We explained to the officer that it had been a prank.
   (Add PARTICIPLE modifying *officer*)

3. The zebra ran from the smoke.
   (Add VERBAL PHRASE modifying *smoke*)

4. The government gave the people free medical care.
   (Add VERBAL PHRASE modifying *government*)

   (Add VERBAL PHRASE modifying *people*)

Exercise *3.4*   Dangling Modifiers

A.   In the space at the right, indicate whether each sentence is correct (C) or contains a dangling modifier (DM). Then revise each incorrect sentence to eliminate the dangling modifier.

Example Walking over the bridge, a car almost struck us.   *DM*

Walking over the bridge, we were almost struck by a car.

1. Driving through the Everglades, a flamingo was seen.

   1. _____

2. To reach the broadest possible audience, we advertised in magazines and newspapers and on radio and television.

   2. _____

3. Listening to WXYZ, the "Top Forty" rock hits were heard.

   3. _____

4. When sleeping in the tent, his dreams terrified him.

   4. _____

5. To obtain a place on the Olympic team, practice must be intensive.

   5. _____

6. Dialing the telephone frantically, the police were called.

   6. _____

7. To become a professional musician, dedication is necessary.

   7. _____

8. To describe a Van Gogh painting, colors must be mentioned.

   8. _____

9. Gliding through the sky, the parachutist was seen.   9. _____

10. Cautiously peering around the corner, a bullet   10. _____
    struck just above the officer's head.

B. Add a main clause to each of the following modifiers; be sure that the
resulting sentences contain no dangling modifiers or misplaced
modifiers.

Example Sliding into third base,

the runner beat the throw.

1. Watching *The Tonight Show,*

2. To impress a member of the opposite sex,

3. To destroy a werewolf,

4. Smelling a foul stench,

5. Growling deep in its throat,

C. Provide the type of modifier indicated for each sentence—infinitive
phrase (INF P) or participal phrase (PART P); be sure to avoid dangling
modifiers and misplaced modifiers.

Example (PART P) *Working all day,*
            he became exhausted.

1. (PART P)
            her parents gave her a new sports car.

2. (INF P)
            a politician must project a favorable image.

58

3. (PART P)

the Loch Ness monster was sighted.

4. (PART P)

the driver stopped the bus suddenly.

5. (INF P)

the promoter sold more tickets than there were seats.

Review Exercise 3   Verbals

A. Revise each sentence to eliminate dangling and misplaced modifiers, unidiomatic expressions, *the* and *of* in gerund phrases, and awkward split infinitives. If a sentence is correct, do not revise it. (Be careful not to confuse the absolute modifiers and dangling modifiers.)

1. Attempting to completely live up to his nickname, "the Sun King," the court of Louis XIV was one of artistic and cultural splendor.

2. The receiving of a box of paints initiated in me the desire of being an artist.

3. The baby was fed by his father in a highchair.

4. To go to college, two jobs were held so that I would be able to completely pay for my education.

5. To tell the truth, the reading of classical literature does not appeal to me.

6. In a large cage swinging on a rope, we saw a gorilla.

7. Having gotten into the habit to eat a large breakfast, oversleeping this morning was particularly annoying.

8. In a wooden cask, lying deep in the ground, Captain Pegley was able to completely hide his treasure.

9.   Everything considered, our party last night was successful to get our
     new neighbors acquainted with the other people in the complex.

10. Having been a Boy Scout, the tying of knots comes easily to me now.

11. Swinging on a chain, the locket attracted our attention.

12. To open this bottle, the cover should be pressed down and turned to
     the right.

13. Keeping a diary, a book would be written when after the war was over I
     returned.

14. Speaking out boldly, his point of view differed from that of the majority.

15. The guard sitting in the cell saw the prisoner.

B. Combine the ideas expressed into a sentence, paying particular attention
     to effective modification.

Example after mowing the lawn
        a cold drink tastes good

After mowing the lawn, I enjoy a cold drink.

OR:

*A cold drink tastes good to me after I have
mowed the lawn.*

1. while tuning up the engine
   my clothes got covered with grease

2. to please his mother
   medical school was necessary

3. after a hard day at the office
   the ride home was frustrating
   it did nothing to relieve Ramid's frustration

4. scratching on the door
   my grandmother heard the cat

5. while stopped for a traffic light
   a shaggy dog leaped on the hood

C. Write five sentences which contain clear and correct modification. Use each of the models below at least once.

Models Slipping on the ice, the coach fell on his dignity.

To take excellent photographs, you must use fresh film.

While dealing the cards, Juana noticed that everyone had become silent.

1.

2.

3.

4.

5.

D. Rewrite the following passage to eliminate modification errors, unidiomatic expressions, *the* and *of* in gerund phrases, and awkward split infinitives. You may combine sentences or move phrases from one sentence to another, if it would improve the sentences. And you may revise the paragraphs to improve them.

(1) Traveling in Transylvania, the opportunity arose to visit what I thought was an abandoned castle. (2) Covered with wilted vines, I saw the crumbling walls. (3) The opening of the thick wooden door made the hinges screech in protest. (4) After I was able of opening the door, a musky odor struck my face coming from inside the castle. (5) Stepping inside, cobwebs and dust covered the walls, ceiling, and floor of a long, dark corridor. (6) One small window I saw lighting the hall.

(7) Although I was not eager of going down the hall, I could not help to go. (8) From the floor, lying to one side of the door, I picked up an ancient lantern, proceeding down the corridor. (9) As I slowly made my way, I was able to carefully glance to the right and left. (10) On the walls, I discovered several ancient portraits. (11) Depicting mysterious evil beings, I shuddered.

(12) Approaching the end of the corridor, a heavy door of black metal stood directly in front of me, having a large iron ring for a handle. (13) Grasping the ring, I was successful to get the door to swing open. (14) The clasping of the iron ring made my flesh crawl. (15) Suddenly a blur flew by my head coming from inside the chamber. (16) Startled, the lantern flew from my hand. (17) Shaking, I managed to eventually strike a match, in picking up the lantern, and in getting it going again. (18) Looking apprehensively around, nothing was seen or heard.

(19) Carefully edging past the door and into the chamber, the lantern was able to dimly illuminate the small, windowless room. (20) Covering the walls, hanging on long metal spikes, I perceived grinning human skulls. (21) The stone floor was bare except for a long object in the center. (22) Although I had a strong desire of leaving, I moved closer and discovered that the object was a coffin made of highly polished dark wood. (23) The opening of the cover revealed a lining of crimson velvet which seemed to faintly have

in it an imprint of a body. **(24)** Moving to read the nameplate at the head of the coffin, a noise was heard.

(25) Dropping the lantern, I rushed blindly from the chamber and ran up the corridor. **(26)** As I neared the open door of the castle, I was horrified in hearing a rush of wings behind me. **(27)** Glancing over my shoulder, a large bat was approaching. **(28)** Stumbling outside, the door was slammed and then a soft thud was heard. **(29)** Incapable to speak, I left the castle as fast as my trembling legs would carry me. **(30)** Considering what could have happened, my visit to the abandoned castle turned out to have been an exciting moment which I lived to tell about.

4

COMMON SENTENCE ERRORS

Four kinds of serious sentence errors commonly occur: fragmentary sentences, comma splices, run-on sentences, and mixed constructions.

4.1 Sentence Fragments (FRAG)

A *sentence fragment* occurs—

1. When a group of words which is not a clause is left to function as a complete sentence:

    I enjoy reading mystery stories. **By authors such as Rex Stout, Emma Lathen, and Ellery Queen.** [FRAG, not a clause]

2. When a subordinate clause is left to stand as a complete sentence:

    I enjoy reading mystery stories. **Because I find them relaxing.** [FRAG, subordinate clause standing alone]

A sentence fragment can be corrected—

1. By joining it to another sentence:

    I enjoy reading mystery stories by authors such as Rex Stout, Emma Lathen, and Ellery Queen.

2. By making it into a complete sentence:

    I enjoy reading mystery stories. I find them relaxing.

3. By rewriting the passage:

    I find reading mystery stories to be enjoyable and relaxing.

4.2 Comma Splices (CS)

A *comma splice* occurs when two or more main (independent) clauses are linked by a comma, but no coordinating conjunction (*and, but, or, for, nor, so, yet*) is used:

> The dog heard a noise, he barked. [CS, no word links clauses]
> The dog heard a noise, therefore he barked. [CS, conjunctive adverb links clauses]

A comma fault can be corrected—

1. By making it into two sentences:

> The dog heard a noise. He barked.

2. By using a semicolon to link the clauses.

> The dog heard a noise; he barked.

3. By adding a coordinating conjunction:

> The dog heard a noise, **so** he barked.

4. By rewriting the passage:

> The dog barked when he heard a noise.

4.3 Run-On Sentences (RO)

A *run-on sentence* occurs when two or more main clauses are joined with no coordinating conjunction and no punctuation between them.

> He rushed to the dock the ship had sailed. [RO, no word links clauses]
> He rushed to the dock however the ship had sailed. [RO, conjunctive adverb links clauses]

A run-on sentence can be corrected in the same ways as a comma fault:

> He rushed to the dock. The ship had sailed. [two sentences]
> He rushed to the dock; the ship had sailed. [semicolon added]
> He rushed to the dock, **but** the ship had sailed. [conjunction added]
> Although he rushed to the dock, the ship had sailed before he arrived. [passage rewritten]

4.4 Mixed Constructions (MIX)

A *mixed construction* occurs when two types of standard sentences are combined into one sentence, or when independent and dependent clauses are joined incorrectly.

She tried to sneak into the house, but when she encountered her father, a real problem. (MIX, inappropriately combines independent and subordinate clauses with *but,* a coordinating conjunction used to join two independent clauses together]

Take two examination books and will you put your name on the cover of each one? [MIX, shifts from command to question]

A mixed construction can be corrected only by rewriting the passage:

Take two examination books and put your name on the cover of each one. [both clauses are commands]

She tried to sneak into the house, but when she encountered her father, she had a real problem. [two independent clauses appropriately linked by *but]*

Although she tried to sneak into the house, she encountered her father. [dependent and independent clauses appropriately linked together]

Exercise *4.1*   Sentence Fragments

A. Indicate whether each passage contains a sentence fragment (FRAG) or is correct (C) by writing FRAG or C in the space at the right. Then revise each sentence fragment using a method for correction that seems most appropriate.

> **Example** Colorful flowers filled the garden. Such as mari-
> golds, zinnias, and mums.

FRAG

Such colorful flowers as marigolds, zinnias, and mums filled the garden.

1. A number of strange animals exist. Animals such as aardvarks, armadillos, and Tasmanian devils.

   1. _____

2. When Congress adjourns for the holidays, the senator will come home.

   2. _____

3. The pioneers who crossed the continent in covered wagons. The West was settled.

   3. _____

4. His rifle filled with lead bullets was useless. Because werewolves can be killed only with silver bullets.

   4. _____

5. The kangaroo, like the opossum, carries its young in a pouch. Both animals are mammals.

   5. _____

6. We did not go swimming. The reason being that the water was too cold.

   6. _____

7. He spoke with bitterness of his experience. Adding a note of cynicism to the discussion.

7. _____

8. The room is intimate. An intimacy that is enhanced by subdued lighting.

8. _____

9. He has worked hard since he entered college. He has made the Dean's List every semester.

9. _____

10. Our encounter group will be successful if one thing happens. That being for each woman to see herself as she really is.

10. _____

B. Indicate whether each sentence is fragmentary (FRAG) or correct (C) by writing FRAG or C in the space at the right. Then revise the passage, correcting each fragmentary sentence. In your revision, try to combine some of the sentences to produce a smoothly written paragraph.

(1) Autumn is my favorite season of the year. (2) The reason being the sports. (3) Which are played in autumn. (4) Sports such as football and soccer which match one time of highly skilled athletes against another. (5) Probably no other sport can match in excitement a football game. (6) With brass bands, cheering fans, and brave participants. (7) Particularly if the game is an evenly fought contest. (8) the outcome being in doubt until the final gun. (9) That's why I prefer autumn. (10) As my favorite season.

1. _____

2. _____

3. _____

4. _____

5. _____

6. _____

7. _____

8. _____

9. _____

10. _____

C. Rewrite each of the following passages in which sentence fragments appear. In your revisions, use a variety of corrective methods, including combining sentences together. If a passage is correct, do not rewrite it.

Example Although she is conceited. Alicia is the best singer in the group.

Although she is conceited, Alicia is the best singer in the group.

1. We moved to the country. To get away from the noise in the city and the congested highways. And to avoid the high taxes. We were glad we did.

2. Poland is a country. Which is about the size of New Mexico. Lying between the Carpathian Mountains and the Baltic Sea.

3. When they reached the door, she turned and looked at him. Her gaze causing him to stammer.

4. Over the years, a number of inventions critical to the development of humanity have been created. For example, the wheel, the telescope, and the internal combustion engine.

5. She burst through the open doorway. Not caring that she knocked a woman down. She excused her actions to herself. Being in a hurry.

Exercise *4.2/4.3* Comma Splices and Run-On Sentences

A. Indicate whether each sentence contains a comma splice (CS) or is correct (C) by writing CS or C in the space at the right. Then correct each
comma splice, using the method of correction that seems appropriate. In
revising the sentences, correct the comma splices by using a variety of
methods (making two sentences, using a semicolon to link the clauses,
adding a coordinating conjunction, or rewriting the passage by using a
subordinate clause or an appositive.

Example At the battle of Shiloh more than 13,000 men were   _CS_
killed fighting for the Union, more than 10,000 were
killed fighting for the Confederacy.

*At the battle of Shiloh, more than
13,000 men were killed fighting for the Union;
more than 10,000 were killed fighting for the
Confederacy.*

1. The Cincinnati Red Stockings were the first profes-   1. _____
sional baseball team, in 1870 they won 130 games in
a row.

2. Only an informed electorate can vote intelligently,   2. _____
therefore each citizen should keep informed.

3. When supply increases and demand decreases,   3. _____
prices drop, when supply decreases and demand
increases, prices rise.

4. Winter often seems endless, however spring even-   4. _____
tually arrives.

5. Buy Foam Flakes for your wash, there are no flakes   5. _____
like Foam.

6. Reducing the speed limit has helped conserve gaso- 6. _____
line, it has also decreased highway fatalities.

7. The Declaration of Independence was signed on 7. _____
July 4, 1776, a new nation was born.

8. Ron broke his arm, but he still managed to take the 8. _____
examination.

9. It was the night before Christmas, the children 9. _____
were excited.

10. It rained for several hours, the game was postponed. 10. _____

B. Indicate whether each sentence is a run-on sentence (RO) or is correct (C)
by writing RO or C in the space at the right. Then correct each run-on
sentence, using the method for correction that seems appropriate. In
revising the sentences, correct the run-ons by using a variety of methods
(making two sentences, using a semicolon to link the clauses, adding a
coordinating conjunction, or rewriting the passage by using a subordinate clause or an appositive.

Example A plant is a living thing it responds to stimuli. _____*FS*_____

A plant is a living thing which responds to stimuli.

1. The Anchovy Alligator is a popular rock group it 1. _____
has sold over ten million records.

2. When I arrived at the box office, the tickets had all   2. _____
   been sold the next time I will arrive earlier.

3. The Civil War ended over one hundred years ago   3. _____
   although some people seem to be still fighting it.

4. *West Side Story* is an excellent musical it is based on   4. _____
   Romeo and Juliet.

5. Before we go camping, Mr. Stecher will show us   5. _____
   how to pitch a tent he used to be in the Boy
   Scouts.

6. I thought you were in Detroit consequently I was   6. _____
   surprised when I saw you in Dallas.

7. At the end of the business meeting, Mr. Broyles   7. _____
   moved to adjourn and Mr. Sherwin seconded the
   motion.

8. The boy does not sketch very well if he wants to   8. _____
   learn he will have to practice.

9. The fishing boat was surrounded by sea gulls as it   9. _____
   entered the harbor they were after scraps of fish.

10. I plan to tour the country on my motorcycle how-   10. _____
    ever I need a companion.

NAME . . . .   SCORE . . . .

C. Indicate whether each sentence contains a comma splice (CS), is a run-on sentence (RO), is a fragment (FRAG), or is correct (C) by writing CS, RO, or C in the space at the right. Then revise the passage to correct all comma splices and run-on sentences. Try to use a variety of methods in your revision, including combining sentences.

(1) One of the most popular novels of all time is *Gone With the Wind* by Margaret Mitchell, it was originally titled *Tomorrow Is Another Day*. **(2)** It was subtitled *A Story of the Old South* it was first published in 1936. **(3)** After selling over one million copies in its first year, it won the Pulitzer Prize for Fiction in 1937 soon it was made into a motion picture. **(4)** The picture starring Vivian Leigh and Clark Gable. **(5)** The world premiere was held in Atlanta. (6) The date December 15, 1939, which the Governor of Georgia declared a state holiday. **(7)** The movie was directed by George Cukor it was over three and one-half hours long. **(8)** It won ten Academy Awards, included in its honors were Oscars for Best Picture, Best Actress, and Best Supporting Actress. **(9)** It was later shown on television the year was 1976. **(10)** Generations of people have seen the film either in the theater or on television however, the novel still sells well.

1. _____
2. _____
3. _____
4. _____
5. _____
6. _____
7. _____
8. _____
9. _____
10. _____

Exercise *4.4* **Mixed Constructions**

A. Indicate whether each sentence is correct (C) or contains a mixed construction (MIX) by writing C or MIX in the space at the right. Then rewrite each incorrect sentence to eliminate the mixed construction.

Example The population is increasing and will we be able to feed the growing numbers?   *MIX*

Will we be able to feed the increasing population?

1. Clean your room and I want you to mow the lawn.   1. _____

2. The beach is enjoyable and when the tide is high.   2. _____

3. I am moving, and I have packed my books in a large box which is difficult to carry.   3. _____

4. Would the fire trap me or I would be saved.   4. _____

5. She wondered if she would get a raise and because she worked hard.   5. _____

B. Indicate whether each sentence in the passage is correct (C) or contains a mixed construction (MIX) by writing C or MIX in the space at the right. Then rewrite the passage to eliminate all mixed constructions.

(1) Trying out for a play is a harrowing experience. **(2)** First the decision must be made should you try out? **(3)** Then you need to choose a part, you must practice speeches from the play basing your selections on the character you wish to portray. **(4)** After you practice, tryout day arrives and although you are sure you are not

1. _____

2. _____

3. _____

4. _____

76

ready. **(5)** You are fourth in line, and you are sure you will never get the part. **(6)** When your name is called, and you walk nervously to the center of the stage. **(7)** Deliver your lines in a raspy, halting manner, and you move off the stage. **(8)** The next candidate comes forward wondering how could you make such a fool of yourself?

5. _____

6. _____

7. _____

8. _____

Review Exercise 4   Common Sentence Errors

A.   In the space at the right, indicate whether each passage is correct (C) or contains a sentence fragment (FRAG), comma splice (CS), run-on sentence (RO), or mixed construction (MIX). Then revise each incorrect passage, using a variety of methods to eliminate the errors.

1.   The electoral process is basically simple. When an election is held, the person who receives the greatest number of votes.

1.   _____

2.   The whale population has been hunted almost to extinction, if nations do not band together and stop the slaughter of whales, those noble sea mammals will cease to exist.

2.   _____

3.   My father had a large number of friends and acquaintances. He was a fun-loving man and who enjoyed making people laugh.

3.   _____

4.   We spent our vacation in an isolated spot. The cabin was located deep in the woods it was very difficult to find.

4.   _____

5.   We were reluctant to attend the convention. The reason for our reluctance being that we were not sure we would be welcome.

5.   _____

6.   Trying to repair the roof, Carol slipped and fell, breaking her leg in two places. She was in a cast for six weeks.

6.   _____

7. Coming down the stretch, his horse was bumped. The jockey lodged a protest, however he was unable to convince the stewards that his mount had been fouled.

7. _____

8. Such laws as we choose to pass. Everyone will have to obey them.

8. _____

9. Although Delaware was one of the smallest colonies, it was the first to ratify the Constitution. The other twelve colonies followed soon after.

9. _____

10. We had been climbing since early morning. Late in the afternoon we reached the top of the mountain, we looked down into the valley below.

10. _____

11. Although he had a criminal record, he was hired. But he was caught with his hand in the money drawer consequently he was fired.

11. _____

12. History has much to teach us. By studying history carefully, we hope to apply the lessons of the past to the present and the future.

12. _____

13. Will you have a hamburger and the french fries are good. I can also recommend the shakes.

13. _____

14. The cowboy was thrown from his horse he suffered three broken ribs. But he was riding again the next day.

14. _____

15. The rocket ships of the future will carry men and women with their powerful engines to the distant planets, they will allow us to explore other galaxies. We may even find other forms of life.

15. _____

B. Rewrite the following paragraph, eliminating all sentence fragments, comma splices, run-on sentences, and mixed constructions. In your revision, use a variety of corrective methods, including combining sentences.

(1) Commuting to school can be a nerve-wracking experience for three reasons, first there is the car itself. **(2)** Will it start will it hold together or fall apart on the trip. **(3)** Or will it run out of gas on the way to school, then there is the commuting trip itself. **(4)** Which is often frightening, because dangerous intersections lie in wait. **(5)** Herds of cars clog the roads a series of obstacles in the form of traffic lights, stop signs pedestrians, dogs. **(6)** Finally, with the car still whole, and the obstacles overcome. **(7)** There is the worst part of commuting to face finding a parking space.

C.   Rewrite the following paragraph, correcting all common sentence errors. You should, where appropriate, combine sentences to eliminate errors.

(1) Although it is classified as a mammal. (2) The duckbilled platypus is an unusual creature, it appears to have been put together from the leftover parts of other animals. (3) It seems to be part mammal and part reptile it also seems to be part aquatic bird. (4) It has webbed forepaws and partially webbed hind ones, its snout is shaped like the bill of a duck its tail is similar to that of a beaver, it lays eggs like a reptile, but it suckles its young like a mammal. (5) Like cold-blooded reptiles the platypus is sensitive to changes in environmental temperature, however like warm-blooded mammals it can produce a limited amount of body heat. (6) It can spend nearly five minutes submerged under water, it hunts by day along the bottoms of streams and lakes, it uses its snout to root out larvae, worms, and crustaceans. (8) Although it eats most of its catch immediately. (9) It does store some in cheek pouches. (10) It enjoys snacking when it returns to its underground den for the night. (11) This strange mammal was once plentiful but trappers seriously depleted the population therefore, the platypus is now protected by strict laws however it is still in danger of being extinct. (12) For it has a low rate of reproduction. (13) Man also has encroached on its natural habitat. (14) If conservation efforts work though, the duckbilled platypus will survive.

5

AGREEMENT OF
SUBJECT AND VERB

Verbs should agree in number with their subjects. A singular subject requires a singular verb; a plural subject requires a plural verb. Problems in subject-verb agreement are most likely to occur when verbs have compound subjects, when collective nouns are subjects, and when other nouns or pronouns come between the subject and the verb.

5.1 Verbs with Compound Subjects

A *compound subject* consists of two or more words, phrases, or clauses joined by *and, or, nor.*

Subjects Joined by *and* usually take plural verbs:

> **South Carolina, Georgia,** and **Mississipi** [compound subject] **were** [plural verb] among the first states to secede from the Union.

However, when the words of a compound subject form a unit or refer to the same person, place, or thing, the verb is usually singular:

> John's closest **friend** and constant **companion** [compound subject] **was** [singular verb] Harry. [*friend* and *companion* both refer to Harry]

Subjects Joined by *or, nor* (or by *either . . . or, neither . . . nor*) sometimes take singular verbs and sometimes plural verbs.

1. When both subjects are singular, the verb usually is singular:

> Either **Ralph** or **Tom is** [singular] to blame.

2. When both subjects are plural, the verb is plural:

> No **children** or **pets are** [plural] allowed.

3. When one subject is singular and the other plural, the verb usually agrees with the subject nearer the verb:

The **teachers** or the **principal is** [singular] responsible.
The **principal** or the **teachers are** [plural] responsible.

4. When the subjects are pronouns in different persons, the verb agrees with the nearer subject:

Neither **you** nor **he is** liable for the damage.

In some cases making the verb agree with the nearer pronoun creates an awkward or unnatural construction. Therefore, it is usually acceptable to use a plural verb with *I*.

Awkward   Neither **you** nor **I am** liable for the damage.
Acceptable   Neither **you** nor **I are** liable for the damage.

HINT: Such awkwardness with pronouns can usually be avoided by substituting a different subject for the compound subject.

Better   **Neither** of us **is** liable for the damage.

Singular Subjects Followed by *as well as* (or *together with, along with, in addition to*) usually take singular verbs:

The **bald eagle as well as the whale is** in danger of extinction.

However, when the addition is intended to form a compound subject, a plural verb is often used:

The **development** of fast forms of transportation **along with** the **improvement** of communication techniques **have** made the world smaller.
The **bald eagle and** the **whale are** in danger of extinction.

5.2 Verbs with Collective Nouns as Subjects

A *collective noun* is a word which refers to a group but is singular in form. Among the common collective nouns are these words: *army, audience, choir, committee, crowd, faculty, gang, group, government, jury, mob, orchestra, public, team.* Verbs and pronouns used with collective nouns are either singular or plural, depending upon the meaning of the group word.

When Referring to the Group as a Unit collective nouns take singular verbs:

The **army is** ready to defend the country.
The **orchestra is** going to perform without an intermission.

When Referring to Individuals in a Group collective nouns take plural verbs:

> The **jury are** debating the verdict.

HINT: Since such sentences sometimes sound unnatural, it is often better to substitute a clearly plural subject:

> The **members** of the jury **are** debating the verdict.

Thus agreement with collective nouns often depends on the context, since some collective nouns may be either singular or plural:

> The **public** [whole group] **is** my concern.
> The **public** [individual members] **are** asked to complete the questionnaire.

Data may be either singular or plural, depending upon its use. (The singular form *datum* is rarely used.)

> Do not form a conclusion until the **data** [individual facts] **have been gathered.**
> That **data** [the whole body of facts] **is** conclusive.

The number (a unit) takes a singular verb; *a number* (individual items) takes a plural verb.

> **The number** of states **has** increased to fifty.
> **A number** of states **have** passed bottle return laws.

Verbs with Measurements and Figures. Words signifying quantity or extent *(dollars, miles, days, pounds)* take singular verbs when the amount is considered as a unit.

> **Three days is** a long time to wait.
> **Three cups** of milk **is** all the recipe requires.

But a plural verb is used when the amount is considered as a number of individual units:

> The next **three days are** all we have for practice.
> **Three cups** of milk **are** left in the bottle.

Words Ending in *-ics*. Words ending in *-ics* that refer to a science, art, or body of knowledge *(economics, physics, civics)* generally take singular verbs:

> **Economics is** my major field.

Words ending in *-ics* that refer to activities or qualities *(athletics, acrobatics)* usually take plural verbs:

> The clown's **acrobatics were** popular with the crowd.

Some words ending in *-ics* (*ethics, politics*) may have either a singular or a plural meaning:

> **Ethics** [a body of knowledge] **is** a branch of philosophy.
> His **ethics** [qualities or activities] **were** deplorable.

5.3 Blind Agreement

Errors in subject-verb agreement frequently occur when the verb is made to agree with a nearby noun or pronoun rather than with its actual subject. This error, called *blind agreement*, usually occurs in the following situations.

Plural Nouns Between Subject and Verb. When a singular subject is followed by a phrase or clause containing plural nouns, the verb is still singular:

Incorrect	If the crime rate cannot be controlled, a **city** such as Boston, Detroit, and others **are** in trouble. [verb agrees with *others*]
Correct	If the crime rate cannot be controlled, a **city** such as Boston, Detroit, and others **is** in trouble. [verb agrees with *city*]

one of those who (or *one of those that*) are plural and take a plural verb:

> *Midnight Cowboy* is **one of those** movies **that appear** infrequently.

However, *the only one of those who* takes a singular verb:

> Scott is **the only one of those** players **who is** in condition.

Verb and Complement. A verb agrees with its subject, not with its complement or object:

> The **tourists were** the biggest problem.
> The biggest **problem was** the tourists.

Inverted Word Order. When the word order is inverted, the verb must still agree with its subject:

> Pressed between the pages **was** a faded **rose.**

Sentences Beginning *there is, there are.* When a sentence begins with an introductory *there*, the number of the verb is determined by the subject which follows the verb:

> **There are** several **reasons** for our action.
> **There is** a **reason** for our action.

In this construction, a singular verb is often used before a compound subject:

There is food and shelter for everyone.

HINT: When you use the contraction *there's*, be particularly careful to avoid an error in agreement.

Incorrect	**There's** many **ways** to solve this problem. *[there's* is singular; *ways* is plural]
Correct	**There are** many **ways** to solve this problem.

Subjects *series, portion, part, type* usually take singular verbs:

A **series** of lectures on investments **was** held last month.

Exercise 5.1   Verbs with Compound Subjects

In each sentence, select the verb that agrees with the subject.

Example Either a cat or a dog (make, makes) a good pet.   *makes*

1. In discussing physical laws, one should note that friction and gravity (works, work) together.   1. _____

2. I do not know if the scenery or the climate (attracts, attract) the most tourists.   2. _____

3. Neither Paula nor I (am, is, are) prepared to discuss the bond issue.   3. _____

4. The high cost of supplies as well as the increase in the cost of labor (prevents, prevent) us from building another factory.   4. _____

5. Neither the guru nor his followers (has, have) caused any disruptions on campus.   5. _____

B. For each sentence provide a verb (v)that agrees with the subject.

Example The secretary of defense, the secretary of state, and the secretary of agriculture (v) among the members of the Cabinet.   *are*

1. Neither cattle barons nor disease (v) able to drive the homesteaders from their land.   1. _____

2. (v) the diplomats and other dignitaries been as-signed seats in a special section?   2. _____

3. When the vagabond appeared, a hue and cry (v) raised.   3. _____

4. One large filing cabinet or two smaller ones (v) needed for our personnel files.   4. _____

5. Neither of you (v)qualified for a promotion at this time.   5. _____

Exercise 5.2   Verbs with Collective Nouns as Subjects

A.   In each sentence, select the verb that agrees with the subject.

Example A number of stores (has, have) summer sales.   _____*have*_____

1.   The public (is, are) asked to refrain from smoking   1. _____
     in the lecture hall.

2.   The census reports that the average American   2. _____
     family (is, are) composed of two adults and two
     children.

3.   Seven years (has, have) passed since we moved to   3. _____
     Circleville.

4.   A number of automobile owners (has, have) re-   4. _____
     placed their large, expensive vehicles with small,
     economical ones.

5.   Genetics (is, are) becoming increasingly important   5. _____
     in biological research.

6.   Once the data (has, have) been analyzed, the popu-   6. _____
     lation trends will be apparent.

B.   For each sentence provide a verb (v) that agrees with the subject.

Example Fourteen dollars (v) too much to pay for a blouse.   _____*is*_____

1.   After nineteen hours of deliberation, the jury (v)   1. _____
     reached a verdict.

2.   Even people in the last row can hear well because   2. _____
     the acoustics in the theater (v) excellent.

3.   The quality of performance has declined in profes-   3. _____
     sional athletics because the number of teams (v)
     increased.

4.   We are trying to raise money because the ski club   4. _____
     (v) to visit Switzerland next winter.

5.   The faculty (v) individual parking spaces assigned   5. _____
     to them.

6.   The public (v) the freedom to vote either for or   6. _____
     against the proposed amendment.

Exercise 5.3   Blind Agreement

A.   In each sentence, select the verb that agrees with the subject.

Example She is one of those individuals who always (understand, understands) the situation.   *understand*

1. A marsupial such as the kangaroo and opossum   1. _____
    (has, have) a pouch.

2. Because of the power failure, the most exciting part   2. _____
    of the Super Bowl game (was, were) not seen.

3. The conclusion I reached when I studied the statis-   3. _____
    tics (agrees, agree) with yours.

4. The owl is one of those birds that seldom (appear,   4. _____
    appears) in the daylight.

5. There (is, are) several reasons for postponing our   5. _____
    trip to Lake Louise.

6. Following the Pied Piper (was, were) several thou-   6. _____
    sand rats, five hundred mice, and three hungry
    cats.

7. The major portion of each of the speeches (was,   7. _____
    were) concerned with the problems of aging.

8. When we were trapped in the cave, our major con-   8. _____
    cern (was, were) explosions which could have
    buried us under tons of rocks.

9. (Does, Do) any one of these movies appeal to you?   9. _____

10. *Hard Times* is the only one of those novels that (has, 10. _____
    have) been translated into seven languages.

11. Throughout world history, a military leader such as   11. _____
    Alexander, Napoleon, and Hitler (has, have) ap-
    peared when a civilization would welcome such a
    leader.

12. In the east gallery there (is, are) an exquisite paint-   12. _____
    ing by Chagall.

B. For each sentence provide a verb (V) that agrees with the subject.

Example There (V) a number of issues to discuss.   _____

1. Dr. Hardly is the only one of those physicians who   1. _____
    (V) able to diagnose my ailment.

2. The least reliable part of the machine (V) the gears.   2. _____

3. Throughout the world (V) strange events which   3. _____
    seem to have no rational explanation.

4. From time to time, a psychiatrist such as Freud,   4. _____
    Jung, or Frankel (V) a new psychiatric theory.

5. There (V) books to read and fine wines to drink.   5. _____

6. A series of three matches (V) being held today.   6. _____

7. Lying under the rock (V) several beetles and a   7. _____
    worm.

8. The fire that drove them from their homes and into   8. _____
    the streets (V) not brought under control for several
    hours.

9. Chung is one of those individuals who always (V)   9. _____
    a kind word for everyone.

10. There (V) a portion of the records that you need   10. _____
    special permission to see.

11. (V) any one of these animals been checked by the   11. _____
    veterinarian?

12. The evidence that was most conclusive (V) the let-   12. _____
    ters written by the deceased to the defendant.

Review Exercise 5   Agreement of Subject and Verb

A. Correct each sentence in which the subject and verb do not agree or in which the subject-verb agreement could be improved. Cross out the word or words you wish to change and write the correct word(s) in the space at the right. If a sentence is correct, write C in the space.

Example A number of battles has already been won.   *have*

Either you or I am going to speak.   *One of us is*

1. A series of meetings are being held next week to discuss the pollution problem.   1. _____

2. Unemployment together with inflation has created complex economic problems.   2. _____

3. Although the number of books in my collection are small, each one is a classic.   3. _____

4. You and I am required to take this course before the end of the year.   4. _____

5. A bouquet of roses make a nice Mother's Day gift.   5. _____

6. Although some of my friends prefer economics, mathematics is my favorite subject.   6. _____

7. The orchestra are taking a break but should return soon.   7. _____

8. Twenty dollars are not too much to pay for a pair of loafers.   8. _____

9. Her biggest admirer and staunchest defender was her husband.   9. _____

10. The series of deadlines place a lot of pressure on the staff.   10. _____

11. Carrying the banner was the two most decorated veterans.   11. _____

12. The entertainment at the reception were a trio and a violinist.   12. _____

13. Your suggestion is one of those solutions that only causes more problems.   13. _____

14. Mark Twain, Sigmund Freud, and Henry James was among the first owners of typewriters.   14. _____

15. The club have agreed to contribute five dollars each for the party.   15. _____

B. Write sentences using the subjects given. All verbs should be in the present tense, and subject-verb agreement should be correct. If necessary, you may alter the subject to improve subject-verb agreement.

Example choir

The choir is rehearsing tonight.

1. a loaf of bread and a jug of wine

2. neither the faculty nor the student body

3. portion

4. public

5. family

6. eleven liters

7. the only one of those beaches

8. a student who is not used to taking essay examinations

9. a number of peacocks

10. one novel or several short stories

11. data [in a sentence beginning *There is* or *There are*]

12. astrologers along with fortune tellers

C. For each set below, write sentences using the subjects given. All verbs should be in the present tense, and subject-verb agreement should be correct. If necessary, you may alter the subject to improve subject-verb agreement. Then, combine each set of sentences into one sentence by turning one of the sentences into a subordinate clause, a verbal phrase, or an appositive. Pay careful attention to subject-verb agreement and to modification.

Example army

The army recruits actively in high schools.

each

Each junior and senior is given information on careers in the service.

(Combined)

When the army recruits actively in high schools, each junior and senior is given information on careers in the service.

1. the student body as well as the faculty

   the dean

   (Combined)

2. forty dollars

   sixty dollars

   (Combined)

3. one of those accidents

   they

   (Combined)

4. committee

   members

   (Combined)

5. neither Gwen nor Bill

   ghosts

   (Combined)

6. physics

   politics

   (Combined)

7. a number

the number

(Combined)

8. the river along with the lake

environment

(Combined)

6

VERBS

Verbs indicate action *(build, jump)*, condition *(am, feel)*, or process *(become, grow)*. English verbs have three principal parts: infinitive, past tense, and past participle. *Regular verbs* add *-ed* to form the past tense and past participle; *irregular verbs* change form in other ways.

	Regular verb	Irregular verb
Infinitive	(to) talk	(to) throw
Present participle	(talking)	(throwing)
Past tense	talked	threw
Past participle	talked	thrown

6.1 Tense

Tenses indicate time (past, present, future) and show continuity. In English, tenses are built from the three principal parts of a verb, the present participle (the *-ing* form), and auxiliary verbs *(am, is, are, was, were, have, had, will)*. The formation of the most frequently used tenses may be illustrated by the regular verb *talk*.

Tense	*I*	*he, she, it*	*we, you, they*
Present	talk	talks	talk
Present Progressive	am talking	is talking	are talking
Perfect	have talked	has talked	have talked
Past	talked	talked	talked
Past Progressive	was talking	was talking	were talking
Past Perfect	had talked	had talked	had talked
Future	will talk	will talk	will talk
Future Progressive	will be talking	will be talking	will be talking
Future Perfect	will have talked	will have talked	will have talked

Sequence of Past Tenses. The various past tenses should be used accurately to express differences in past time:

> We **have arrived home** [perfect] and **are preparing** dinner [present progressive].
> We **had arrived** home [past perfect] and **were preparing** dinner [past progressive].
> We **had arrived** home [past perfect] when the call **came** [past].
> The call **came** [past] when we **arrived** home [past].

When the verb of a main clause is in the past or past perfect tense, the verb in a subordinate clause is also past or past perfect:

Incorrect	We **understood** [past] what he **has said** [perfect].
Correct	We **understood** [past] what he **said** [past].
	We **understood** [past] what he **had said** [past perfect].

A present infinitive is usually used after a verb in a past tense.

> I **tried** [past] **to understand** [not *to have understood*] him.
> I **had tried** [past perfect] **to understand** him.

Consistent Use of Tenses. Unnecessary shifts in tense (as from the present to the past or from the past to the future) confuse time. Verbs should be consistent in tense.

Unnecessary shifts	We **went** to the shore and **hear** the waves pounding the sand. We **saw** the sunlight dancing on the water and **listen** to the seagulls screeching overhead. [shifts from past to present to past to present]
Consistent	We **went** to the shore and **heard** the waves pounding the sand. We **saw** the sunlight dancing on the water and **listened** to the seagulls screeching overhead. [all in past]

6.2   Irregular Verbs and Auxiliaries

Forming the tenses of irregular verbs may cause problems. The list on page 98 shows the principal parts of many common irregular verbs. When two forms are given, both are acceptable; however, the first form given is usually preferred. Consult a dictionary for the principal parts of irregular verbs not listed here.

Troublesome Verbs. *Can* is used for ability and *may* to express permission:

> With the lantern lit, we **can** [have the ability to] see.
> You **may** [have permission to] enter now.

Lie (lay, lain, lying) means "to recline" and does not take an object:

> The book **lies** on the table. Yesterday the book **lay** on the table. The book **has lain** on the table for three weeks. The book **is lying** on the table.

Common Irregular Verbs

Infinitive	Past tense	Past participle	Infinitive	Past tense	Past participle
arise	arose	arisen	lie (recline)	lay	lain
bear (carry)	bore	borne	light	lighted, lit	lighted, lit
bear (give birth to)	bore	borne, born	lose	lost	lost
			pay	paid	paid
begin	began	begun	prove	proved	proved, proven
bid (offer)	bid	bid			
bid (command)	bade	bidden	ride	rode	ridden
			ring	rang, rung	rung
bite	bit	bitten, bit	rise	rose	risen
blow	blew	blown	roar	roared	roared
break	broke	broken	run	ran	run
bring	brought	brought	see	saw	seen
burst	burst	burst	set	set	set
catch	caught	caught	shake	shook	shaken
choose	chose	chosen	shine	shone, shined	shone, shined
come	came	come			
dig	dug	dug	show	showed	showed, shown
dive	dived, dove	dived, dove			
do	did	done	shrink	shrank, shrunk	shrunk
drag	dragged	dragged			
draw	drew	drawn	sing	sang, sung	sung
dream	dreamed, dreamt	dreamed, dreamt	sink	sank, sunk	sunk, sunken
drink	drank	drunk	sit	sat	sat
drive	drove	driven	slide	slid	slid, slidden
eat	ate	eaten	speak	spoke	spoken
fall	fell	fallen	spring	sprang, sprung	sprung
fly	flew	flown			
forget	forgot	forgotten	stand	stood	stood
freeze	froze	frozen	steal	stole	stolen
get	got	got, gotten	swear	swore	sworn
give	gave	given	swim	swam, swum	swum
go	went	gone			
grow	grew	grown	take	took	taken
hang (person)	hanged	hanged	tear	tore	torn
			throw	threw	thrown
hang (object)	hung	hung	wake	waked, woke	waked, woke
know	knew	known			
lay (place)	laid	laid	wear	wore	worn
lead	led	led	wring	wrung	wrung
lend	lent	lent	write	wrote	written

Lay (laid, laid, laying) means "to put or place" and takes an object:

> He **lays** the book [object] on the table. Yesterday he **laid** the book on the table. He **has laid** the book on the table. He **is laying** the book on the table.

Sit (sat, sat, sitting), as in a chair, does not take an object:

> She **sits** by the window. Yesterday she **sat** by the window. Often she **has sat** by the window. She **is sitting** by the window.

Set (set, set, setting) means "to put down" and takes an object:

> They **set** the piano [object] in the den. Yesterday they **set** the piano in the den. They **have set** the piano in the den. They **are setting** the piano in the den.

6.3 Active and Passive Voice

If the subject of a verb is performing the action, the verb is *active;* if the subject is being acted upon, the verb is *passive:*

Active   **Kay saw** a swan. [The subject *Kay* was doing the seeing.]
Passive   A **swan was seen** by Kay. [The subject *swan* was being seen.]

Appropriate Passives. The passive is appropriate (1) if the actor is unknown or unimportant, or (2) if the writer wants to emphasize the thing acted upon or the act rather than the actor:

> The house **was built** two hundred years ago. [actor unknown]
> The lecture **was cancelled** because of the storm. [actor unimportant]
> The eclipse **was observed** by thousands. [object emphasized]

Inappropriate Passives. In nearly all other instances the passive is weak, awkward, or wordy. Revise such sentences by making the subject the actor:

Passive   **It was decided** by me to go to college.
Active   **I decided** to go to college.

6.4 The Subjunctive Mood

The *subjunctive mood* consists of a few untypical verb forms (such as *if I were* instead of *I was* and *that you be there* instead of *you are).* Use of the subjunctive in modern English is limited and inconsistent. Since an alternative construction is almost always available, writers seldom need to use the subjunctive. The subjunctive mood is most frequently used in the following situations:

Subjunctive Conditions. The subjunctive is sometimes used to express a condition contrary to fact:

> If I **were** a king [I'm not], I'd make you a queen.

In *that* Clauses. The subjunctive is sometimes used in *that* clauses which express recommendations, demands, and the like:

Subjunctive   I require **that** you **be** in my office at 9:00 A.M. tomorrow.
Alternative   I require you **to be** in my office at 9:00 A.M. tomorrow.

Subjunctive in Idioms. The subjunctive is found in several idioms and set expressions:

> **Be** that as it may   as it **were**

6.5 Idioms with Verbs

Many idiomatic expressions that are acceptable in informal conversation are not acceptable in formal writing. The following list should help you use idioms appropriately in writing.

> **able to be:** Avoid *able to be;* use *can be* instead.
> **being that:** Avoid *being that* as a substitute for *because, since* or *for.*
> **do:** Avoid informal expressions using *do (done* in, *did* them out of). Some other expressions using *do* are acceptable (*do* away with, *do* without, make *do*).
> **enthuse:** Avoid *enthuse;* use *be enthusiastic about* or *show enthusiasm.*
> **fix:** Avoid *fix* in the sense of "get even with."
> **get:** Avoid informal expressions using *get (gets* on my nerves, that *gets* me, *get* away with). Other expressions using *get* are acceptable (*get* ahead, *get* along with).
> **leave:** Avoid using *leave* for permission; use *let* instead.
> **try and, try to:** Although both are acceptable, *try to* is preferred in writing.
> **want to, want that:** Avoid *want to* used in the sense of "ought" or "should" (You *should* [not *want to*] finish). Use *want to* in statements of desire (I *want* you *to* [not *want that you*] visit me).

Exercise 6.1 Tense

A. Write the tense of each italicized verb in the space at the right.

Example He *ran* all the way home   *past*

1. Before the trial ends, I *will have convinced* the jury   1. _____
    that my client is innocent.

2. Warren *had mastered* three languages by the time he   2. _____
    was twenty.

3. Both the sea and the air *are* moving constantly.   3. _____

4. We *were exploring* the hidden room when the door   4. _____
    slammed shut.

5. Our ninth president, William Henry Harrison,   5. _____
    served in office only thirty-one days.

6. After you finish your talk, I *will introduce* the next   6. _____
    speaker.

7. The tiger *paces* back and forth in its cage.   7. _____

8. We *have visited* Cape Cod every year since 1948.   8. _____

9. As he *was reaching* for the hammer, he knocked   9. _____
    over the box of nails.

10. She *will have arrived* in Sweden before we leave for   10. _____
    work tomorrow.

11. Because we left early, we did not know until we   11. _____
    arrived home that the game *had ended* in a tie.

12. I *am considering* moving to Hawaii.   12. _____

13. In 1936 and 1937, Luise Rainer *won* Oscars for   13. _____
    her performances in *The Great Ziegfeld* and *The
    Good Earth.*

14. Sleeping pills seldom *snore*.   14. _____

15. If you come to my apartment, I *will show* you my   15. _____
collection of chiroptera.

B. Select the verb form that follows the proper sequence of tenses.

Example She went to the market and (is buying, bought) her   *bought*
groceries for the week.

1. When you (have finished, had finished) painting   1. _____
the fence, you should have put away the paint.

2. He has been told of the problem and (is trying,   2. _____
tries) to find a solution.

3. We started to comprehend what we (have done,   3. _____
had done).

4. If I had known that the bridge was out, I would   4. _____
have tried (to have stopped, to stop) the train.

5. The travel agent has planned our trip and (is pur-   5. _____
chasing, was purchasing) our tickets.

6. By the time they reach the station, the train (was   6. _____
leaving, will have left).

7. Until that moment, I had never seen George when   7. _____
he hadn't, hasn't tried to borrow something.

8. They (have heard, had heard) the explosion and   8. _____
were rushing to the scene.

9. I had already decided (to resign, to have resigned)   9. _____
myself to my fate.

10. The rescue party had already found the plane when   10. _____
I (had heard, heard) that it had crashed.

C. Revise each sentence in which the tense of verbs is inconsistent or does
not follow the proper sequence. If a sentence is correct, do not rewrite
it.

Example Because she had prepared thoroughly for the examination, she is not afraid to take it.

Because she had prepared thoroughly for the examination, she was not afraid to take it.

1. The telephone had stopped ringing when I had picked it up.

2. We would have attempted to have launched the life raft, but the waves would have swamped it immediately.

3. The storm has passed Cape Hatteras and was heading toward Long Island.

4. When the jury has reached a verdict, we should have been informed.

5. They attempted what no person has tried before.

6. Ahmed had sealed the envelope and was looking for a stamp when the doorbell rang.

7. Because of engine trouble, she did not complete the race until all of the other cars have crossed the finish line.

8. The horses had broken out of their corral and are running away.

9. I had planned to have argued against the motion, but Ed persuaded me not to do so.

10. Until then we had not visited a city in which we have wanted to live permanently.

D. Rewrite the following sentences, changing the verb tense as indicated.

Example Vampira enjoyed mystery novels. [change to present tense]

Vampira enjoys mystery novels.

1. A campfire creates an atmosphere that is perfect for telling ghost stories.

2. Although the opportunities for anthropologists are limited, I am convinced that I can find a job. [change to past]

3. I finished mowing the lawn in time to go to the movies. [change to future]

4. I imagine myself existing on a desert island. [change to past]

5. I demand that you attend the lecture. [change to past]

Exercise **6.2**   **Irregular Verbs**

A.   Select the proper verb form and write it in the space at the right.

Example It was so cold I almost (freezed, froze).   *froze*

   1.   We (have paid, have payed) for our mistakes.   1. _____

   2.   The unsuspecting commander (lead, led) his troops   2. _____
        straight into a trap.

   3.   She (would have borne, would have bore) her se-   3. _____
        cret to the grave.

   4.   Yesterday I (lay, laid) the car keys on the mantle.   4. _____

   5.   When the falling snow sounded like elephants on   5. _____
        the roof, I knew that I (had drank, had drunk) too
        much last night.

   6.   She (can, may) think more clearly when it's quiet.   6. _____

   7.   Harry Houdini (was borne, was born) in Appleton,   7. _____
        Wisconsin.

   8.   We were (setting, sitting) the chair on the porch.   8. _____

   9.   I (would have swore, would have sworn) that I left   9. _____
        the brake on.

10.   They (hung, hanged) the tapestry on the wall.   10. _____

B.   Correct each sentence in which the verb form is faulty. Cross out the
     word or words you wish to change and write the correct word(s) in the
     space at the right. If a sentence is correct, put a C in the space.

Example We swimmed across the lake.   *swam*

1.   The sergeant had bid me to go on guard duty.   1. _____

2.   I would have rang the doorbell, but I saw that the   2. _____
     door was open.

3. He was so ill that he laid in bed three weeks.   3. _____

4. She sat her trophies in a display case.   4. _____

5. According to one Greek myth, Athena has sprang   5. _____
fully grown out of the head of Zeus.

C. Write sentences using the verb given in the form indicated.

Example drive [past participle]
They had driven miles out of their way before they found the restaurant.

1. lie (recline) [past tense]

2. sit [past participle]

3. bear (carry) [past participle]

4. grow [past tense]

5. hang (person) [past participle]

6. set [past tense]

7. slide [past tense]

8. freeze [past tense]

9. ring [past participle]

10. draw [past participle]

11. prove [past tense]

12. rise [past participle]

D. Rewrite the following sentences, using the verb form indicated.

Example We eat quickly. [past participle]

We had eaten quickly.

1. The honor comes not in winning the election but in serving the public. [past participle]

2. You grow taller nearly every day. [past tense]

3. Leroy pays for his textbooks with cash. [past participle]

4. The clerk swears in the witness. [past participle]

5. The leopard springs into the tree. [past tense]

6. We arise long before dawn. [past tense]

7. The crowd roars. [past participle]

8. The falcon dives toward its prey. [past participle]

Exercise 6.3   Active and Passive Voice

A.   Identify each italicized verb as active or passive.

Example The mayor *was asked* several questions at the press
        conference.   *passive*

1.   The song *was sung* by the popular recording artist   1. _____
    Mac Macho.

2.   Frank *is working* by the mill today.   2. _____

3.   That question *is asked* more often than any other.   3. _____

4.   She *has been studying* medicine for two years.   4. _____

5.   Our ladder *has been stolen*.   5. _____

6.   Harriet *was approached* by a salesperson.   6. _____

7.   Black cats *have been avoided* for centuries.   7. _____

8.   We *were swimming* in the pond when we saw the   8. _____
    alligator.

9.   Next, the nut *is screwed* onto the bolt.   9. _____

10.   The decorations *had been hung* before the guests   10. _____
    arrived.

11.   The monkey *was swinging* from tree to tree.   11. _____

12.   That abstract painting seems *to have been turned* up-   12. _____
    side down.

13.   Those vultures *have been circling* for several minutes.   13. _____

14.   The streets *are covered* with ice.   14. _____

15.   The children *are finding* most of the hidden pennies.   15. _____

B.   Some of the following sentences could be improved by changing the
voice from active to passive or from passive to active. Decide which
sentences could be improved and revise them. If changing the voice
would not improve a sentence, do not rewrite it.

Example Somebody built that stone wall a long time ago.

That stone wall was built a long time ago.

1. Allen Stewart Konigsberg's name was changed by him to Woody Allen.

2. From his hiding place, Tom was seen by the troll.

3. The workers will complete the bridge by August.

4. People for several miles saw the flames.

5. The jury found Senator Walters guilty and he was sentenced to four years in prison.

6. The last three innings were played in a steady downpour.

7. Three sea bass were caught by Carl on his deep-sea fishing expedition.

8. The pine cones were made by Edna into a wreath which hung on the door.

9. Luckily for her, Sharon was carrying her rifle when the rhino charged.

10. This award will be given to that individual who best exemplifies the ideals of the college.

11. On April Fool's Day, her father's toothbrush was coated with soap by Kim.

12. The cat is curled up in front of the fireplace.

13. When the courtroom was entered by the judge, everyone rose.

14. Why is "Ho! Ho! Ho!" said by the Jolly Green Giant?

15. A distinction is made by students between the teacher who treats them as adults and the instructor who treats them as children.

C. Write sentences using the verb indicated. First, write a sentence in which the verb is *passive;* then change the sentence so that the verb is *active;* finally, put an asterisk (*) next to the sentence you think is more effective.

Example *bring*

Passive *The mistake was brought to my attention by the vice-president.*

Active *The vice-president brought the mistake to my attention.*

1. *batter*
Passive

Active

2. *reveal*
Passive

Active

3. *tremble*
Passive

Active

4.   *confuse*
Passive

Active

5.   *lose*
Passive

Active

6.   *watch*
Passive

Active

7.   *choose*
Passive

Active

8.   *dig*
Passive

Active

Exercise 6.4   The Subjunctive Mood

A.   Identify each verb in the subjunctive mood and write it in the space at the right.

Example If I were in your place, I would view the situation   *were*
differently.

1.   If the guilty party be present, let him step   1. _____
forward.

2.   If Shakespeare were alive today, he would probably   2. _____
be writing scripts for motion pictures.

3.   Come what may, we intend to remain on this land.   3. _____

4.   It is necessary that every student register on time. 4. _____

5.   I recommended that he be more cautious.   5. _____

6.   If the time for death be now, then let it come.   6. _____

7.   The court ordered that she pay alimony.   7. _____

8.   Be that as it may, I still think that a secret ballot 8. _____
should be taken.

9.   If it were a bear, it would have bitten you.   9. _____

10. She stated that if she were running the country, all 10. _____
millionaires would pay taxes.

B.   Using the subjunctive mood, write sentences of the types indicated.

Example (condition) *If it were summer, we could swim.*

(that clause) *I suggest that you be more careful.*

1.   (condition)

2.   *(that* clause)

112

3.   *(that* clause)

4.   (condition)

5.   (condition)

Exercise 6.5 Idioms with Verbs

A. For each sentence, select the proper idiomatic form.

Example Critics (enthused over/were enthusiastic about) Chekhov's *Three Sisters*.

were enthusiastic about

1. She (was able to, could) place the blame on someone else.

   1. _____

2. I (want for you to go, want you to go) away.

   2. _____

3. A stray fist (got, struck) him in the face.

   3. _____

4. We (have got, got) to finish this project soon.

   4. _____

5. Red paint (is able to, can) be mixed with yellow to produce orange paint.

   5. _____

6. You (should, want to) eat balanced meals.

   6. _____

B. Each sentence contains an inappropriate idiom. Cross out the word(s) you wish to change and write the correct word(s) in the space at the right.

Example This wood is able to be used again.

can

1. I will leave you get the mail today.

   1. _____

2. We were done in after the election.

   2. _____

3. I'll fix you for breaking my bicycle.

   3. _____

4. Your constant chatter gets on my nerves.

   4. _____

5. His air of innocence gets me.

   5. _____

6. Try and knock that can off the fence.

   6. _____

114

Review Exercise **6** Verbs

A. Rewrite each passage, correcting all errors in verb tense, form, voice, and mood, and all inappropriate idioms.

1. I had been laying under the car fixing the tail pipe when some rust falls off the bottom of the car and aggravates my eyes.

2. The steak which he has grilled out was ate by Arthur.

3. After he has been captured by the sheriff, Deadeye was hanged by the vigilantes to fix him for being a train robber.

4. Can you be payed in full now by me for the stereo which had been bought last week at the auction?

5. If you should stop setting in the rocker, the picture could be able to be hanged by you before the doorbell has been rang by Aunt Theodora.

6. I had drew a picture of our cabin and left it lieing on the table. I think that I had sat it there, so someone has took it. If it be you, I want for you to find it and return it.

7. When I remember that I had forgot to have wrote a letter home, the telephone was picked up and dialed. I had chose to contact my parents before they had began to worry about me.

8. Our shopping shall be done tomorrow. We should be able to find all of the items we need if we will drive to the new shopping plaza which has been builded on the edge of town. When we shall arrive there, we will have over thirty different stores we may visit.

9. The sun has not rose when we have began our trip to the shore. As the early morning rays came over the horizon, we have drove into the parking area. We get out of the car and went to the water. Because we had wore our swimsuits under our clothes, we may dive right in. After we had swam for about an hour, we have grown tired and leave the ocean for the beach. We lay our blanket on the sand and lie in the warm summer sun.

10. Inspector Cramer suspicioned that it was Mr. Waterhouse who has took the jewelry out of the safe and threw it into the cigar box. However, Nero Wolfe had knew all along that the jewelry was stole by Mr. Waterhouse himself. When the accusation was made by Wolfe, Mr. Waterhouse had arose from the yellow leather chair in which he had been setting, let his hand slid into his pocket, and had got out a gun. But Mr. Waterhouse had not saw that Archie Goodwin, Wolfe's trusted assistant, has rose from his desk and has came around behind him. Goodwin catches Mr. Waterhouse by the arm and hanged on until he has been drawn to the floor and the gun had been shook out of his hand. The gun flew over the floor where it come to rest at the feet of Inspector Cramer.

B. Complete the following sentences by adding the material indicated.

1. After Charlotte _____ (a past tense of *eat*)too much _____ (noun) and _____ (past tense of *drink*) too much _____ (noun), she _____ (correct tense of *dream*) of _____ (plural noun).

2. When the _____ (noun) _____ (past tense of *ring*), Arnold _____ (correct tense of *spring*) from the _____ (noun) on which he _____ (correct tense of *lie*), _____ (correct tense of *throw*) on his _____ (noun), and _____ (correct tense of *fly*) to the _____ (noun).

3. Because Stella _____ (past tense of *lose*) the _____ (noun) that _____ (proper noun) _____ (correct tense of *lend*), her, _____ (proper noun or pronoun) _____ (correct tense of *aggravate* or *irritate*).

4. He _____ (*will* or *shall*) _____ (proper form of *know*) whether or not he _____ (*should* or *would*) _____ (proper form of *speak*) to the general about the _____ (noun) which we _____ (*will* or *shall*) _____ (proper form of *lead*) tomorrow.

5. When he _____ (past perfect of *grow*) weary of the _____ (noun) which he _____ (correct tense of *bear*) for three days, he _____ (correct tense of *set*) it down in the _____ (noun) and _____ (correct tense of *lie*) down beside it.

6. I _____ (*shall, will, would* or *should*) be enthusiastic about the _____ (noun), if I _____ (proper tense of *know*) that it _____ (*would be able to* or *could*) be _____ (proper tense of *return*) if it _____ (*should, did, does,* or *would*) not fit.

7. The _____ (noun) _____ (past tense, passive, of *steal*) by _____ (proper noun) and _____ (correct tense, passive, of *drive*) by _____ (pronoun) to the _____ (noun) where _____ (*a* or *an*) _____ (noun) _____ (correct tense, passive, of *find*) by _____ (pronoun).

Using your own paper, change what you have written in 7 from passive to active.

7

NOUNS

A *noun* indicates a person *(mother, Ralph Bunche)*, place *(garage, Puerto Rico)*, thing *(table, apple)*, quality *(beauty, ugliness)*, action *(fishing, cooking)*, or idea *(democracy, infinity)*. Nouns function in sentences in several ways—

Subject of a verb: The **garage** burned down.
Direct object of a verb: She ate an **apple.**
Indirect object: We gave **Mother** a new lamp.
Complement: The most powerful emotion is **love.**
Object of a preposition: He parked the car in the **garage.**
Appositive: Mrs. Neal, my **mother,** hopes to visit Florida.
Modifier of a noun: They held a **garage** sale.
Modifier of a statement: Every **week** we visit the museum.

7.1 Plurals of Nouns (See 17.2, Spelling Troublesome Plurals.)

7.2 Possessive Case

In English, nouns have only two case forms, the *common* form *(mother, table, poet)* and the *possessive* form *(mother's, table's poet's)*. An *of* phrase *(of the table, of the poet)* can also function as a possessive form.

Most Singular Nouns form the possessive by adding *'s,* as do the few plural nouns that do not end in *-s.*

the **queen's** throne (the throne *of the queen*)
the **women's** lounge (the lounge *of the women*)

Plural Nouns Ending in *-s* form the possessive by adding only an apostrophe:

the **kings'** meeting (the meeting *of the kings*)
the **tables'** price (the price *of the tables*)

118

Singular Nouns Ending in *-s* may form the possessive either by adding an apostrophe alone or by adding *'s* if an extra syllable would be pronounced. (Either form is correct, but be consistent in whichever form you use.)

    the **poetess'** [or *poetess's*] talk   **Charles'** [or *Charles's*] idea

HINT: In store names, firm names, and advertising, an apostrophe is often omitted when it should appear (*Joes Bar, Friedas Dresses, Angelos Bakery*). Be careful not to do the same thing in your writing.

Group Words or Compound Nouns are made possessive by adding *'s* to the last term:

    the **King of France's** policy   his **brother-in-law's** car

Nouns in a Series (joined by *and, but,* or *nor*) are made possessive by adding the apostrophe only to the last noun if there is joint possession. When there is individual possession, the apostrophe is used with both nouns:

    Bob and Brad's father   **Bob's and Brad's** cars

Plural Nouns as Modifiers. The apostrophe is not used in some expressions in which the plural noun is considered a modifier:

    teachers convention   **United States** Information Agency

Awkward Use of *'s* **Forms.** An *of* phrase may be preferable to an *'s* form—

1.   When a possessive noun is separated from the word to which it refers:

    The palace **of the king** who led the army was captured. [not *The king who led the army's palace* nor *The king's palace who led the army*]

2.   When you need to distinguish between the doer and recipient of an act. *The queen's paintings* could mean either paintings *by* the queen, paintings *belonging* to the queen, or paintings *picturing* the queen; but *the paintings of the queen* usually means that the queen was the subject of the paintings.

7.3 Use of *a* and *an* with Nouns

The indefinite article *a* is used before words beginning with a *consonant sound,* whether the first letter is a consonant or a vowel:

    a table   **a** *B*   *a* European vacation   **a** useful tool

The indefinite article *an* is used before words beginning with a *vowel sound,* whether the first letter is a vowel or a consonant:

    an apple   **an** ear   **an** *F*   **an** honorable person

7.4 Noun Modifiers

Usually adjectives rather than nouns are used to modify nouns:

French [not France] literature   **dental** [not dentist] work

But when nouns do not have exact adjectival equivalents, the noun forms are used as modifiers:

a **detective** story   the **kitchen** sink   a **television** antenna

Noun modifiers—particularly units of measurement—are ordinarily singular:

a **ten-gallon** [not ten-gallons] hat   a **three-mile** [not three-miles] run

Exercise *7.2/7.3*   **Possessive Case/Use of *a* and *an* with Nouns**

A.   In each sentence select the proper possessive form.

Example (Charlies', Charlies, Charlie's) aunt   *Charlie's*
         was asked to speak at the luncheon.

1.   The (lawyer's, lawyers, lawyers')   1. _____
     summation was a powerful defense
     of his client.

2.   (Freud and Jung's, Freud's and   2. _____
     Jung's, Freud's and Jung) theories
     of the subconscious helped to revo-
     lutionize the treatment of mental
     patients.

3.   Stephen A. Douglas defeated Abra-   3. _____
     ham Lincoln and was elected to the
     (United States, United State's, Uni-
     ted States') Senate.

4.   The (speakers, speaker's, speakers')   4. _____
     mannerisms distracted her audi-
     ence.

5.   When Tom fell, he spilled his drink   5. _____
     on the (hostess', hostesses, host-
     esses') dress.

6.   It was (Copernicus' and Galileo's,   6. _____
     Copernicus and Galileo's, Coper-
     nicus's and Galileo's) belief that the
     sun was at the center of our solar
     system.

7.   To assist with her education, she re-   7. _____
     ceived benefits from the (Veterans,
     Veteran's, Veterans') Administra-
     tion.

8. We have orders to paint the (men and women's, mens' and womens', men's and women's) locker rooms.   8. _____

B. Rewrite each sentence, correcting any errors in possessive form and in the use of *a* and *an* with nouns.

Example The kings' death came at a hour we least expected.

The king's death came at an hour we least expected.

1. When he put a ear to the ground, he heard the train's approaching.

2. The witches cauldron contained a bat, an owl, a eagles feather, and an hornets' eye.

3. An unusual event occurred when we were at Helens party.

4. Toms' instructor gave him a *F* in biochemistry.

5. Neither Frank nor Sue's coat could be found.

6. From the castles towers they could see the enemys spearpoints glistening in the sunlight.

7. To receive the kings praises would be a honor indeed.

8. If the clubs' effort is an united one, we can raise enough money to purchase Mr. Lanes collections' of stamps and coins.

9. The United States' government regulates interstate commerce.

10. His mother-in-laws entries in the flower show won several prizes including an horticultural blue ribbon.

NAME . . . .   SCORE . . . .

C.   Write the possessive form of each of the following nouns, and then
        write a sentence using the possessive form.

Example *eagle* (singular)   Possessive form *eagle's*

The eagle's nest was high on the side of a cliff.

1.   nation (plural)   Possessive form _____

2.   actress (singular)   Possessive form _____

3.   teacher (singular)   Possessive form _____

4.   lawyer (plural)   Possessive form _____

5.   witch (plural)   Possessive form _____

6.   dog and cat (singular)   Possessive form _____

7.   chair and table (plural)   Possessive form _____

8.   Fred and Bertha (singular)   Possessive form _____

Review Exercise 7   Nouns

A. Write each noun in the following sentences in the first column on the right. In the second column indicate whether the noun functions as a subject (S), direct object (DO), indirect object (IO), complement (C), object of a preposition (OP), appositive (AP), or modifier (M).

Example The truck carried chickens to the

     marketplace.

              truck   S

              chickens   DO

              marketplace   OP

1. The electrician wound tape around the wire.

1. _____ _____

     _____ _____

     _____ _____

2. When he began his career, Stanley Applebaum changed his name to Robert Goulet.

2. _____ _____

     _____ _____

     _____ _____

     _____ _____

3. She is a person who understands politics.

3. _____ _____

     _____ _____

4. Bali, a tropical island in the South Pacific, is a good spot for a vacation.

4. _____ _____

     _____ _____

     _____ _____

     _____ _____

     _____ _____

5. He generously gave the orphanage his country estate.

5. _____ _____

     _____ _____

     _____ _____

B. Rewrite each sentence, correcting all errors in noun form, in awkward use of 's forms, in the use of *a* and *an*, and in nouns used as modifiers.

1. The performer who won the award's family was present at the ceremony.

2. Neither Napoleon nor Hitler's plan to invade Russia was successful.

3. The woman on the train's face is still vivid in my mind.

4. When we visited the barons castle, a mystery event occurred.

5. The Massachusetts' National Guard assisted in evacuating the floods victims.

6. Jonah's records all sold over one million copies.

7. The man's great-grandfather who bought the estate was a slave.

8. The intelligent report pinpointed the locations of the enemies troops.

9. My uncles brother-in-laws pet is a unusual creature.

10. To have a prestige library, Rodney insisted that all of his books covers be of fine leather.

11. Story's about Charlemagne present the ancient France king as a myth figure.

12. The team that won the championship's star had decided to study veterinarian medicine rather than sign a professional contract.

C. Combine each of the following groups of sentences into a single sentence by using appositives.

Example His father-in-law is an electrician. His favorite hobby is fishing.

Fishing is the favorite hobby of his father-in-law, an electrician.

1. The drug industry is one of the largest industries in the country. It is being investigated by the attorney general.

2. John Glenn is a United States senator. He was formerly an astronaut.

3. The landscape was prominently displayed in the den. It was her favorite painting.

4. Trigger was Roy Rogers' horse. He was called the smartest horse in the movies.

5. The Lincoln Highway was the first coast-to-coast paved road in the United States. It opened in 1913.

6. John Creasey was a writer of mystery novels. He used twenty-eight pseudonyms. He wrote 560 books.

7. Honey glides are birds. They are relatives of woodpeckers. They enjoy eating honeycomb.

8. Copernicus was a Polish astronomer. He developed the theory that the sun is the center of the solar system.

8

PRONOUNS

A *pronoun* functions as a noun but does not name a specific person, place, thing, quality, action, or idea. A pronoun usually refers to a previously stated noun, which is called its *antecedent*.

8.1 Reference of Pronouns

A pronoun must refer clearly to its antecedent. If it does not, the reference is faulty. To provide accurate reference, either change the pronoun, substitute a noun for the pronoun, or revise the sentence.

Pronouns Referring to a Definite Antecedent. The antecedent must be clearly stated, not just implied:

Faulty	She had wished for good weather, but **it** did not come true. [no antecedent for *it*]
Accurate	She had wished for good weather, but her **wish** did not come true. [noun *wish* substituted for pronoun *it*]

The antecedent should not be a noun used as a modifier:

Faulty	When the new **kitchen** stove is installed, **it** will be completely redorated. [*kitchen* is a noun modifying *stove*]
Accurate	When the new stove is installed, the **kitchen** will be completely redecorated.

The antecedent should not be a noun in the possessive form:

Faulty	The doctor put a cast on the **boy's** arm **who** fell. [*boy's* is *possessive*]
Accurate	The doctor put a cast on the arm of the **boy who** fell.

Ambiguous Reference. If a pronoun could refer to either of two different antecedents, the reference is ambiguous. Eliminate the ambiguity either by substituting a noun for the pronoun or by clarifying the antecedent:

<table>
<tr><th colspan="4">Kinds of Pronouns</th></tr>
<tr><th></th><th>Subjective</th><th>Objective</th><th>Possessive</th></tr>
</table>

Personal pronouns
First Person

	Subjective	Objective	Possessive
Singular	I	me	my, mine
Plural	we	us	our, ours

Second Person

	Subjective	Objective	Possessive
Singular	you	you	your, yours
Plural	you	you	your, yours

Third Person
Singular

	Subjective	Objective	Possessive
Masculine	he	him	his
Feminine	she	her	her, hers
Neuter	it	it	its
Plural	they	them	their, theirs

Relative pronouns

Subjective	Objective	Possessive
who	whom	whose
which	which	whose, of which
that	that	

Interrogative pronouns

Subjective	Objective	Possessive
who	whom	whose
which	which	whose, of which
what	what	

Reflexive and intensive pronouns
Singular: myself, yourself, himself, herself, itself, oneself
Plural: ourselves, yourselves, themselves

Demonstrative pronouns   this, these, that, those

Indefinite pronouns

all	both	everything	nobody	several
another	each	few	none	some
any	each one	many	no one	somebody
anybody	either	most	nothing	someone
anyone	everybody	much	one	something
anything	everyone	neither	other	such

Reciprocal pronouns   each other, one another
Numerical pronouns   one, two, three . . ., first, second, third . . .

Ambiguous	When Gloria visited Edith, **she** learned that **she** was pregnant.
Accurate	When **she** visited Edith, **Gloria** learned that **Edith** was pregnant.

Avoid identifying the antecedent by repeating it after the pronoun:

Awkward	Ralph first met Ned when **he** (Ned) needed legal advice.
Accurate	When Ralph first met **him,** Ned needed legal advice.

128

Pronouns Referring to Ideas and Statements. When *this, that, which,* and *it* refer to ideas expressed in previous statements, the idea to which the pronoun refers should be obvious:

> Please put papers, glass, and metal into separate containers. **This** will help our recycling effort.

HINT: To avoid possible ambiguity entirely, use a noun or rewrite the passage:

> Please put papers, glass, and metal into separate containers. **This procedure** will help our recycling effort.
> **Putting papers, glass, and metal into separate containers** will help our recycling effort.

Use of *who, which, that.* *Who* refers to persons (the speaker *who*). *Which* usually refers to things (the lamp *which*) or to impersonal organizations (the Chandler Corporation *which*). *That* refers to either persons (the individual *that*) or things (the wind *that*).

Use of *he or she.* The masculine pronoun *(he, his, him)* has traditionally been used to refer to persons of both sexes. (Everyone will correct *his* paper; A doctor is dedicated to *his* patients). Although such usage is gramatically correct, it may offend some individuals. As a result, many people have modified their usage to one of two alternatives—

1. The use of two pronouns to signify both sexes:

    > **Everyone** who wants to see *The Emperor Jones* should buy **his or her** ticket in advance.

2. The use of a plural construction:

    > **All** who want to see *The Emperor Jones* should buy **their tickets** in advance.

A third alternative is the use of *they (their, them)* as a common-gender singular:

> **Everyone** who wants to see *The Emperor Jones* should buy **their** ticket in advance.

Although this alternative solves the gender problem, it forces a plural form *(their)* to agree with a singular form *(Everyone)*. Such constructions can usually be avoided by employing one of the two forms above or by eliminating the second pronoun:

> **Everyone** who wants to see *The Emperor Jones* should buy **a ticket** in advance.

8.2 Agreement of Pronoun and Antecedent

A pronoun must agree in number with its antecedent. When a pronoun serves as a subject, its verb must agree with the pronoun's antecedent.

Personal Pronouns. Errors in agreement most often occur when a pronoun is separated from its antecedent:

Faulty:	After reading her **poems** on death, I found that I was moved by **it**. [the antecedent *poems* is plural; the pronoun *it* is singular]
Accurate:	After reading her **poems** on death, I found that I was moved by **them**. [Both the antecedent *poems* and the pronoun *them* are plural.]

When a pronoun's antecedent is a collective noun, the pronoun may be either singular or plural, depending on the meaning of the noun:

The **committee** issued **its** report. [singular, refers to the group as a unit]
The **committee** brought **their** lunches. [plural, refers to individuals]

When a pronoun refers to nouns joined by *and,* it is usually plural. When singular nouns are linked by *or* or *nor,* the pronoun is singular:

After **Barbara and Tammy** finished the examination, **they** left for the ski lodge.
Neither Barbara nor Tammy lost **her** way.

Relative Pronouns. When a relative pronoun is used as a subject, its antecedent determines the number of the verb and of all related words:

Peter is one of those **individuals who have** made **their marks** in the world before **they were** forty. [*Individuals* is the antecedent of *who;* therefore, *have, their marks* and *they were* are all plural.]
Peter is the only **one** of those individuals **who has** made **his mark** in the world before **he was** forty. [*One* is the antecedent of *who;* therefore, *has, his mark,* and *he was* are all singular.]

Indefinite Pronouns. *Each, everyone, anybody, somebody, someone, neither, no one,* and *nobody* are singular and take singular verbs:

Someone is coming.   **Each** of the boys **hopes** that **he** will be chosen.

None, all, any, some, most, and *more* may be either singular or plural, depending upon the meaning of the statement:

Some of the pie **is** left. [singular, refers to a quantity]
Some of the boxes **are** empty. [plural, refers to individual items]
None of our friends **is** more welcome than Joe. [singular]
None of our friends **are** bigots. [plural]

8.3 Case of Pronouns

Pronouns change form according to their functions in sentences. Pronouns may take three different forms or *cases:* subjective (or nominative) case, objective case, and possessive case.

Subject and Object Pronouns. Most personal pronouns (and the relative or interrogative pronoun *who*) have one form when used as *subjects.* (*I, she, he, we, they, who*) and another form when used as *objects* (*me, her, him, us, them, whom*). Although the distinction between these cases is often disregarded in speech, it should be maintained in writing.

After prepositions use the objective form:

> This is a secret just between **you** and **me**.

After *than* or *as* in comparisons, use the form of the pronoun that would be used in a complete clause:

> He trusts you more than [he trusts] **her**.
> He trusts you more than **she** [trusts you].
> He trusts you as [he trusts] **her**.

For complements, formal English prefers the subject form after the linking verb *be (it is I, that is she),* but the objective form is frequently used as well *(it's me, that's her).*

Choice of *who, whom*. Although the distinction between *who* and *whom* has nearly disappeared in speech, it is usually maintained in writing. Use *who* for subjects, *whom* for objects:

> **Who** can go? [subject]   **Whom** did you bring? [object or verb]
> To **whom** are you referring? [object of preposition]

Possessive Pronouns. Possessives of *personal pronouns* have two forms: one is used (as a modifier) *before* a noun *(your dog, her cat);* the other is used (by itself or in a phrase) *after* a noun (the dog is *yours,* that cat of *hers).* Note that no apostrophe is used with personal pronoun possessives.

Confusion of *its, it's*. *Its* (without an apostrophe) is the possessive form of *it; it's* (with the apostrophe) is the contraction of *it is* or *it has:*

> **It's** a long time until September. [contraction for *it is*]
> The team lost **its** first game. [possessive]

Possessives of indefinite pronouns. *All, any, each, few, most, more, some* are used only in *of* phrases for the possessive:

> the leader **of most**   the best **of all**

Other indefinite pronouns *(anyone, someone, somebody, another,* and so on) form the possessive by adding *'s:*

> **anyone's** position   **someone's** coat

Confusion of *whose, who's*. *Whose* is the possessive form of *who; who's* is the informal contraction of *who is* or *who has:*

> This is Uncle Fred, **whose** sense of humor is highly developed. [possessive]
> This is Uncle Fred, **who's** highly humorous. [contraction for *who is*]

8.4 Reflexive and Intensive Pronouns

Reflexive pronouns are used when the doer and recipient of an act are the same:

She burned **herself** on the stove.

Intensive pronouns (which have the same form as the reflexive) are used to make other words more emphatic:

Survival **itself** was the issue.

Hisself and *theirselves* are not standard English forms.

8.5 Choice of Personal Pronoun Form

Use of *I* and *we*. Use *I* rather than an awkward phrase designed to avoid *I:*

Awkward	**This writer** believes that life in our cities must be improved.
Revised	I believe that life in our cities must be improved.

Use *I* rather than the editorial *we:*

Awkward	**We** are suggesting that **our** solution will work.
Revised	I am suggesting that **my** solution will work.

Use *we* for general reference:

We must solve a number of problems before **we** can call **ourselves** civilized.

Use of *you*. Avoid *you* for general reference, unless the generalization actually does apply to everyone:

Awkward	When **you** first try out for the team, **you** are nervous.
Revised	When **I** first tried out for the team, **I** was nervous.

Use of *one*. *One* refers either to people in general or to the writer:

To comprehend Einstein's view of the universe, **one** must understand the concept of relativity.

One is, however, often impersonal and stiff and can usually be replaced by other personal pronouns:

To comprehend Einstein's view of the universe, **you** must understand the concept of relativity.

8.6 Avoiding Shifts in Pronoun Form

Be consistent in your use of pronouns, particularly when using pronouns for general reference:

Inconsistent	Before **one** gets behind the steering wheel, **you** should understand how a car works. **We** should also study the traffic laws.
Consistent	Before **you** get behind the steering wheel, **you** should understand how a car works. **You** should also study the traffic laws.

Exercise *8.1*   Reference of Pronouns

A.   Identify the antecedent of each numbered pronoun; then write the antecedent in the space at the right.

Example Because Carl was having difficulty making a doghouse, **(a)** *he* asked **(b)** *his* father to help **(c)** *him* build **(d)** *it*.

a. _____Carl_____
b. _____Carl_____
c. _____Carl_____
d. _____doghouse_____

1. George knew that if **(1)** *he* did not reach the barn in time **(2)** *it* would be lost, as would the horses **(3)** *which* were stabled in **(4)** *it*.

1. _____
2. _____
3. _____
4. _____

2. Achilles learned that the gods would not save **(5)** *him* from the punishment **(6)** *which* **(7)** *he* deserved and **(8)** *which* **(9)** *they* **(10)** *themselves* ordained.

5. _____
6. _____
7. _____
8. _____
9. _____
10. _____

3. When Lin Li returned from **(11)** *her* vacation, **(12)** *she* knew that **(13)** *she* would always remember the moonlight **(14)** *that* reflected off the waves, the brilliant sun **(15)** *which* warmed the sand, and the natives **(16)** *themselves* **(17)** *who* offered friendship.

11. _____
12. _____
13. _____
14. _____
15. _____
16. _____
17. _____

4. When Linda began **(18)** *her* campaign, **(19)** *she* presented **(20)** *herself* as a political newcomer **(21)** *who* did not make deals.

18. _____
19. _____
20. _____
21. _____

5. Alex was embarrassed by the mistake **(22)** *which* **(23)** *he* made **(4)** *himself.*

22. _____

23. _____

24. _____

25. _____

B. Rewrite each sentence, using pronouns to replace unnecessarily repetitious nouns.

Example When the knight saw the unicorn, the knight attempted to capture the unicorn.

When the knight saw the unicorn, he attempted to capture it.

1. Maureen hoped to catch a leprechaun so that Maureen could make the leprechaun reveal to Maureen the location of the leprechaun's treasure.

2. The responsibility was a responsibility which few people could accept without having the people's values tested.

3. Because Gina's art work was exceptional art work, the personnel director was impressed with Gina's art work, and the personnel director offered Gina the position.

4. The refugees, to repay the farmer for the farmer's kindness to the refugees, helped the farmer harvest the farmer's crops.

5. The senator told the crowd that the senator had served the crowd well during the senator's first term in office and that the crowd should reelect the senator to a second term.

6. When Jed examined the engine, Jed saw that Jed's expertise was needed to repair the engine.

7. Because the car gathered too much speed as the car went down the hill, the car was unable to negotiate the curve at the bottom of the hill and the car crashed into a tree.

8. The old prospector had spent three days and nights crawling over the sand before the old prospector glimpsed an oasis through the old prospector's tired eyes.

C. Revise each sentence so that the reference of all pronouns is clear and accurate.

Example When the officers confronted the bank robbers, they shot at them.

When the officers confronted the bank robbers, the criminals shot at them.

1. Although he spoke with authority about the problems of leadership, he had never been one.

2. Vern told Ed that he would pick him up when he finished work that evening.

3. The Indians which had roamed the prairies and woods for centuries were systematically robbed by the white man.

4. Each lawyer must ask himself if he would be able to defend a person whom he knew was guilty.

5. During the Civil War, many speculators robbed the soldiers at every op-
    portuity, not caring if they were cheated but only whether they were
    making a large profit.

6. Doris knew Claire long before she (Claire) became a famous neuro-
    surgeon.

7. To build a stone wall without mortar, stack them as closely together as
    possible.

8. Because they could not find their way to my cabin, I had to dictate it
    over the telephone to them.

9. When we were trapped in the cottage without any heat, we found an
    old blanket in a trunk and put it over us. It warmed us for a while but
    soon we could hardly stand it.

10. All parents can register his or her children on Friday afternoon.

11. Although he was relatively unknown, his story reached nearly everyone
    in town.

12. When Brenda met Gail in the restaurant, she did not believe that she
    had gone to elementary school with her thirty years ago.

D. Rewrite the following passages, combining sentences, eliminating unnecessary words, and using pronouns to replace repetitious nouns.

1. The plane stood on the end of the runway. The pilot waited for the control tower to give the pilot permission for the plane to take off. The pilot
received permission from the control tower for the plane to take off. The
pilot revved up the plane's engines. The plane started to move down
the runway. At first the plane moved slowly down the runway. Then
the plane began to move faster and faster down the runway. The plane
reached a tremendous speed. The pilot pulled back on the stick. The
plane left the runway. The plane headed toward the sky. The pilot
pushed a button. The landing gear on the plane folded up. Flight 802
was airborne.

2. The coyote wanted to catch the road runner. The coyote strapped the coyote to a rocket and the coyote sat on the rocket by the side of the road. The coyote was waiting for the road runner to pass. The road runner zoomed by the coyote. The coyote ignited the rocket. The rocket and the coyote took off with a roar. The rocket and the coyote moved closer and closer to the road runner. The coyote was about to grab the road runner. The road took a sharp turn to the left. The road runner turned left. The rocket and the coyote went straight ahead. The rocket and the coyote went over a cliff. The rocket sputtered out in mid-air. The rocket turned the rocket's nose toward the ground far below. The coyote got a horrified look on the coyote's face. The coyote and the rocket plunged toward the ground. The coyote and the rocket made a whistling sound as the coyote and the rocket fell. The coyote and the rocket hit the ground with a thud. The road runner went "beep! beep!"

Exercise *8.2*   Agreement of Pronoun and Antecedent

A. Select the proper pronoun to go with the antecedent or the proper verb to go with the pronoun.

Example Each of us wants (her, our) own way.   *her*

1. None of the attempts I made (was, were) suc-   1. _____
   cessful.
2. The jury announced that (it, they) had reached a   2. _____
   verdict.
3. Eunice or Helen will let you stay at (her, their)   3. _____
   house tonight.
4. Millard Fillmore was one of our presidents who   4. _____
   (has been, have been) virtually ignored since (he,   _____
   they) left office.
5. All of the dessert (has, have) been eaten.   5. _____
6. Neither poverty nor disease can leave (its, their)   6. _____
   mark on a courageous individual.
7. No one (has, have) the right to take the life of   7. _____
   another individual.
8. The typical student believes that a college education 8. _____
   will help (him or her, them, him) lead a full life.
9. I asked at least fourteen people, but no one (was,   9. _____
   were) able to give me an answer.
10. After studying your plans to invade the island, I do 10. _____
    not think that (it, they) will work.
11. Franklin D. Roosevelt was the only one of our pres- 11. _____
    idents who (was, were) elected to (his, their) office   _____
    four times.
12. In Pablo Pantasa's new volume of verse, some of   12. _____
    the poetry (is, are) excellent, but most of the poems   _____
    (is, are) horrible.

B. Rewrite each sentence, correcting all errors in pronoun-antecedent agreement and subject-verb agreement.

Example Some of the senators has indicated that they will support the bill.

Some of the senators have indicated that they will support the bill.

1. None of our states are larger than Alaska.

2. Golf is one of those sports that does not lose its appeal as one grows older.

3. Bermuda is one of the resort areas which has little trouble attracting its share of tourists.

4. Most of the club is content but some of the membership is complaining.

5. By the time I reached the stage, I thought that everyone was staring only at me, and I could not ignore him or her.

6. Your suggestion about lower taxes seems sound and I am impressed by them.

7. Each of the cages at the zoo are designed so that each of the animals appear in their natural surroundings.

8. Before a child can run, they must learn to walk.

9. All of the important questions was asked, but most were left unanswered.

10. Neither Jim nor Pete passed their examination.

Exercise 8.3/8.4   Case of Pronouns / Reflexive and Intensive Pronouns

A. In each sentence, select the proper pronoun.

> **Example** To fertilize the garden properly we need to have   *its*
> (its/it's) soil analyzed.

1. Walt is stronger than (he, him).
2. Dr. Jonas Salk is a scientist (who's, whose) work helped conquer polio.
3. You are the one (who, whom) I promoted.
4. The rocket left (it's, its) launching pad at 9:00 A.M.
5. They managed to invite (theirselves, themselves) to dinner.
6. All that you have heard about (we, us) longshoremen is not true.
7. William Harvey was an English physician (who, whom) discovered that blood circulated in the human body.
8. We found (somebodys, somebodies, somebody's) wallet on the sidewalk.
9. You have only (you, yourself) to consider.
10. The awards were presented to (she and I, her and I, her and me, she and me).
11. John is better at mathematics than (I, me).
12. Antônio Gonçalves Dias was a nineteenth century Brazilian author to (who, whom) the people gave the name "the Poet of the Indians."
13. I shook hands with President Coolidge (himself, hisself).
14. The townspeople erected a monument to the saint (who, whom) they revered.
15. The parrot opened (its, it's) cage and escaped.

1. _____
2. _____
3. _____
4. _____
5. _____
6. _____
7. _____
8. _____
9. _____
10. _____
11. _____
12. _____
13. _____
14. _____
15. _____

B. Rewrite each sentence in which there are errors in pronoun case and form. If a sentence is correct, do not rewrite it.

Example I want to hire the woman who you recommended, not the one who he suggested.

I want to hire the woman whom you recommended, not the one whom he suggested.

1. One man's poison is anothers meat.

2. Us executives have to take some of our work home.

3. Giacomo Puccini was an Italian composer who's most popular operas are *La Bohème, Tosca,* and *Madame Butterfly.*

4. The turtle is able to pull it's head, limbs, and tail into its shell.

5. Ricardo asked Juan and myself if he could pick us up after dinner.

6. Who did you bring with yourself?

7. The immortal gods theirselves cry out at this injustice of your's.

8. They are also in college as you and me.

9. Were you able to communicate with the extraterrestrial being who left the spaceship?

10. Before you and me can vote intelligently, we must examine the issues theirselves and decide who we should support.

11. Although she is more talented than me, she herself has said that there is no one for who she has more respect than myself.

12. If you are trying to decide which of we candidates should get the job, you should examine each's strengths and weaknesses to determine whom is more qualified, her or I.

Exercise 8.5   Choice of Personal Pronoun Form

A.   For each passage, select the proper words and write them in the spaces
at the right.

Example When (I entered, you enter) college,   *I entered*

(I felt, you feel) apprehensive.   *I felt*

1.   It is (this writer's, my) conclusion   1. _____
that the *Pequod* functions as a sym-
bol of human society.

2.   It is discouraging when (one studies,   2. _____
you study, I study) hard only to fail
(his, your, my) exams.   _____

3.   When (one, you) destroy(s) a per-   3. _____
son's confidence, (one, you, he)
destroy(s) (him, her, the person).   _____

_____

4.   Through (his, our, my) research,   4. _____
(the author has, we have, I have)
shown that the artifacts (he, we, I)   _____
found in the ruins are at least 3000
years old.   _____

5.   After (you, I) have looked at several   5. _____
examples of contemporary art, (you
are, I am) not sure what (you, I)   _____
have seen.   _____

6.   When (one visits, you visit, I visit)   6. _____
a bird sanctuary (one, you, I) may
need (one's, your, my) field glasses   _____
and camera.   _____

B.   Revise each passage so that the choice of personal pronoun form is consistent.

Example Although one can ask for help, you should be prepared to complete the task
alone.

*Although you can ask for help, you should be prepared
to complete the task alone.*

1. If one wishes to trace their family history, they should be prepared for a long chore. First, you should talk with your parents and grandparents. One's living relatives often can provide quite detailed accounts of several generations of their family.

2. After reading the works of Wordsworth, Shelley, and Keats, this writer is able to conclude that you find a particularly close relationship between the Romantic poets and nature. One is able to find many references to nature in their poems, and if we examine those references closely, you discover that nature meant something particular to Romantic poets.

3. We are of the opinion that most people do not use their time wisely. One can, for example, use odd bits of their time to think over their problems and formulate plans. If you are waiting in line to buy your lunch, one can choose a topic for their next paper. We can also use the time when one waits for a traffic light to turn green to plan an activity for tomorrow.

Review Exercise 8   Pronouns

A.   Rewrite each sentence, correcting all errors in the use of pronouns (agreement, case, reference, and form).

1. Linda was unable to give Sarah the message because she was talking with the person who the message concerned.

2. Although both of them have been asked to help, neither Vernon nor Elizabeth are able to donate their time to the project.

3. Although the average citizen believes firmly in democracy, they often do not bother to cast their ballots at election time.

4. None of the nations lack flags, ideologies, and patriots who they honor on holidays.

5. When the scene of the crime was shown to Sherlock and I, we found that all of the books was lying on the floor and the statue of Venus was gone from it's pedestal.

6. Aunt Rosita took seriously the citizenship for whom she had waited so long, and she instilled in each of us the desire to be good ones.

7. Some of the class is interested in studying those artists who's works are realistic; most of them wants to explore those artists whom painted in a naturalistic style; and all of it hopes to learn about the ones who were impressionists.

8. Although my son is taller than me, that jacket fits both he and I.

9. The specialist who I consulted last week suggested hisself that an operation would be necessary.

10. Mark Twain was one of those humorists who was able to make people laugh nearly every time he opened his mouth.

11. Businesses have often deceived consumers, not caring if they received inferior products at inflated prices, but only if they made a profit.

12. Andy and me hoped to convince the mayor hisself to speak at the ceremony honoring the woman who the club named Citizen of the Year.

B. Rewrite the following paragraph, correcting all errors in the use of pronouns (agreement, case, reference, and form), and using consistent pronoun and verb forms.

(1) All of us has seen speakers whom we knew were no better than we at public speaking. (2) One reason why you and me felt this way may have been that the speakers who we heard did not know how to use ones gestures properly. (3) When speakers face the members of an audience, they must use gestures carefully so that they will not be distracted. (4) One should not be one of those speakers who gestures continuously; rather you should be sure that your gestures are effectively spread out and that each of them are appropriate responses to specific points in your talk. (5) One should also vary their gestures rather than repeat the same one again and again, for they will bore them. (6) Speakers should control their gestures and not move mechanically. (7) And one should consider the audience themselves to determine the appropriateness of them to them. (8) For example, most of an adult audience does not appreciate a speaker who they see gesturing throughout one's talk. (9) However, an audience of children enjoy them. (10) Therefore, if we want to be an effective speaker, you should control and vary their gestures, and use them appropriately and sparingly. (11) If a speaker follows this advice, they will be one who's talks people will enjoy. (12) For when a speech has it's meaning enhanced by effective gestures, neither a young audience nor an older one find that their time has been wasted.

9

ADJECTIVES
AND ADVERBS

An *adjective* modifies a noun or a noun equivalent; an *adverb* modifies a verb, an adjective, another adverb, or a whole statement.

9.2 Predicate Adjectives

A *predicate adjective* follows a linking verb *(be, seem, appear, become, taste, feel, look,* etc.) and refers to the subject.

> The tree is **tall.** [modifies *tree*]

Some verbs, however, may be used both as linking verbs and as action verbs. Thus both adjectives and adverbs may be used after such verbs. To determine whether to use a predicate adjective or an adverb after a verb, decide whether the word modifies the subject or the verb. If it modifies the subject, use an adjective:

> The **sky** appeared **cloudy.** [*appeared* is a linking verb]

If it modifies the verb, use an adverb:

> The car **appeared quickly.** [*appeared* is an action verb]

Choice of *good, well.* *Good* is an adjective (a *good* dog); *well* is either an adjective (she is a *well* child) or an adverb (she hears *well*). Both *good* and *well* may be used as predicate adjectives, but with different connotations:

> He feels **well.** [refers to a physical condition]
> I feel **good** about our agreement. [refers to a state of mind]

Good should not be used in place of the adverb *well:*

> The chorus sang **well** [not *good*]

Choice of *bad, badly.* Although *badly* is sometimes used after a linking verb if the emphasis is on the verb (I feel *badly* about your illness), it is better to use *bad* with linking verbs:

148

The liver tastes **bad.**

I felt **bad** about your illness.

Choice of *most, almost.* *Most* is an adjective meaning "the greatest number"; *almost* is an adverb meaning "very nearly." Do not use *most* as an adverb:

Incorrect	He is **most** always ready on time.
Correct	He is **almost** always ready on time.

9.4 Forms of Adverbs

Although some adverbs (*now, quite, even, there, too,* and so on) have no distinctive form, most adverbs are formed by adding *-ly* to an adjective (*peculiar, peculiarly; real, really; constant, constantly*). A few adjectives ending in *-ly* are also used as adverbs (*early, likely*). Adverbs can be made by adding *-wise* to a noun (*lengthwise, endwise*), but this practice has been greatly abused (*moneywise, dictatorwise*). Such words are better avoided.

Some adverbs have two forms, one with the *-ly* and one without (*slow, slowly, quick, quickly*). Although the two forms are usually interchangeable, the *-ly* form is used between *to* and a verb and between the subject and verb:

He wore his gunbelt **loose.** [*Or* He wore his gunbelt **loosely.**]
to **closely** observe [not to *close* observe]
she **brightly** said [not she *bright* said]

When adverbs have only the *-ly* form (*considerably, really, seriously, surely*), do not drop the *-ly* ending:

They dressed **differently** [not *different*] from everyone else.

9.5 Position of Adverbs

Unlike adjectives, which usually appear immediately before or after the words they modify, adverbs can appear in various places in a sentence (He *quickly* stopped the car; he stopped the car *quickly; quickly* he stopped the car).

Misplaced Adverbial Modifiers (MM). Problems arise if adverbs are not placed so that the meaning of a statement is clear. A misplaced adverb could (1) seem to modify one word when it is supposed to modify another or (2) seem to refer to either of two elements in the sentence:

MM	We have **almost** planted every available acre. [seems to modify *planted;* should modify *every*]
Revised	We have planted **almost** every available acre.

MM	Because it seemed that the roof would collapse **quickly** we removed all of the occupants. [could modify either *removed* or *collapse*]
Revised	Because it seemed that the roof would collapse, **quickly** we removed all of the occupants.
	Because it seemed that the roof would collapse, we **quickly** removed all of the occupants.

Position of *only* and Similar Adverbs. Limiting adverbs (*only, merely, hardly, just*) should be placed immediately before the elements they modify. Note the difference in meaning of the following:

> **Only** I like you.
> I **only** like you.
> I like **only** you.

9.6 Double Negatives

Double negatives are statements in which a second negative needlessly repeats the meaning of the first negative. Double negatives should be avoided.

Incorrect	**No** individual has **not** wished for ill health.
Correct	**No** individual has wished for ill health.
Incorrect	He has**n't** got **no** money.
Correct	He has **no** money.
	He has**n't** any money.

Can't hardly, couldn't scarcely, wasn't barely and similar constructions are double negatives to avoid. *Irregardless* is also a double negative; use *regardless* instead:

Correct	From the balcony, you **can hardly** [not *can't hardly*] hear the actors.
Correct	I will speak **regardless** [not *irregardless*] of the consequences.

9.7 Comparison of Adjectives and Adverbs

Most adjectives and adverbs have three different forms to indicate degrees of the characteristics they name: *positive, comparative,* and *superlative*. Most adjectives and adverbs are compared either by adding *-er, -est* to the positive form or by placing *more, most* (or *less, least*) before the positive form. A few common modifiers form the comparative and superlative degrees irregularly.

	Positive	Comparative	Superlative
Adjectives	cold	colder	coldest
	intelligent	more intelligent	most intelligent
	bad	worse	worst

150

Adverbs	near	nearer	nearest
	intelligently	more intelligently	most intelligently
	well	better	best

The Comparative Form is generally used to compare two things:

You are **smarter** than I am
San Francisco is **farther** from New York than Detroit is.

The Superlative Form is used to compare three or more things:

You are the **smartest** person in class.
San Francisco is the **farthest** I have traveled from home.

Avoid using the superlative to indicate nothing more than general approval:

Weak	He has the **nicest** smile.
Better	He has a **nice** smile.

Comparison of *unique* and Similar Words. *Unique, perfect, dead, empty, full* and other words that express absolute states are usually not comparable. Nothing can be *more empty* or *most dead*.

Comparing Like Items. Things compared must be of the same kind and must be able to be compared:

Incorrect	Let us compare Monet's **paintings** to **Van Gogh.** [*paintings* and *Van Gogh* are not comparable]
Correct	Let us compare Monet's **paintings** to **Van Gogh's.**
	Let us compare Monet's **paintings** to **those** of Van Gogh.

Completing Comparisons. Statements involving comparisons should be written out in full; otherwise the meaning may be ambiguous:

Ambiguous	She enjoys Mozart more than **other** composers.
Clear	She enjoys Mozart more than **she enjoys other composers.**
	She enjoys Mozart more than **other composers do.**

Double Comparisons (*as . . . as, if . . . than*) should also be stated completely:

Incomplete	He can run **as** fast, **if** not faster **than,** Alex.
Complete	He can run **as** fast **as, if** not faster **than,** Alex.
Better	He can run **as** fast **as** Alex, **if** not faster.

Use of *other* in Comparisons is used only in comparing things of the same class, not in comparing things of different classes:

Incorrect	Our cat makes a better pet than any **other** dog.
Correct	Our cat makes a better pet than any dog.
	Whiskers makes a better pet than any **other cat** I know.

Use of *like* or *as* in Comparisons. *Like* is a preposition and is followed by a noun or noun equivalent; *like* introduces a *prepositional phrase* of comparison:

> She sings **like** her mother.

As (as if, as though) is a conjunction and is followed by a *clause* of comparison:

Weak	He wanted to become a lawyer **like** his mother had been.
Preferred	He wanted to become a lawyer **as** his mother had been.

Exercise 9   Adjectives and Adverbs

A.   In the first column on the right, write each adjective and adverb in the
following sentences. In the second column, indicate whether it is an adjective (ADJ) or adverb (ADV). Then write the word it modifies in the
third column (if an adverb modifies an entire sentence, write *statement* in
the third column.)

Example

	Modifier	ADJ/ADV	Modifies
The blue car swerved	*blue*	ADJ	*car*
sharply.	*sharply*	ADV	*swerved*
	Modifier	**ADJ/ADV**	**Modifies**

1.   The harried officer fran-   1. _____

tically attempted to un-   _____

tangle the chaotic traffic.   _____

2.   Being of unquestionably   2. _____

sound mind, I hereby   _____

will to my only worth-   _____

while relative my black   _____

cape and my silk spats.   _____

3.   Unfortunately, the sec-   _____

ond explosion ignited   _____

the wooden structure   3. _____

which proceeded to burn   _____

furiously.   _____

4.   Because we are quite   _____

certain that all of the   4. _____

problems have been   _____

solved, we are prepared   _____

to initiate the project.

5. They saw a very playful   5. _____

otter cavorting in the   _____

warm sun.   _____

B. Cross out all of the adjectives and adverbs in each sentence, noting how they made the meaning of the sentence more specific. Then rewrite each sentence, adding different adjectives and adverbs to change the specific meanings.

Example Please hand me the ~~blue~~ book on the ~~second~~ shelf.

Please hand me the large book on the bottom shelf.

1. A broken arrow hung from the charred wall.

2. The conceited woman laughed caustically.

3. The persistent salesman talked glibly about the easy payments.

4. The timid knight stood fearfully before the mouth of the forbidding cave.

5. A rubber duck floated aimlessly among toy frogs and plastic lily pads.

C. Develop each sentence by adding adjectives and adverbs to make the meaning more specific. Do not, however, overload your sentence with adjectives and adverbs.

Example The hornet attacked the child.

The angry hornet attacked the frightened child.

Not The very angry hornet madly attacked the frightened, crying child.

1. The surfer swam to avoid the teeth of the shark.

2. Osceola was a Seminole chief.

3. The face of the ruler was carved in marble.

4. An artist, poet, and inventor, the professor was acclaimed as a genius.

5. You have hair, eyes, a nose, a mouth, ears, arms, legs, and a body.

Exercise 9.2/9.4/9.5   Choosing Adjective and Adverb Forms/Position of Adverbs

A.   Select the proper adjective or adverb form and write it in the space at the right.

Example They talked (calm, calmly).   *calmly*

1. Her doctor feels (good, well) about   1. _____
    the fact that Anita feels (good, well)   _____
    now.

2. Charlie Brown (most, almost) always   2. _____
    strikes out.

3. Lucretia Borgia thought that her   3. _____
    wine tasted (bad, badly).

4. William Blake viewed the universe   4. _____
    (different, differently) from others.

5. Roland's horn sounded (clear, clear-   5. _____
    ly) in the distance.

6. I am (slow, slowly) accepting my   6. _____
    (recent, recently) acquired respon-   _____
    sibilities.

7. Because Mike paints (good, well),   7. _____
    his work was (quick, quickly) se-   _____
    lected for the exhibit.

8. Eight dollars is a (considerable, con-   8. _____
    siderably) large amount to pay for a
    frankfurter without mustard.

9. *The Sound of Music* was a (real,   9. _____
    really) fine family film.

10. Her (exceptional, exceptionally) performance on the uneven bars won
her a standing ovation from the
(usual, usually) indifferent crowd.

10. _____

_____

11. It was (sure, surely) nice to see you
again.

11. _____

12. The situation proved (seriously, serious) when we discovered that our
food supply had dwindled (most,
almost) (complete, completely).

12. _____

_____

_____

13. Although the slope did not look
(easily, easy), we were able to negotiate it (easily, easy).

13. _____

_____

14. Because he was (serious, seriously)
hurt in the fall, he was moved
(quick, quickly) to the hospital
where surgeons attempted to repair
his (severe, severely) injuries.

14. _____

_____

_____

15. (Lucky, Luckily), they were able to
(complete, completely) repair the
damage.

15. _____

_____

B. Revise each sentence to correctly place misplaced modifiers.

Example You have nearly eaten all of the candy.

You have eaten nearly all of the candy.

1. The children looked in the bakery window and saw gingerbread figures
staring back at them hungrily.

2. As the door opened slowly she moved into the room.

3. I am so sentimental that the most trivial things even move me to tears.

4. With Marshal Dillon watching carefully the gambler dealt the cards.

5. Vera's team has almost won all of the games.

6. When the giant turned quickly the elf hid behind the saltshaker.

7. Dennis had nearly collected all of the coins minted since he was born.

8. When the audience broke into applause spontaneously he wept.

9. Sneakily we saw the cat eyeing the goldfish.

10. We found ourselves on the beach somehow still alive.

Exercise *9.6/9.7* Comparison of Adjectives and Adverbs/Double Negatives

A. Revise each sentence: correct any errors in degree; make all comparisons idiomatic; and eliminate all double negatives.

Example My frog can hop farther than Alice.

My frog can hop farther than Alice's.

1. Isn't Skipper the smartest dog?

2. My piece of possum pie is as small or smaller than yours.

3. I can't hardly wait until I am more big than I am now.

4. Claudia's saw seems to be sharper than you.

5. With ice in your hair and beard, you look as the Abominable Snowman.

6. As we moved closer, the light grew brillianter and brillianter until it was as bright if not brighter than the sun.

7. She enjoys Tolstoy more than other Russian novelists.

8. Try a Big Rat Sandwich! It's better than other restaurants.

9. They respect her more than you.

10. He has feet nearly as attractive as a camel.

NAME . . . .   SCORE . . . .

B. Fill in the spaces with the form of the word given which is appropriate to the comparison being made.

Example Of all your reasons for being late, the _most plausible_
(plausible) one is the last.

1. You will view the situation differently when you are _____
    (emotional) than you are now.

2. Pluto is the planet _____ (far) from the sun.

3. To disarm the bomb successfully, you need to work _____
    (delicately) than you are.

4. Although your problem is a strange one, it is not _____
    (unique).

5. George was not selected to be a cheerleader because his cheers were
    _____ (dynamic) than Ralph's.

6. When the time expired, she had _____ (almost)
    finished the examination.

7. Occasionally the mail contains an interesting letter, but _____
    (often) it is filled with bills and circulars.

8. The lighting in the cafe was the _____ (dim) I
    had ever seen.

9. He wandered _____ (errantly) from the path of truth.

10. That statue is _____ (shapely) than this one.

11. The comedian at The Gazebo this week is _____
    (funny) than the one who appeared last week.

12. She has a _____ (deep) mind than he does; in
    fact, it is the _____ (intricate) I have seen.

13. Paul is a _____ (good) cook; Fred is
    _____ (good) than Paul; Frank is the
    _____ (good) of the three.

14. Although your muscles may be _____ (strong)
    than mine, your mind is _____ (weak).

Review Exercise 9 Adjectives and Adverbs

A. Rewrite the following paragraph (1) so that the forms, positions, and degrees of all adjectives and adverbs are correct, (2) so that all comparisons are idiomatic, and (3) so that all double negatives are eliminated.

(1) My dream was a most unique one in which everything seemed nearly a distortion of reality. **(2)** I was walking careful down a corridor that had as many if not more twists and turns than a maze. **(3)** The dim lighted corridor was lined with strange shaped doors. **(4)** Then three long-haired eggplants brandishing sharper swords burst through a door and danced ballet-wise around me, swinging lusty their swords as executioners. **(5)** The blade carried by the smaller eggplant sliced a piece of material even out of my sleeve. **(6)** I was real scared, but terrorwise the worse was yet to come. **(7)** From the next door appeared a brightly red rose as tall or taller than a telephone pole and giving off an odor as pungently as a skunk. **(8)** Its stems covered with the sharpest thorns writhed like a snake does. **(9)** That fantastic flower snapped open its petals quick and spoke to me. **(10)** "You have done good to make it this far along the corridor," it said, "but this is all the farther you can go safe." **(11)** Irregardless of what the rose said, I knew intuitive-like that I couldn't scarcely go back. **(12)** Although the rose's stems were thrashing wild as the arms of an octopus and it blocked the corridor like a net blocks the sea, waiting to catch me fishwise, I charged brave. **(13)** Although it was my fonder wish that I could get past the reeking monster somehow those dread claws impaled me. **(14)** I couldn't hardly breathe because the rose's stench affected me more than any other anesthetic. **(15)** Just as I reached those thorns which could tear me into as many if not more pieces than a paper shredder suddenly I woke up.

B. For each sentence, first correct any errors involving adjectives and adverbs. Then add the material indicated.

1. The cat couldn't hardly squeeze into the box.
   (Correct any errors.)

   (Add adjectives modifying *cat* and *box*.)

2. A woman can think.
   (Correct any errors.)

(Add an adjective modifying *woman* and an adverb modifying *think.*)

(Add *only.*)

(Move *only* to a different place in the sentence.)

3. He seeks trouble like an actor seeks applause.
    (Correct any errors.)

    (Replace *an actor seeks applause* with something else.)

    (Add an adverb modifying each verb.)

4. He is sly as a fox.
    (Correct any errors.)

    (Replace *is sly* with an action verb and an adverb.)

C. Write the sentences described.

1. a sentence using *serious* and *seriously*

2. a sentence using *bad* and *badly*

3. a sentence using *look* as a linking verb with a predicate adjective

4. a sentence using *look* as an action verb with a modifying adverb

5. a sentence using *only*

6. Move *only* to a different place in the previous sentence to change the meaning.

7. a sentence using all three degrees of *well* (adverb)

8. a sentence in which you compare your ability in your first attempt to do something (bowl, fish, ride a bicycle, drive a car) with your proficiency now

9. a sentence using *as . . . as,* or *if . . . than* to compare the ways in which two living creatures eat or drink

10. a sentence in which you compare two things, using *these* and *those, less* or *more,* and *like* or *as*

Further Practice Exercise 1   Grammar and Usage
(Chapters 1-9)

A.   Answer the questions following each sentence; write your answers in the spaces at the right.

The dishonest alchemist completely convinced the gullible townsfolk that he could turn lead into gold.

1.   What part of speech is *lead?*   1. _____

2.   What part of speech is *completely?*   2. _____

3.   Is *that he could turn into gold* an adjective, adverb,   3. _____

or noun clause?

Kismet is a Turkish word which means "fate" or "destiny."

4.   What is the subject of the sentence?   4. _____

5.   What type of verb is *is?*   5. _____

6.   What is the complement?   6. _____

After we had built our fortifications, we waited for the enemy to attack us.

7.   What type of phrase is *to attack us?*   7. _____

8.   Of what is *enemy* the object?   8. _____

9.   What kind of clause is *after we had built our fortifica-*   9. _____

tions?

Tarzan is one of those individuals who are real swingers.

10.   What is the antecedent of *who?*   10. _____

11.   What kind of clause is *who are real swingers?*   11. _____

12.   What kind of phrase is *of those individuals?*   12. _____

The forbidden fruit was eaten proudly by Eve.

13.   What voice is *was eaten?*   13. _____

14.   What part of speech is *proudly?*   14. _____

15.   What modifies *fruit?*   15. _____

Trying to catch a plane, we were delayed in very heavy traffic.

16. What kind of phrase is *trying to catch a plane?*   16. _____

17. What part of speech is *very?*   17. _____

18. What does *very* modify?   18. _____

If I were you, I would not give Ralph your telephone number.

19. What mood is *were?*   19. _____

20. What is the indirect object of *give?*   20. _____

21. What case is *your?*   21. _____

The security guard was sleeping at his post when an explosion violently awakened him.

22. What tense is *was sleeping?*   22. _____

23. What case is *him?*   23. _____

24. What is the subject of *awakened?*   24. _____

Will Raoul recover from his sore arm in time to pitch in the league play-offs?

25. What type of sentence is it (purpose)?   25. _____

26. What tense is the verb?   26. _____

27. How many prepositional phrases are there?   27. _____

Although Jack the Ripper is gone, he is not forgotten.

28. What type of sentence is it (clause structure)?   28. _____

29. What voice is *is forgotten?*   29. _____

30. What is the antecedent of *he?*   30. _____

B.   Rewrite each passage, correcting all errors in grammar and usage.

1.   A number of mountain climbers has encountered a yeti, only a few has survived.

2. He had the habit to spend each of his weekends almost at the chalet where he was not aggravated by the sounds of the city. Such as the noise of the traffic, the wailing of sirens, and the barking of dogs.

3. She could see perfect as she approaches her eightieth birthday however, she had to admit that her hearing was not as keen as it was.

4. To adequately discuss the poetry of Keats, several images must be mentioned by this writer. Particular those of birds, flowers, and water.

5. When us guys took a boat trip through the Everglades, we had been careful not to let our hand trail in the water. Because alligators and snakes are reptiles and which lurk in the swamp.

6. I sure got a eerie feeling as a shortcut was took through the cemetery. Whistling in the dark graveyard silently tombstones and crypts appeared from among the shadows.

7. In the criticizing of the play, one reviewer has wrote that Ms. Sterling had gave such an inept performance as the Duchess that she was not capable to describe how badly it was. Using venom rather than ink, Mr. Holden was attacked for having been inepter as Bosola. And that she couldn't hardly be blamed because of the atrocious acting for leaving at intermission.

8. Riding the bus downtown, a poster announced that a series of lectures were to be held at Parthenon College by the Benevolent Union of Radiology Professors open to the public.

9. I have ate the last sled dog. I have long ago abandon the sled because it could not be dragged through the snow by myself. I set in the snow watching the sun sink three wolves appear on the horizon. I have wrote this note, lay it in a jar, digged a hole and mark the spot with my empty rifle. Whomever has found this will also find my bones.

10. Him and me has been together for a long time. We growed up together, tasting each others lollipops and chasing each others girls. None of the other guys was as close as us, although a number was pretty close. We went to even the same college. Graduating, that business was joined by he and I. And now us two is retiring together with identical gold watches. Whomever said friendship was temporary spoke wrong.

C. Write the sentences described, using correct grammar and usage.

1. a sentence using the superlative degree of *sincerely*

2. a sentence including an infinitive phrase

3. a sentence including a subordinate clause beginning *whose*

4. a sentence using *some* as the subject

5. a sentence using *whomever*

6. a question including two main clauses joined by *or*

7. a statement with two main clauses joined by a conjunctive adverb

8. a complex sentence with these ingredients:
   a) a subordinate clause beginning *although* which states a comparison between two things
   b) a main clause which states a comparison of more than two things

9. a compound-complex sentence with these ingredients:
   a) a subordinate clause beginning *when* with a compound subject
   b) two main clauses
   c) a subordinate clause beginning *because*

10. a complex sentence with these ingredients:
    a) a verbal phrase including *having spoken* and an adverb
    b) a main clause with an indirect object and a direct object
    c) an adjective clause modifying the direct object

D. Combine the material given into a complete, gramatically correct sentence. You may correct errors, change clauses to phrases or phrases to clauses, make appositives, add words, and the like.

1. Ulysses Simpson Grant was the eighteenth president of the United States.
   Harry Morgan portrayed him in the movie *How The West Was Won*.
   Harry Morgan played Colonel Potter on the television program *M*A*S*H*.

2. Beethoven had wrote his Third Symphony between 1803 and 1805.
   Being called the Eroica Symphony, Beethoven dedicated the work to Napoleon.
   Napoleon was the Emperor of France at the time.

3. George Hay was known as the "Solemn Ole Judge."
   The Grand Ole Opry began on November 28, 1925.
   George Hay founded this.
   Being heard on radio station WSM, which was in Nashville, Tennessee.

4. Don Larsen was a pitcher, he pitched for the New York Yankees.
   He pitched the only perfect game in World Series history.
   Being on October 8, 1956, he pitched it at Yankee Stadium.
   It was against the Brooklyn Dodgers.
   The Yankees won, 2-0.

5. Michael Landon played Little Joe Cartwright.
   He did this in the television series *Bonanza*.

Having a real name of Eugene Orowitz, the character Charles Ingalls
was also played by Landon.
It was in *Little House on the Prairie.*
Little House on the Prairie was another television series.

6. Luther "Bill" Robinson was an extraordinary black tapdancer.
    It was in the 1920's and 1930's.
    He played Shirley Temple's dancing partner in four films, these in-
    cluded *Rebecca of Sunnybrook Farm.*
    He was known as Mr. Bojangles.

E. Make each of the following passages one gramatically correct sentence.
    In your revision, eliminate unnecessary and repetitious words.

1. Regarding the behavior of societies' members, rules are forming. Every
    society does this.

2. Being formed by society, criminal behavior is delineated by these rules.
    Which also delineate antisocial behavior.

3. There's prohibitions regarding criminal behavior these are codified. They
    are codified in the written criminal laws.

171

4. Being unwritten, antisocial behavior has prohibitions against it. It appears in the unwritten social code that code is established by society.

5. Engaging in criminal behavior, it is not necessarily the same. As engaging in antisocial behavior because they are not necessarily the same.

6. An act can be criminal. It may also be antisocial. Another act might be antisocial it can not be criminal. Another act may be criminal, it may not be antisocial.

7. Beating and robbing senior citizens, criminal acts are being committed by individuals. It is also antisocial.

8. An individual continually being sarcastic and insulting others, this is antisocial behavior. But committing a crime is probably not being done.

9. Probably stealing food, the act being did to feed a family, is committing a crime. It is perhaps not antisocial.

10

END PUNCTUATION

Every sentence requires a punctuation mark at the end—a period (.), a question mark (?), or an exclamation mark(!).

10.1 Periods

Periods are used—

1. After statements and commands:

    The sky is clear tonight. [statement]
    Go home. [command]

2. After indirect questions and courtesy questions:

    She wondered where they had gone. [indirect question]
    May we receive payment soon. [courtesy question]

3. After abbreviations (see 16, Abbreviations and Numbers):

    Ph.D.   etc.   i.e.   A.M.   Mr.

A period after an abbreviation may be followed by other punctuation marks if necessary, but is not followed by another period at the end of a sentence:

    After she earned her Ph.D., she received a postdoctoral fellowship.
    Did he earn a Ph.D.?
    He earned a Ph.D.

4. With figures:

    .667   74.8% $28.17 $.72 [but: 72 cents or 72¢]

(See 14.3 for periods used as ellipses to mark the omission of words.)

10.2 Question Marks

Question marks are used—

1. After direct questions:

   Will the economic conditions improve?

2. After questions within a sentence:

   "Have you eaten yet?" she asked.

When a question mark and quotation marks occur together, the question mark goes *inside* the quotation marks if only the quotation is a question. If the whole sentence is a question, the question mark appears *outside* the quotation marks:

> She asked, "Can music sooth the savage breast?" [Only the quotation is a question.]
> Do you believe that "music has charms to sooth a savage breast"? [The whole sentence is a question.]

3. To indicate a doubtful statement (with or without parentheses):

   Manor House, built in 1540**?,** was recently destroyed by fire.
   Manor House, built in 1540 **(?),** was recently destroyed by fire.

HINT: Avoid the use of a question mark in parentheses to indicate humor or sarcasm:

   He put up a brave **(?)** front.

10.3 Exclamation Marks

An exclamation mark is used—

1. After emphatic interjections:

   Help!   Ow!

2. After exclamatory statements:

   What a terrifying experience you had!

HINT: Except in dialogue, you will seldom need to use an exclamation mark. Use an exclamation mark only if a statement is genuinely emphatic.

Exercise 10   End Punctuation

A.   Provide periods, question marks, and exclamationmarks where needed. Write in the space at the right the correct punctuation mark, the word or abbreviation that goes with it, and any relevant quotation marks.

Example "Did you know that Susan Howe earned a Ph D in
      biochemistry" she asked

            Ph. D.
     biochemistry?"
        asked.

1.   Mr C K Berowne of Mt Pleasant, Alabama, escaped injury when his car slammed into a guardrail on Rt 62.

1.   _____

   _____

   _____

2.   Ms Wilson asked the clerk to tell her where the sale items were

2.   _____

2.   _____

3.   Do you believe that "absence makes the heart grow fonder?"

3.   _____

4.   After winning the game with two free throws in the last second, Al leaped around the court screaming, "I did it We won We're champs"

4.   _____

   _____

   _____

5.   May we receive by Oct 15 at least 333% of the balance due

5.   _____

   _____

   _____

6.   Dr Murphy responded, "Didn't you know that the average normal body temperature of humans is 986°"

6.   _____

   _____

7.   "Egad" said Igor. "The Cyclops has escaped"

7.   _____

   _____

8.   With our $24 we were able to buy wood for $1780, varnish for $198, and a brush for $279, leaving us 43¢ in change

8.   _____

   _____

   _____

B. Correct each sentence, crossing out faulty punctuation and providing periods, question marks, and exclamation marks where needed. Also add or delete capital letters if you divide or combine structures to make the sentences correct. (Review 4, Common Sentence Errors, before completing this exercise.)

Example We were unable to plant our garden until late spring，̶ B̶ecause of the severe winter.

1. Walking briskly in the cool evening air, Arnold passed the T L Hardy Co where he worked he turned down St James Ave and came to the river

2. Have you washed the wall yet I am ready to start painting

3. "What a catastrophe" said Elmo. When he returned from the site of the train wreck

4. She had been sentenced to serve five years however, her sentence was suspended

5. 'Why have you asked me to perform" said Harold "You know that I get stage fright"

6. Get out of the kitchen don't you know that "too many cooks spoil the broth"

7. The committee chairperson asked the mayor where he got his campaign funds, the mayor answered, "I don't have to reveal those names, do I"

8. "Help I'm stuck in quicksand" screamed Jane desperately "That's nice, dear," said Tarzan as he rolled over and went back to sleep.

9. Does a ruler have the right to force citizens to act in a manner contrary to their moral beliefs this issue is explored in Sophocles' *Antigone*.

10. To the reporter who asked her where she had been held captive, the recently released heiress could only respond, "I haven't the foggiest notion," she then entered the limousine and was driven to the family's estate on Mt Mendacity

11

COMMAS

A comma marks a slight separation between grammatical elements which is similar to a pause in speech. Since commas contribute to the meaning of sentences, it is important to know when to use commas and when not to use them.

11.1 Commas Between Coordinate Clauses

Commas are generally used between coordinate clauses joined by coordinating conjunctions.

HINT: To remember the coordinating conjunctions, use the mnemonic device *fanboy*—**for, and, nor, but, or, yet.**

> The decision was reached after careful deliberation, **and** we all agreed to abide by it.
> The decision had been reached early in the day, **but** it was not announced until late afternoon.

Exception—The comma may be omitted before *and, or, nor* if the clauses are short and closely related in thought:

> I round the corner **and** I am home.

11.2 Commas After Conjunctive Adverbs

In joining two coordinate clauses with a conjunctive adverb *(however, nevertheless, therefore, consequently, also)*, the adverb is preceded by a semicolon and followed by a comma:

> The auctioneer looked my way; **however,** I did not have enough money to bid again.
> You are the best qualified applicant; **therefore,** I am happy to offer you the position.

11.3 Commas After Long Introductory Elements

An adverb clause or a long modifying phrase placed at the *beginning* of a sentence is usually separated from the main clause by a comma:

> **Because she was not able to find a piece of paper,** she wrote the list on the back of an old envelope. [adverb clause]
> **Clinging precariously to the limb,** the kitten mewed helplessly. [long modifying phrase]

Exception—If the introductory adverb clause or modifying phrase is short and closely related to the main clause, the comma may be omitted:

> **After she left** she drove directly home. [adverb clause]
> **At this time** we are not hiring workers. [introductory phrase]

An adverb clause or a modifying phrase placed *after* the main clause usually is not separated by a comma:

> She drove home **before the police arrived.** [adverb clause]
> One must read *Finnegan's Wake* **to understand the depths of Joyce's genius.** [modifying phrase]

Exception—If a following adverb clause or modifying phrase is only loosely related to the main clause, a comma is used:

> Some gourmets find hot dogs delicious, **although they can't explain why.** [adverb clause]
> We hoped for victory, **encouraged by the early election returns.** [modifying phrase]

11.4 Commas with Nonrestrictive Modifiers

A *nonrestrictive modifier* is a subordinate clause or a phrase that does not limit the meaning of the term it modifies; if it were omitted, the meaning of the sentence would not change much. A *restrictive modifier* limits (or restricts) the meaning of the term it modifies; if it were omitted, the meaning of the sentence would change or become obscure.

Nonrestrictive modifiers are set off by commas; *restrictive modifiers* are not:

> Senior citizens, **who have been largely ignored for decades,** need to maintain their dignity as people. [nonrestrictive clause; simply adds information about *senior citizens*]
> Senior citizens **who lack adequate health care** should receive assistance from the government. [restrictive clause; specifies one group of *senior citizens*]

> The scene, **painted by Tintoretto,** is one of serenity. [nonrestrictive phrase; simply adds information about the *scene*]
> The scene **painted by Tintoretto** is one of serenity. [restrictive phrase; specifies which *scene*]

Note the different meanings of the last two sentences.

Appositives are usually nonrestrictive modifiers and are set off by commas:

> Valley Forge, **site of Washington's winter headquarters,** is visited by thousands of tourists each year.

Appositives that are restrictive or that are used as part of a name require no commas:

> He was proud of his daughter **the surgeon.** [specifies which *daughter*]
> Attila **the Hun** was called the Scourge of God. [part of the name]

11.5 Commas to Set Off Interrupting, Parenthetical, and Contrasting Elements

A word, phrase, or clause that interrupts a sentence is usually set off by commas or other appropriate marks:

> The United States, **on the other hand,** has existed for only two hundred years.

Adverbs appearing in the middle of a sentence that compare or contrast some preceding idea (*however, therefore, nevertheless, too, also, consequently, conversely*) are usually set off by commas:

> He knew, **however,** that his luck could not hold.

When such an adverb introduces a main clause and links it to a preceding main clause, the adverb is preceded by a semicolon and followed by a comma (see 12.1 for the use of semicolons with conjunctive adverbs):

> She ran to answer the telephone; **however,** it stopped ringing as she reached it.

When adverbs that compare or contrast appear at the beginning of a sentence, they may or may not be followed by a comma, depending on the emphasis desired:

> **Thus** the war ended not with a bang but with a whisper.
> **Therefore,** many who might have been killed in battle survived.

Adverbs that modify the verb or the entire sentence (*perhaps, so*) and conjunctions are not set off by commas when they begin the sentence:

> **Perhaps** we can go to the theater on Friday.
> **But** some instinct warned him of the danger.

Weak exclamations (*well, say, oh*) and *yes* and *no* are separated by commas:

> **Well,** you'll have to try again.
> **Yes,** you may visit for a while.

Names that interrupt direct address are set off by commas:

> I come to you, **my fellow Americans,** with a solemn message.
> I was trying to explain, **Ed,** that our checks will not arrive until Monday.

11.6 Commas to Separate Items in a Series

Words, phrases, or clauses in a series are traditionally separated by commas. Modern usage, however, often omits the comma before *and*, particularly in series of words or phrases:

> **Dolphins, porpoises, and seals** (*or* **Dolphins, porpoises and seals**) are among the sea creatures which perform at Marine World. [words]
> Our forces are supreme **on the land, on the sea, and in the air** (*or* **on the land, on the sea and in the air**). [phrases]
> **Because I trust in democracy, because I have faith in the people, and because I believe in a judicial system,** I am sure that the jurors will find me innocent. [clauses]

Exception—If all the items in a series are joined by conjunctions, commas are usually not used:

> We visited **Rome and Paris and Frankfurt and Madrid.**

Coordinate adjectives in a series that all modify the same word are separated by commas. In a coordinate series the adjectives could be joined by *and*, and the order of the adjectives is not important.

> He was **short, heavy, and balding.** [or *short, heavy and balding*]

Exception—Commas are omitted when the adjectives are placed so that each adjective modifies the entire phrase that follows. Such adjectives cannot be reversed in order and cannot be joined by *and*.

> She served a **fine old French** wine. [not a *fine, old, French wine*]

HINT: If you omit the comma before *and*, be sure that *and* indicates the last item of the series:

> She served **salad, corn and potatoes, and roast beef.** [not *salad, corn and potatoes and roast beef*]

11.7 Commas to Separate for Clarity

When a word has two possible functions, a comma may guide the reader:

Unclear   **We have nothing to fear but people who** live farther north do.

Clear   **We have nothing to fear, but people who** live farther north do.

1. Use a comma for clarity when the *subject* of a clause can be mistaken for the *object* of a verb or preposition that precedes it:

| *Unclear* | **As you know our plans** include a side trip to Hong Kong. |
| *Clear* | **As you know, our plans** include a side trip to Hong Kong. |

2. Use a comma when one expression might be taken for another:

| *Unclear* | After **he lost his bicycle racing** was impossible. |
| *Clear* | After **he lost his bicycle, racing** was impossible. |

3. When the same word occurs consecutively, a comma may be used:

Each of you who **works, works** well.

11.8 Commas in Conventional Places

Commas are used in the following conventional places—

1. To group numerals into units of three:

7,829   18,716,329   3,800,000,000

Exception—Commas are not generally used in round numbers of four figures, in serial numbers, or in street addresses:

7000   serial number 7J-441831   21907 Poplar Street

2. To separate the day of the month from the year:

October 8, 1940   May 24, 1964

A comma is optional when only the month and year are given:

July, 1963   July 1963

3. To separate elements in addresses:

Ogden, Utah   Washington, D.C.   Melrose, Middlesex County, Massachusetts

4. To separate proper names from titles and degrees:

Walter Stevens, Jr.   Penelope Quigley, A.B., M.S., J.D., Ph.D.

Within a sentence, the final element in dates, addresses, and titles is followed by a comma:

He traveled to Vienna, Austria, during the spring of 1972.

5. After the salutation of an informal letter. (A colon is used after the saluation in a formal or business letter.)

Dear Hank,   Dear Aunt Emma,   Dear Ms. Waters: Dear Sir:

6. After expressions that introduce direct quotations:

He said, "I think we've met before."

Exception—No comma is used with very short quotations, exclamations, or phrases built closely into a sentence:

He faced adversity by reminding himself that "this too shall pass."

11.9 Misused Commas

Do *not* use a comma—

1. Between main sentence elements (subject and verb, verb and object, verb and complement, preposition and object):

Incorrect	The lessons I learned in school, were not as important as the ones I learned after school. [comma between subject and verb]
Correct	The lessons I learned in school were not as important as the ones I learned after school.

2. Between two words or phrases joined by *and* or another coordinating conjunction, such as between the two parts of a compound subject or a compound verb:

Incorrect	In her spare time she made flower arrangements, and climbed mountains. [comma between two parts of a compound verb]
Correct	In her spare time she made flower arrangements and climbed mountains.

3. Between main clauses without a coordinating conjunction (see 2.2, Comma Faults):

Incorrect	The taxi was waiting, she had to leave.
Correct	The taxi was waiting; she had to leave.
	The taxi was waiting. She had to leave.

4. With restrictive modifiers:

Incorrect	The elephant, that escaped from the zoo, was seen running down Elm Street.
Correct	The elephant that escaped from the zoo was seen running down Elm Street.

5. After the last item in a series:

Incorrect	The plays of Shakespeare, Jonson, Marlowe, and Webster, are still being performed nearly four hundred years after they were written.
Correct	The plays of Shakespeare, Jonson, Marlowe, and Webster are still being performed nearly four hundred years after they were written.

Comma Usage

Commas Are Used:

Between coordinate clauses (11.1)
a. when joined by *and, or, nor* if the clauses are long or not closely related.
b. when joined by *for, but, yet.*

After conjunctive adverbs which join coordinate clauses (11.2)
In such cases, the adverb is proceeded by a semicolon and followed by a comma.

After long introductory elements (11.3)
An adverb clause or a long modifying clause which precedes the main clause is followed by a comma. (The comma is optional if the adverb clause or main clause is short and closely related to the main clause.)

With nonrestrictive modifiers (11.4)
a. to set off a subordinate clause or a phrase that does not limit the meaning of the term it modifies.
b. to set off appositives that do not limit the meaning.

To set off interrupting and parenthetical elements (11.5)
Words, phrases, and clauses which interrupt a sentence are usually set off by commas.

To separate items in a series (11.6)
a. in a series of words, phrases, or clauses not all joined by conjunctions.
b. in a series of coordinate adjectives which all modify the same noun.

To separate for clarity (11.7)
a. when the subject of a clause can be mistaken for the object.
b. when one expression might be taken for another.
c. when the same word appears consecutively.

In conventional places (11.8)
a. in numbers, dates, and addresses.
b. with titles and degrees.
c. with the salutation of an informal letter.
d. with expressions that introduce direct quotations.

Commas Should Not Be Used:

Between main sentence elements (11.9):
subject and verb, verb and object, verb and complement, preposition and object

Between two words or phrases joined by *and* (11.9)

Between two main clauses without a coordinating conjunction (11.9)
Use a semicolon.

With restrictive modifiers (11.9, 11.4)

After the last item in a series (11.9)

With an adverb clause or modifying phrase placed after the main clause (11.3)
unless it is only loosely related to the main clause and would be preceded by a pause in speech.

With adverbs that modify the verb or the entire sentence (11.5)

To separate items in a series if the items are all joined by conjunctions (11.6)

Exercise 11   Commas

A. Each sentence contains numbered places where commas might be inserted. If a comma should be used in a numbered space between coordinate clauses, after conjunctive adverbs, or after long introductory elements, put a comma in the appropriate space at the right. If a comma is unnecessary, leave the space at the right blank.

Example He asked **(a)** her to go **(b)** but **(c)** she declined.

a. _____
b. _____
c. _____

1. Working in the fields **(1)** from dawn to dusk **(2)** they developed **(3)** deep tans.

2. The telephone **(4)** rang **(5)** but **(6)** no one was there **(7)** to answer it.

3. After the fire broke out **(8)** and the alarm was sounded **(9)** a crowd gathered; therefore **(10)** the police had **(11)** to work hard **(12)** to keep the street clear.

4. Winning a gold medal **(13)** is my dream **(14)** and I train every day **(15)** to make that dream **(16)** become real.

5. Reaching into his pocket **(17)** he pulled **(18)** out a battered wallet **(19)** crammed with money.

6. When you think **(20)** that life **(21)** has given you a lemon **(22)** you should make lemonade.

7. Because we like the neighborhood **(23)** we bought the house **(24)** but we did not know **(25)** that it was haunted.

1. _____
2. _____
3. _____
4. _____
5. _____
6. _____
7. _____
8. _____
9. _____
10. _____
11. _____
12. _____
13. _____
14. _____
15. _____
16. _____
17. _____
18. _____
19. _____
20. _____
21. _____
22. _____
23. _____
24. _____
25. _____

B. Each sentence contains numbered places where commas might be inserted. If a comma should be used in a numbered space to indicate a nonrestrictive modifier, to set off interrupting or parenthetical elements, or to separate items in a series, put a comma in the appropriate space at the right. If a comma is unnecessary, leave the space at the right blank.

Example Orange juice **(a)** which many people **(b)** drink every morning **(c)** is rich **(d)** in vitamins.

a. _____
b. _____
c. _____
d. _____

1. Economics **(1)** which many students find **(2)** a difficult subject **(3)** deals with such matters **(4)** as cost **(5)** and price **(6)** savings **(7)** and investments **(8)** and supply **(9)** and demand.

2. The questions **(10)** that he avoided **(11)** and the incomplete answers **(12)** that he gave to other questions **(13)** cause one **(14)** to challenge his competence.

3. The wheel **(15)** which is vital to civilization **(16)** was invented by an unknown **(17)** but brilliant **(18)** primitive **(19)** human.

4. The wheel **(20)** however **(21)** has become a bane to humanity. Automobiles now **(22)** clog the highways **(23)** tankers spill oil into the sea **(24)** and **(25)** airliners crash into mountains.

1. _____
2. _____
3. _____
4. _____
5. _____
6. _____
7. _____
8. _____
9. _____
10. _____
11. _____
12. _____
13. _____
14. _____
15. _____
16. _____
17. _____
18. _____
19. _____
20. _____
21. _____
22. _____
23. _____
24. _____
25. _____

C. Each sentence contains numbered places in which commas might be inserted. If a comma should be used in a numbered place, put a comma in the space at the right. If a comma is unnecessary, leave the space at the right blank.

Example The dress **(a)** in the store window **(b)** was appealing **(c)** but **(d)** I had no money.

a. _____
b. _____
c. _____
d. _____

1. The scientists **(1)** who helped develop the atomic bomb **(2)** urged the government **(3)** not to use it.

2. Lorenzo **(4)** the Magnificent **(5)** who is generally considered to have been the most brilliant **(6)** of the

1. _____
2. _____
3. _____
4. _____
5. _____
6. _____

Medici rulers of Florence **(7)** built a fine library **(8)** which contained volumes **(9)** by Sophocles **(10)** Homer **(11)** and Pindar **(12)** among others.

3. Looking up **(13)** at the clear sky **(14)** we saw the full moon **(15)** and thousands of stars.

4. Because her interest in crime was detached **(16)** scientific **(17)** and dispassionate **(18)** she was able to study **(19)** the cases **(20)** of Jack **(21)** the Ripper **(22)** Thomas Neill Cream **(23)** and Hawley Harvey Crippen **(24)** without having nightmares.

5. Wearing garlic **(25)** around the neck **(26)** is an old **(27)** Transylvanian **(28)** method **(29)** of preventing attacks by vampires **(30)** and werewolves **(31)** although werewolves **(32)** at least **(33)** seem not to fear the garlic.

6. After finishing second **(34)** two years in a row **(35)** we finally won **(36)** the league title **(37)** and entered the regional tournament.

7. Concentration **(38)** which can be developed **(39)** with practice **(40)** is of great value **(41)** whether you are taking an examination **(42)** or composing a song **(43)** or building a bridge.

8. William Howard Taft **(44)** our twenty-seventh President **(45)** served as **(46)** chief justice of the Supreme Court **(47)** after his term **(48)** in the White House.

9. Yes **(49)** you may borrow my car **(50)** but you will have to fill the gas tank.

7. _____
8. _____
9. _____
10. _____
11. _____
12. _____
13. _____
14. _____
15. _____
16. _____
17. _____
18. _____
19. _____
20. _____
21. _____
22. _____
23. _____
24. _____
25. _____
26. _____
27. _____
28. _____
29. _____
30. _____
31. _____
32. _____
33. _____
34. _____
35. _____
36. _____
37. _____
38. _____
39. _____
40. _____
41. _____
42. _____
43. _____
44. _____
45. _____
46. _____
47. _____
48. _____
49. _____
50. _____

D. Correct each sentence, adding commas where necessary and crossing out unnecessary commas.

Example His shirt was red~~,~~ and black,and~~,~~ his tie was red, gray, and silver.

1. The Rawlings Corporation which has its main office in Rawlings Alaska, and branch offices in Minneapolis Minnesota Dallas Texas and Newark New Jersey, did a gross business of $327018449, during the last year.

2. After we had registered for the course, and paid our lab fees we were issued our dissecting kits, and our frogs.

3. The paintings, of Thomas Cole, who ranks as one of America's greatest Romantic artists depict, the nation's landscape as wild primitive and free.

4. The feature event, on this evening's card, features Mazilla, the Masked Marvel, the current, world, heavyweight champion and Lord Lightly the ranking challenger in a two-out-of-three-falls match, with a sixty-minute time limit.

5. Walter, and I were both born, under the sign of Aries although neither of us, really, believes in astrology.

6. Dr. Wong on the other hand has had, great success in treating her patients partly because of her ability to set them, at ease, and partly because of her awareness, of the latest advances in medicine.

7. Because she had reached the top of her profession, Doris had nothing to gain but self-respect drove her to work toward perfection.

8. Because we had studied the history, of astronomy, we were aware of the contributions of Copernicus, Galileo, Kepler, Newton, and Einstein, to the modern view, of the universe.

9. "If we, who are aware of the facts, do not speak out" he said "and inform those, who are unaware, we fail to meet our responsibilities."

10. On our vacation trip, last fall, we visited, a number of very, historic places including Boston Massachusetts, Gettysburg Pennsylvania Winchester Virginia Atlanta Georgia, St. Augustine Florida and New Orleans Louisiana.

E.   Create the sentences described; be sure to use commas correctly and appropriately.

Example a. Write a main clause using *build* as a verb.

They built a tree house.

   b. Add an introductory adverb clause.

After they got permission, they built a tree house.

1.   **a.** Write a main clause using *open* as a verb.

   b. Add an introductory participial phrase.

2.   **a.** Write a main clause using *police officers* as the subject.

   b. Use *who sometimes are called upon to risk their lives* to modify *police officers.*

3.   To the introductory adverb clause *When she went to the shopping mall* add a main clause which uses *visit* as a verb and which indicates three or four places she went at the mall.

4.   **a.** To *He said* add a direct quotation indicating what he said.

   b. Add an introductory adverb phrase beginning *When.*

5.   **a.** To the main clause *young adults are often reluctant to seek advice* add a restrictive modifier.

   b. Add an introductory clause or phrase.

12

SEMICOLONS AND
COLONS

The functions of semicolons and colons are distinctly different. A semicolon separates coordinate (or equal) elements; a colon introduces or indicates what is to follow.

12.1 Semicolons

Semicolons, which separate coordinate elements, are used—

1. To separate main clauses *not* joined by a coordinating conjunction *(and, but, or, for, nor, yet):*

    The ship had been battered by the sea for three days; on the fourth day it sank.

    HINT: The use of a comma rather than a semicolon in such places results in a *comma splice.* Failure to use any punctuation mark creates a *run-on sentence.* (See 4, Common Sentence Errors.)

2. To separate main clauses joined by a conjunctive adverb *(however, therefore, nevertheless,* and so on):

    We had hoped to cross the river before the flood season; **however,** the heavy spring rains came early that year.

3. To separate main clauses connected by a coordinating conjunction

    (a) if the clauses are unusually long:

    We all know people who care only for themselves and who are ignorant of or unsympathetic to the needs of others; and we all know people who care only for others and who are seemingly oblivious to their own needs. [long clauses]

    (b) if the clauses are not closely related:

    The sun was shining brightly over the water; and our engine would not start. [clauses not closely related]

    (c) if one or more of the clauses contain commas:

The lions, fierce and proud even as they obeyed the trainer, thrilled the children; but the clowns, with their painted faces and colorful costumes, were more popular. [commas within clauses]

(d) if there is an emphatic contrast between statements:

You have the advantage for now; but that advantage will not last forever. [emphatic contrast between clauses]

4.   To separate clauses or phrases that contain other punctuation marks:

In the haunted house, we encountered a ghost, flying through the air; an evil-looking pirate, swinging his sabre and hopping on his peg leg; a vampire, drooling blood from his fangs; and a werewolf, howling ferociously and clawing at the air.

12.2 Colons

Colons, which introduce or indicate what is to follow, are used—

1.   After a main clause to indicate that a list, an illustration, or a summation follows:

My collection consists of stamps from the following nations: Denmark, Iceland, Sweden, Finland, and Norway.

HINT: Use a colon only after expressions that are grammatically complete. Do not use a colon between verbs and their objects or complements, or between prepositions and their objects:

Incorrect	My collection has stamps from: Denmark, Iceland, Sweden, Finland, and Norway. [colon between preposition and objects]
Correct	My collection has stamps from Denmark, Iceland, Sweden, Finland, and Norway.
Incorrect	My favorite poets are: Robert Frost, Gwendolyn Brooks, and Imamu Amiri Baraka. [colon between verb and objects]
Correct	My favorite poets are Robert Frost, Gwendolyn Brooks, and Imamu Amiri Baraka.

2.   Between main clauses when the second clause is an illustration, a restatement, or an amplification of the first:

He was a dreamer: he built castles in the air.

3.   Before a quotation that is grammatically complete, especially if the quotation is more than one sentence:

A pessimistic philosopher once said: "Life is meaningless. It is merely a moment in time in which one performs a series of meaningless actions while waiting to die."

4.   In conventional places:

   a) Between hours and minutes expressed in figures (7:45, 1:18).
   b) Between volume and page in formal footnotes and bibliographies
      James Joyce Quarterly, 12:476).
   c) Between the title and subtitle of a book *(From Corporal to Commander-in-Chief: A Life of Hitler).*
   d) Between chapter and verse of a book of the Bible (Genesis 3:16).
   e) After the salutation in a formal letter (Dear Admiral Jackson:**).**

Exercise 12   Semicolons and Colons

A. Indicate whether a semicolon (S) or colon (C) belongs in each numbered place by writing S or C in the space at the right. If neither punctuation mark is needed, leave the space blank.

Example We have searched all of the rooms except the kitchen **(a)** therefore, it must be hidden there.

a. _____S_____

1. *The Golden Bough* by Sir James George Frazer is an excellent work on classical mythology **(1)** it studies the origins and historical importance of **(2)** cults, myths, and rites.

2. There are three primary colors **(3)** red, yellow, and blue.

3. He practiced the guitar **(4)** for several hours each day **(5)** because he hoped to play professionally.

4. On July 8, 1889, John L. Sullivan and Jake Kilrain fought the last bareknuckle prizefight in history **(6)** Sullivan retained the heavyweight championship with a TKO over Kilrain in the seventy-fifth round.

5. We bought **(7)** apples picked right from the tree, cider squeezed while we watched, and jelly made that morning.

6. Sir Gerald Gargoyle spoke **(8)** "My lords, it has been several years **(9)** since I had the honor of addressing the House **(10)** but our situation is so desperate that I feel I must break my silence. We simply cannot allow these motorized vehicles to be driven on the roads of England **(11)** they frighten our horses."

7. They wanted revenge **(12)** they wanted blood for blood.

8. Each of our senses was stimulated **(13)** we heard the morning songs of the birds **(14)** we saw the sun rise over the hill **(15)** we felt the dew in the morning air **(16)** we smelled bacon frying over an open fire **(17)** and we tasted coffee out of old mugs.

9. She had almost convinced herself **(18)** that one small bite of apple wouldn't hurt **(19)** however, something about the old lady bothered her.

10. Tigers enjoy immersing themselves in water to cool off **(20)** this fondness for bathing distinguishes them from other cats.

1. _____
2. _____
3. _____
4. _____
5. _____
6. _____
7. _____
8. _____
9. _____
10. _____
11. _____
12. _____
13. _____
14. _____
15. _____
16. _____
17. _____
18. _____
19. _____
20. _____

B. Punctuate each sentence, adding semicolons, colons, and commas where appropriate.

Example Good teachers help their students learn; great teachers force their students to think for themselves.

1. Several ancient people built great civilizations the Incas in Peru, the Egyptians in Africa, the Mayas and Aztecs in Mexico, and the Chinese in the Orient.

2. He pulled frantically at the rip cord however nothing happened.

3. I have crossed the desert on a camel, the mountains in a balloon, and the ocean on a raft however, I have never known fear until I crossed the road on foot.

4. Lead isotopes are formed through the radioactive disintegration of uranium and thorium hence, the age of uranium and thorium minerals can be measured by an isotopic analysis of the lead found in them.

5. Your report should have several parts a preface, an introduction, a body, a conclusion, notes, and a bibliography.

6. Physical afflictions can be overcome although he suffered from epilepsy, Julius Caesar ruled Rome although blind John Milton wrote *Paradise Lost* although deaf Beethoven composed the Ninth Symphony, and although partly paralyzed by a stroke Louis Pasteur developed a vaccine for rabies.

7. We have discovered the cause of those strange sounds in the forest elves dancing in the moonlight.

8. The crowd quieted as the governor said "My fellow citizens, your cause is a just one it is one in which I also believe. I support your efforts."

9. The vampire flew through the open window and landed next to Gwendolyn's bed she awoke, saw the leering face, and screamed.

10. Our basketball team like the United Nations had representatives from nearly everywhere Carlos, a Mexican with a mixture of Spanish and Aztec blood Kunde, an African descended from a Bantu warrior Li, a

second generation American whose ancestors were born in China Stan, an American of Polish descent and Johnny, a Yankton Sioux.

11. The field of anthropology has several areas of specialization. Physical anthropology deals with the biological origins of humanity and with variations in the human species social anthropology explores the social existence of primitive societies cultural anthropology is concerned with the beginnings and development of human culture.

12. When Cheng saw the empty canoe floating aimlessly he called to Quang when Quang saw the markings on the canoe he screamed in agony.

C. Follow the directions given to create sentences which use semicolons and colons correctly. Also, use commas where appropriate.

Example a. Write a main clause using *cats* as the subject.

Cats train people.

b. Write a second main clause using *dogs* as the subject.

People train dogs.

c. Join the two clauses together using a conjunctive adverb.

People train dogs; however, cats train people.

1. To the main clause *She was an optimist* add a main clause which illustrates her optimism.

2. **a.** Write a main clause using *garden* as the subject.

b. Write a second main clause using *yard* as the subject.

c. Join the two clauses together without a connective.

3. **a.** Write a main clause detailing what sports are enjoyed in the fall.

b. Now add a main clause telling what sports are enjoyed in the winter.

c. Now add a main clause telling what sports are enjoyed in the spring and summer.

d. Now add the introductory main clause *Americans enjoy sports in every season.*

4. **a.** Write a main clause using *ceiling* as the subject.

b. Write a main clause using *walls* as the subject.

c. Write a main clause using *floor* as the subject.

d. Combine the three clauses together in one sentence.

5. [You might wish to review 12.1.4 before you write this exercise.]

a. In the dark we heard _____ _____ and _____. [list three things heard]

b. In the dark we heard _____ _____VP_____ _____ _____VP_____ _____ _____VP_____. [add a verbal phrase to each of the three things heard]

c. In the dark we heard _____ _____VP_____ _____ _____VP_____ _____VP_____ _____ _____VP_____. [add a second verbal to one of the things heard]

Review Exercise 10-12   End Punctuation, Commas, Semicolons, and Colons

A. For the following paragraph, indicate the punctuation mark (period, question mark, exclamation mark, comma, semicolon, or colon) that belongs in each numbered place by writing the mark in the space at the right. If no punctuation mark is needed, leave the space blank.

Walking along the beach **(1)** early in the morning **(2)** I

found **(3)** some driftwood **(4)** several varieties of shells **(5)**

and an old **(6)** French **(7)** wine **(8)** bottle **(9)** sealed with

wax **(10)** and containing a note. Eagerly **(11)** I broke the

seal **(12)** took out the note **(13)** and started to read the scrib-

bled words written there **(14)** "Help **(15)**" it began **(16)** "Some

two years ago **(17)** I entered this jungle **(18)** into which few

Europeans had ever come **(19)** I had hoped to civilize the

natives **(20)** teaching them to read and write **(21)** helping

them in their agricultural ventures **(22)** and teaching them

moral and ethical principles **(23)** Although **(24)** at first **(25)**

they greeted me warmly **(26)** things soon began to go

wrong **(27)** I asked them **(28)** if they would give up their

practice of eating the flesh of their neighbors **(29)** they

answered **(30)** 'why should we **(31)**' Our discussions got

1. _____
2. _____
3. _____
4. _____
5. _____
6. _____
7. _____
8. _____
9. _____
10. _____
11. _____
12. _____
13. _____
14. _____
15. _____
16. _____
17. _____
18. _____
19. _____
20. _____
21. _____
22. _____
23. _____
24. _____
25. _____
26. _____
27. _____
28. _____
29. _____
30. _____
31. _____

more and more heated (32) until (33) finally (34) they took

me (35) who had come to help them (36) prisoner (37)

They are now feeding me six meals a day (38) and they are

forcing me to eat (39) When I am sufficiently plump (40)

they will feast (41) I do not want to be forgotten (42) there-

fore (43) if you (44) who have found this (45) have a kind (46)

generous nature (47) erect a small monument to me with

this epitaph (48)

    'In memory of Henly Kidder (49) Something he dis-

agreed with ate him (50)' "

32. _____
33. _____
34. _____
35. _____
36. _____
37. _____
38. _____
39. _____
40. _____
41. _____
42. _____
43. _____
44. _____
45. _____
46. _____
47. _____
48. _____
49. _____
50. _____

B. Write the sentences described, using end punctuation, commas, semicolons, and colons correctly.

1. the words of Little Miss Muffet as she sat on her tuffet and began to eat her curds and whey (use a colon)

2. the words of the spider as he sat down beside Little Miss Muffet (use a question mark)

3. the words of Little Miss Muffet in response to the spider (use a question mark)

4. the words of the spider as Little Miss Muffet disappeared rapidly over the horizon (use a semicolon)

5. a sentence about the opposite sex (use a nonrestrictive modifier)

6. a sentence about the opposite sex (use a restrictive modifier)

7. a sentence listing your four favorite foods

8. a sentence in which you explain to Dracula why he shouldn't want to attack you (use a main clause and a subordinate clause)

9. Dracula's response to you (use a main clause, *however,* and another main clause)

10. a sentence listing three or four reasons why you do not want to spend a night alone in an abandoned mansion in the woods (use a colon and two or three semicolons)

11. two sentences in which you discuss the UFO you saw (use at least one subordinate clause and three main clauses)

12. two sentences in which you discuss a way to rid your neighborhood of dragons (use at least two subordinate clauses and a restrictive modifier)

C. To the following passage add end punctuation, commas, semicolons, and colons as appropriate. (You will also have to add capital letters to begin each sentence.)

Another way to insure longevity which is the subject of this book is to develop hopefully at a young age excellent dietary habits but by heavens in establishing your rules for eating pay no attention to the members of the medical profession after all what do they know how many of them live to be as old as I am the first rule of eating I developed and it was at the age of eight that I developed it is never eat anything green and fuzzy this rule which should form the base for any set of dietary principles was followed quickly by three other rules never eat anything grey never eat anything that is still alive whether plant or beast never eat anything capable of eating you although these rules are few in number if you follow them faithfully you may become a very old person according to me and remember that I am the expert there is only one important rule for the liquid you drink never drink water milk soda pop coffee tea beer or wine drink only whiskey and drink it at least three times each day if you eat and drink according to these rules you will also need to develop good living habits I have some rules even though others scoff at them for you to follow the three most important rules for living are these avoid all physical exercise more strenuous than shuffling cards avoid sitting in objects such as automobiles trains and airplanes which move avoid any activity like shark hunting skydiving and hangliding and alligator wrestling where you could lose your life.

[adapted from Martin "Methuselah" McGinty, *Longevity*]

13

DASHES, PARENTHESES, AND BRACKETS

13.1 Dashes

Dashes are generally used—

1.   To set off parenthetical expressions and abrupt interruptions:

    You are in for trouble—very serious trouble—if you continue to flout authority.

2.   To mark sharp turns in thought:

    Ms. Norman complimented me for my extraordinary competence, my industrious nature, and my honest character—then she fired me.

3.   To give greater emphasis to parenthetical elements that could also be set off with commas:

    Our love of violence—no doubt a characteristic inherited from our simian ancestors—has led us more than once to the edge of destruction.

4.   To set off a statement that summarizes or illustrates the preceding statement:

    The world was made smaller by two ditches—the Suez and Panama Canals.

5.   After introductory words which are to be repeated before each of the lines that follow:

    I promise—
      To seek out injustice.
      To help the downtrodden.
      To support and defend the country.

6.   To indicate interrupted dialogue (two dashes separated by a space are generally used):

    "But if you knew we were gone— —"
    "How could I have known that?"

Dashes should not be used to excess. They should not be used where another punctuation mark (or no mark) would be more appropriate.

Excessive	The weather has been unusual—we've had no snow—but the temperature has been very cold—particularly this past week.
Better	The weather has been unusual. We've had no snow, but the temperature has been very cold, particularly this past week.

13.2 Parentheses

Parentheses are used—

1. To enclose incidental remarks:

   In all of his travels (he had visited four continents) he had never encountered a people as friendly as the Malaki.

2. To enclose details and examples:

   The increases in workers' salaries (figure A) have been more than offset by rises in prices (figure B).

3. To enclose letters or figures used to enumerate points within a sentence:

   The major themes in the novel center on (1) the relationship of the individual to society, (2) the place of the individual in the universe, and (3) the inner tension between an individual's reason and emotion.

No punctuation marks are used before a parenthetical statement that occurs within a sentence. If a punctuation mark is needed after the parenthetical statement, it is put *outside* of the closing mark:

   This vacation (my first in five years) is relaxing.
   This vacation is fun (it ought to be at these prices).

If the parenthetical statement is a separate sentence that comes between sentences, the proper end punctuation is placed *inside* the parentheses:

   One of my first friends was Crusher Kelly. (We called him Crusher because he liked to crush paper cups by stamping on them.)

Dashes and parentheses have similar uses, but dashes set off elements more emphatically than do either parentheses or commas. In some cases a writer may use either dashes, parentheses, or commas, depending on the amount of emphasis desired.

13.3 Brackets

Brackets are used—

1. To insert editorial comments within quoted material:

   "This policy [of not intervening in the social problems of other countries] condemns millions to lives of slavery and injustice."

2. To indicate in quoted statements that the speaker didn't actually say the enclosed words:

   "You are all prejudiced [the audience stirred uncomfortably]."

Exercise *13*   Dashes, Parentheses, and Brackets

A.   Correct each sentence, adding dashes, parentheses, and brackets where needed. In some cases, more than one form of punctuation may be correct.

Example Among the new ideas which have greatly altered civilization are two that

changed radically the place of humans in the universe the heliocentric

universe and the theory of evolution.

1.   Speaking from a handwritten copy he had not had time to get it typed, the governor proclaimed the western half of the state a major disaster area and appealed pleaded, actually for federal assistance.

2.   "We must emerge victorious applause and we shall long applause."

3.   He considers himself a wit and he is half right.

4.   If we fortify the pass figure 1, the enemy will be forced to take the longer road figure 2, and we can deploy forces to meet them figure 3.

5.   That glorious defeat resulted in a rallying cry "Remember the Alamo!" which inspired the troops to future victories.

6.   Someone I believe it was Shakespeare once said: "We are such stuff / As dreams are made of."

7.   The original oil paintings, the shelves of rare books, and the priceless carpets all symbols of her success were thick with dust.

8.   In his own lifetime 1885-1970 he had seen the advent of industrialization, telecommunications, computers, miniaturization, and space exploration all pointing toward the developments of the next two hundred years.

9.   To begin, the speaker should salute those present: "Ladies and gentlemen if both sexes are in attendance, I am honored to have been asked if asked to address you."

10.   'All I want and I do want that is for each of you to try to complete your tasks before Friday the deadline, you will recall, was established by Mr. Frazier."

B. Correct each sentence, crossing out improperly used dashes, parentheses, and brackets, and replacing them with the proper punctuation marks.

Example Elizabeth I̸ of England ̸ enjoyed coursing—the chasing and killing of live quarry by greyhounds.

1. The band members—who spent all day Saturday soliciting funds door-to-door—managed to raise over $2000 for new uniforms—the other $1000 was the gift of an anonymous donor.

2. We enjoy summer (more than winter) because we can be outside (in the fresh air)—rather than cooped up (in the house).

3. My raccoon [I called him my raccoon because it was my trash he raided every evening] was on friendly terms with all of the dogs in the neighborhood—but I don't know how that happened.

4. "I would be happy to engage in such a battle (of wits) with you—however, I never fight an unarmed opponent."

5. We called the Shark Loan Company [which used the slogan—"Don't let others gouge you—come to us"]—our "friendly neighborhood predator."

6. It was a dark—and stormy—night—on board the ship were seven pirates—counting their treasure by candlelight [electricity was unknown at the time].

7. Admiral Drake (the Iron Duck) led his flotilla onto the coral reef—seven ships were lost (including Drake's flagship—*The Mouldy Quacker*).

8. The legacies we wish to leave our children are many—[1] a cure for cancer—[2] a world at peace—[3] the eradication of poverty—[4] a clean environment—and—[5] the ultimate pizza.

9. "We can no longer tolerate (we must no longer tolerate) these abuses—our rights and our bodies are being trampled—we must rally to the call—'Elves of the world, unite—' great applause."

10. He paused at the curb—he checked the traffic light—he looked carefully to the left and to the right—and then stepped briskly into an open manhole.

14

QUOTATION MARKS, ELLIPSIS MARKS, AND ITALICS

14.1 Quotation Marks

Quotation marks are used—

1. To enclose direct discourse:

   Hal said, "I'd rather be a pauper than a prince."

   Do *not* use quotation marks with indirect discourse:

   Hal said that he would rather be a pauper than a prince.

2. To enclose material quoted from others. *Short prose quotations* may be incorporated into the structure of a sentence:

   In considering this piece of legislation, we should be guided by the words of Sir Stuffly Curmudgeon who stated: "I am all for reform—provided that nothing changes."

Long prose quotations (in general, over fifty words or four lines of type) are usually indented, double-spaced, and *not* enclosed in quotation marks:

   In considering this piece of legislation, we should be guided by the words of Sir Stuffly Curmudgeon who stated:

   > All of this talk of reform is rubbish. It is tommyrot. There is nothing wrong with children working in factories or sweeping out chimneys. They learn about life that way. They perform valuable services that way. They earn their keep that way. Do not misunderstand me. I am all for reform—provided that nothing changes.

   For a quotation within a quotation, use single quotation marks if quoted material appears within another quotation enclosed in double quotation marks:

   Arguing against the bill, Representative Pastly stated: "We should be guided by the words of Sir Stuffly Curmudgeon who stated, 'I am all for reform—provided that nothing changes.'"

Use double quotation marks if quoted material appears within a long quotation that is indented and not enclosed in quotation marks.

In quoting poetry, use quotation marks if a phrase or line is incorporated in a sentence:

His "milk of human kindness" has soured.

If three or more lines of poetry are cited, indent, double-space, and omit quotation marks:

In his eulogy to Abraham Lincoln, "When Lilacs Last in the Dooryard Bloom'd," Whitman writes:

O powerful western fallen star!
O shades of night—O moody, tearful night!
O great star disappear'd—O the black murk that hides the star!
O cruel hands that hold me powerless—O helpless soul of me!
O harsh surrounding cloud that will not free my soul.

3.   Around titles of short written works such as short poems, essays, short stories, and magazine articles (see 14.3 for the use of italics with titles of longer works):

Wordsworth's poem "Michael"
his essay "Modern Values"
her article "Environmental Disasters"
Hawthorne's short story "Young Goodman Brown"

4.   To set off words used as words. A word used as a word may be either italicized or enclosed in quotation marks. Whichever you do, be consistent:

The words "gourmand" and "gourmet" [or *gourmand* and *gourmet*] often are used incorrectly.
In the eighteenth century, he would have been "a dandy" [or *a dandy*]; today he is simply "a disco jerk" [or *a disco jerk*].

Weak and Improper Uses of Quotation Marks.

1.   Do *not* use quotation marks for indirect discourse.
2.   Do *not* use quotation marks around quotations that are indented and double-spaced.
3.   Do *not* use quotation marks for nicknames:

Abe Lincoln [not *"Abe" Lincoln*]
Charles the Hammer [not *Charles "The Hammer"*]

4.   The use of quotation marks with slang and colloquial expressions is weak and best avoided:

Weak   He is a "hunk." [slang]
Improved   He is virile.

Quotation Marks with Other Punctuation. A number of conventions govern the use of other punctuation with quotation marks.

1. Commas and periods are always placed *inside* the closing quotation mark:

   "However," Helen said, "we still have time."

2. Semicolons and colons are always placed *outside* the closing quotation mark:

   She believed in "an eye for an eye"; he practiced turning the other cheek.

3. Questions marks, exclamation points, and dashes are placed—
   a) *Inside* the closing quotation mark when they apply to the quotation only:

   She turned abruptly and snapped, "Go to hell!"
   He gasped, "Tell the others——" and fainted.

   b) *Outside the closing quotation marks when they apply to the entire sentence:*

   Do you believe in "an eye for an eye"?

4. End punctuation marks are not doubled. If a quotation ends the sentence, the end punctuation within the quotation marks is sufficient.

Faulty	I asked Tom, "Did you like the play?".
Correct	I asked Tom, "Did you like the play?"

14.2 Ellipsis Marks

An *ellipsis* mark is a punctuation mark of three spaced periods (. . .) used to indicate that one or more words have been omitted from quoted material. If the ellipsis mark comes at the end of a sentence, four periods (. . . .) are used (three for the ellipsis and one for the period):

> His remarks were brief: "I want . . . to do a creditable job. . . . But I need your help . . . and your prayers."

If a paragraph or more than one line of poetry is omitted, a full line of ellipsis marks is used:

> Death, be not proud, though some have called thee
> Mighty and dreadful. . . . [five words omitted]
> . . . . [10 lines omitted]
> One short sleep past, we wake eternally
> And death shall be no more; Death, thou shalt die.
>
> —John Donne, *Holy Sonnet 10*

In narrative, ellipsis marks are sometimes used to indicate interruptions in thought, incomplete statements, or hesitations in speech:

> He panted, "Rejoice . . . we . . . conquer."
> "I can't seem to remember. . . . " His voice trailed off.

14.3 Italics

Italics (represented by underlining in handwritten or typed papers) are used—

1. For titles of newspapers, magazines, books, plays, films, long poems, and works of art:

Time magazine
The Boston Globe [or the Boston *Globe*]
The Naked Ape [book]
Mourning Becomes Electra [play]

Midnight Cowboy [film]
Paradise Lost [long poem]
Madame Butterfly [opera]
Mona Lisa [painting]

Some titles are set off neither by italics nor by quotation marks.

the Bible
the New Testament
the Declaration of Independence

the Gettysburg Address
the Sears, Roebuck Catalog
the Omaha Telephone Directory

2. For names of specific ships, airplanes, and spacecraft:

the *Titanic* [ship]   *Air Force One* [plane]   *Apollo VII* [spacecraft]

3. For words used as words. (They may also be set off by quotation marks.)

Some people confuse *predominate* and *predominant* [or "predominate" and "predominant"].

4. For foreign words, including the following—

a) Foreign words and expressions that are not in common usage:

coureur de bois   *wunderkind*   *deus ex machina*   *hasta luego*

A number of foreign words commonly used in English are not italicized:

bourgeois   laissez-faire   sputnik

b) Scientific names:

the moon fish *(Lampris regius)*   the common opossum *(Didelphis marsupialis)*

c) Uncommon Latin abbreviations and phrases:

quo modo   *quo jure*   *cum grano salis*

Common Latin abbreviations are not italicized:

e.g.   et al.   etc.   ibid.   i.e.   vs.   vis.

5. For emphasis:

Although we are all subject to restraints, we want to live *as free as possible.*

Italics for emphasis should be used sparingly.

Exercise **14**   Quotation Marks, Ellipsis Marks, and Italics

A. In each passage, correct any errors in the use of quotation marks, ellipsis marks, and italics, and add those punctuation marks where needed.

Example He asked ✗if I was familiar with the ~~Bible~~ and with Don Quixote, Cervantes's
novel.✗
$$\underline{Bible}$$

1. Senator Snort was quoted in the Washington Post as saying: At times
    such as these . . our country must stand behind its citizens, not on top
    of them.

2. On February 14, 1952, we sailed aboard the Valentine; on March 15 we
    anchored in Ides Bay. Our voyage was written up in both Newsweek
    and Time.

3. Mr. Hildreth told Keith: You should say She is sentimental, not She is
    sedimental.

4. When Henry explained why he was late, I took what he said "cum
    grano salis."

5. In his book entitled The Otter Cat, Dr. Robbins states:

    "The jaguarundi (Felis jaguarondi), found throughout Central and
    South America, hunts both in the daytime and at night. Although
    its diet consists mainly of frogs, small mammals, and fish, it also
    eats fruit. Adult specimens grow to four feet and weigh up to fifty
    pounds."

6. The announcer urged us "to go to our local theater to see the "horror
    double feature of the year": The Sponge that Soaked up Seattle, starring
    Rock Weakly and Heather Feather, and The Celestial Grave Robbers,
    featuring Claudia Clam and Ab Normal.

7. The first essay "question" on my humanities examination read: Compare
    and contrast the use of color imagery in Shakespeare's poem *Venus and
    Adonis,* Melville's novel "Moby Dick," Verdi's opera "Otello", Matisse's
    painting "The Dessert," and Joyce's short story "The Dead."

8. Matthew Prior's short poem *A Reasonable Affliction* points out that two people may have the same reaction to a given situation although their reasons may differ:

> "On his deathbed poor Lubin lies:
>   His spouse is in despair:
> With frequent sobs, and mutual cries,
>   They both express their care.
>
> "A diff'rent cause, says Parson Sly,
>   The same effect may give:
> Poor Lubin fears, that he shall die;
>   His wife, that he may live."

9. Urging the crowd to vote for her, the candidate insisted: "In the words of "Abe" Lincoln's *Gettysburg Addess*, I am for a government "of the people, by the people, and for the people," and I will listen to your concerns and do something about them."

10. In The Electric Eggplant, Rollie Rock tells the story of the rise to fame and fortune of a modern recording group. At one point Mr. Rock states: While in the tub grilling eggplant for dinner, the lead singer, Hank Gravel, accidentally knocked the grill into the water; yelling jubilantly, he knew he had found *the* name for the group. . . "

B. For each quotation, write a sentence that uses *part* of the quotation. Ordinarily you would not change material you are quoting in any way; in these quotations, however, the punctuation is sometimes intentionally incorrect or left out. In your sentences, and in the parts of the quotations you are using, use quotation marks, ellipsis marks, and other punctuation marks correctly. Underline all words that belong in italics.

Example Humans are, no doubt, descended from a strain of killer apes. As a result, latent within each one of us is an urge to kill.

> Professor Li stated: "Humans are ... descended from ... killer apes. As a result ... [each of us has] an urge to kill.

1. The werewolf is a wise beast which is most adept at stalking its victims until they are alone. This ability usually results in a tasty dinner taken at leisure.

2. The reasons for censorship change from age to age. All copies of the Renaissance play Isle of Dogs were confiscated and destroyed for political reasons. James Joyce's novel Ulysses was banned early in this century for moral reasons.

3. The altitude was beginning to take its toll on us. With little oxygen to breathe, we were finding it difficult to continue.

4. Language is continually changing. Some words such as garth and fey slowly disappear. Others, such as sputnik and input, enter the language.

5. I have been described as a vain and arrogant person. Nonsense. I am not vain; I am humble. I am not arrogant; I am modest. I am, if I do say so myself, a wonderful person.

6. Come live with me and be my love,,
   And we will all the pleasures prove,
   That valleys, groves, hills and fields,
   Woods or steepy mountain yields.
   > —from Christopher Marlowe,
   > "The Passionate Shepherd to
   > His Love"

7. Human history is written in blood on a parchment of human suffering—the blood of a pharaoh's slaves, the blood of Aztec sacrifices, the
   blood of a czar's purges, the blood of Attila's victims, the blood spilled
   at Marathon, Hastings, Jerusalem, Waterloo, Jutland, and Saigon.

8. For all of its faults, the American political system works. In each major
   crisis, the control of the government has passed from one leader to
   another without catastrophe. We have had no aspirant murder a Caesar,
   no War of the Roses, no coup d'etat, no battles for a throne.

9. In an article (The Modern Family) which appeared in The Atlantic
   Monthly last June, thrice-divorced writer Herman H. Holly argues: The
   modern family is not like that of the past. . . . . it has become a group
   of individuals rather than a unit composed of individuals. Holly, whose
   latest book, Society's Garbage, sold over 300,000 copies, goes on to suggest that the word individual has done more to destroy family unity
   than anything else.

Review Exercise *13–14* Dashes, Parentheses, Brackets, Quotation Marks, Ellipsis Marks, and Italics

A. Punctuate each passage, adding dashes, parentheses, brackets, quotation marks, ellipsis marks, and italics where necessary.

1. Should we book passage, asked Alicia, on the Queen Mary? Or should we sail on the Sunken Treasure?

2. The firm's treasurer was quoted last Friday in the Wall Street Journal as saying: Our company is in the best financial position it has been in . . for several years. . . I, for one, am not worried about my future. Indications are that he maintained this position vehemently over the weekend and that early Monday he flew to Brazil.

3. When asked her opinion of the new film Population Explosion, the critic for the Podunk Journal replied. It was a bomb.

4. He said, Of all the books I have ever read he has read at least three Paper Dolls and Rhinos is my favorite.

5. The increase in the number of ships of The Royal Baron's class see chart A has resulted in a proportionate increase in shipping mishaps see chart B.

6. My what sparkling white teeth you have said Dora to Drac. You must have brushed after every meal. That is perspicacious of you, my dear, said Drac as he took from his pocket his toothbrush.

7. The readings for this week, said Professor Shea, will include Conrad's novel Nostromo, Pirandello's play Henry IV, and Poe's short story The Cask of Amontillado. He did not assign the books of Genesis and Exodus from the Old Testament, although he told us that we could read them if we wished to.

8. You have read rather widely for an illiterate.

9. The cost of automobile insurance and a high cost it is prohibits some individuals from owning cars stated Insurance Commissioner Gregorio in an interview published in the Sunday Times.

B. Write the sentences described, correctly using dashes, parentheses, brackets, quotation marks, ellipsis marks, and italics where necessary.

1. a sentence containing the last words of Trigger O'Rourke as he lay in the dust with a bullet in him (use ellipses)

   Trigger gasped,

2. a sentence in which you indicate the last book you read and the last movie you saw

3. a sentence including an incidental remark in parentheses

4. a quotation from a speech by Senator Snort (indicate in brackets how the audience responded to the senator's words)

5. the words of Humpty Dumpty just before he fell off the wall (include a sharp turn in thought)

6. a sentence using part of this quotation: "Onward, soldiers, onward! Do not look back. Do not retreat. Press onward. For our homeland, for our families, for our goddess, onward!"

7. two or three sentences quoting Ms. Shoemaker (the little old lady who lived in the shoe with so many children she didn't know what to do) after a reporter asked her how many children she had

8. two or three sentences describing Jack-Be-Fumble's attempt to jump over a a lighted candle (use at least one dash)

9. two or more sentences presenting the statements of Burt Reynolds and Dolly Parton to each other when they are confronted by placard-bearing demonstrators for women's rights

    Seeing the demonstrators, Burt turned to Dolly and said,

    Dolly replied,

15

CAPITAL LETTERS, HYPHENS, AND APOSTROPHES

15.1 Capital Letters

Capital (upper case) letters are used to mark the beginning of a unit of expression.

1.   The first word of every sentence or expression punctuated with a period, question mark, or exclamation point is capitalized:

Robbery! Do you think I would rob a bank? That would be foolish.

2.   The first word of a direct quotation that is itself a complete sentence is capitalized:

She asked, "Where are you going?"

No capital is used when the quotation is fragmentary or incorporated into the sentence, or for the second part of a quoted sentence interrupted by an expression such as *he said:*

We do not believe that "might makes right."
"After the dance," he said, "we will have a late snack."

3.   The first word of a complete sentence in parentheses when it stands alone, but *not* when it is inserted in another sentence, begins with a capital letter:

No emergency lighting could be found. (We looked in every conceivable place.)
Claudia had been born a Chomley (that family had ancestors who sailed aboard the *Mayflower*), and she was proud of it.

4.   In titles, the first word, last word, all important words, and all prepositions of more than five letters are capitalized:

"America the Beautiful"   *The Last Supper*   "Tranquility Through Meditation"

5.   The person *I* and the exclamation *O* are capitalized:

Tenderly, O my love, I come to you.

Capital letters are used for proper nouns as follows:

1. Names and nicknames of people:

    Jimmy Carter   Satchmo   J. Wellington McNutt   Fats Domino

2. Titles of people when used with the name, but *not* when a title is descriptive:

    Senator Charles Percy   Judge Roy Bean   Doctor M. Clay Vaughan
    Charles Percy is a senator. He is a judge.   She is a doctor.

3. Names of family relationships when used with a name or used to stand for the name, but *not* when used as common nouns or preceded by a possessive:

    Uncle Bob   I told Father that I dented the fender.
    She is my cousin.   My grandfather's name is Ira.
    Grandpa Jones   Will you give this to your father?

4. Names of racial, national, linguistic, political, or religious groups, but *not* names of social and economic groups:

    Caucasian   Dane   Republican
    Moslem   Oriental   Methodist
    Chicano   the intelligentsia the upper class

5. Names and abbreviations of organizations, businesses, and the like:

    General Motors (GM)   Campfire Girls   Phi Kappa Phi
    the Italian-American Club Lions Club   United Mine Workers (UMW)

6. Names of specific places and geographic divisions:

    Europe   Florida   the Bronx   MacArthur Park   Jefferson Place

7. Names of directions when used to identify geogrpahic areas, but *not* when used to indicate direction:

    the South   a Northerner   the Near East   a northern exposure   turn east

8. Names of specific institutions and their divisions and departments, but *not* names that apply to a whole class of institutions:

    Consumer Protection Division of the Attorney General's Office
    Commonwealth Public Library   Jefferson High School   a public library

9. Specific academic courses, but *not* general subjects (except languages):

    Medieval European Literature   Physics 207   Adolescent Psychology
    Spanish literature   physics   psychology

10. Names of specific objects (ships, planes, structures, documents, brand name products, and the like):

H.M.S. *Victory*   Magna Carta   the Great Pyramid   Jello

11. Specific time periods, events, months, days, and holidays:

   the **R**eformation   the **B**attle of **J**utland   the **D**ark **A**ges   **F**ather's **D**ay

   Names of the seasons are *not* capitalized *(spring, summer, autumn, winter).*

12. Abstractions and personifications. (These are seldom appropriate except in poetry and sentimental writing.)

   O **L**iberty, thou art precious.   Clasp me, **N**ature, to thy bosom.

13. To distinguish the proper form from the common form of a word:

   a **D**emocrat [member of the **D**emocratic **P**arty]
   a **d**emocrat [one who believes in democracy]

   Orthodox belief [of the **G**reek **O**rthodox **C**hurch]
   orthodox belief [conventional]

   Romantic literature [of the **R**omantic **P**eriod]
   romantic literature [concerning romance or love]

15.2 Hyphens

There are few firm rules governing the use of hyphens. Whether an expression is hyphenated, written as one word, or written as separate words is based on convention. If in doubt about hyphenating a given expression, consult a good dictionary. There are, however, some conventional places where hyphens are generally used.

1. Names for famliy relationships. Some are hyphenated; others are written as one word or two words:

Hyphenated	mother-in-law, great-grandfather, brother-in-law
One word	grandmother, stepdaughter
Two words	third cousin, half brother

2. Compound numbers from twenty-one to ninety-nine are hyphenated. *Fractions* are hyphenated, except when the fraction already contains a hyphenated number:

   seventy-two   one and two-thirds meters   two twenty-sevenths

   Adjectives indicating age are hyphenated as follows:

   He is twenty-seven
   He is twenty-seven years old.
   He is a twenty-seven-year-old freshman.

3. Compound words with *self* are usually hyphenated; some may be written with or without the hyphen; a few are written as one word:

Hyphenated	self-controlled, self-defense, self-image, self-pity
With or without	self support, self government
One word	selfless, selfsame

4. Some compound nouns are hyphenated; others are written as one or two words:

Hyphenated	bull's-eye, jack-in-the-box, goof-off
One word	newspaper, policyholder
Two words	kitchen sink, murder mystery, science fiction

5. Group modifiers are often hyphenated (*seventeenth-century manuscript*). Use the following guidelines—

a) Compound modifiers formed with *participles* are usually hyphenated when they precede the noun, but are not hyphenated after the noun:

a **well-organized** paper   The paper was **well organized.**

b) When the first word of the group modifier is an adverb ending in *-ly*, no hyphen is used:

secretly hostile actions   **beautifully** carved statue

6. Hyphens are used between prefixes and root words in the following situations—

a) Between a prefix and a proper name:

post-Reformation   pro-Republican   ex-President Ford   anti-American

b) Between some prefixes ending with a vowel and a root word beginning with a vowel:

anti-inflation   re-ink

c) To prevent confusion with a similar term:

re-cover a book   recover from an illness

d) With stressed prefixes:

ex-husband   do-gooder

7. A suspension hyphen is often used to carry the modifying expression from one word to the next:

Most people do not use **three-** and **four-syllable** words in speech.

8. To divide words at the end of lines, use a hyphen. Words are divided into syllables (*par-ty, pres-ti-dig-i-ta-tion*), and a word can be broken at the end of a line only by syllables:

Incorrect	Although she had a headache, she went to the **part-y** with Fred.

Correct	Although she had a headache, she went to the **party** with Fred.
Incorrect	The magician performed feats of **prestidigitation** and legerdemain.
Correct	The magician performed feats of **prestidigitation** and legerdemain.
	The magician peformed feats of **prestidigitation** and legerdemain.

HINT: Consult a dictionary to determine how a word is divided into syllables.

Avoid unnecessary hyphens in terms which are written as one word or as separate words. Common words often erroneously hyphenated include the following:

One word	anybody, percent (or per cent), football, roundabout, bookkeeping, semicolon, footnote, whatever, tonight, nevertheless, overlooked
Separate words	all right, high school, no one, school days, three o'clock, "How do you do?"

15.3 Apostrophes

The apostrophe (') is used—

1. In contractions:

   don't   can't   I'll   I'm   o'clock   hasn't

2. With possessive forms (see 7.2 for possessive nouns and 8.3 for possessive pronouns):

   Paul's book   everyone's favorite   the Queen of England's throne

3. For plurals of letters and figures:

   the late 1800's *or* 1800s   two *a*'s   several size 36's *or* 36s

4. For letters dropped to represent ways of speaking:

   "He was comin' 'round the bend."

Exercise 15   Capital Letters, Hyphens, and Apostrophes

A. Add capital letters, hyphens, and apostrophes as needed in the following words and phrases. If an expression is correct, leave it as it is. If you are uncertain whether an expression is hyphenated, one word, or separate words, use a dictionary.

Example jack o lantern   *jack-o'-lantern*

        base ball   *baseball*

        african violets   *african violets*

1. custom made (ADJ)_____
2. o, the times _____
3. havent_____
4. forty six_____
5. its a long day _____
6. the renaissance _____
7. greek literature _____
8. the 1700s _____
9. searchin _____
10. pre reformation _____
11. aunt sarah _____
12. anybodys belief _____
13. dog kennel _____
14. walk in (ADJ) _____
15. self propelled_____
16. negro _____
17. that is hers_____
18. presbyterian _____
19. hot dog _____
20. girl scouts _____

21. anti ballistic missile _____
22. Freds pen _____
23. three ts _____
24. light-fingered _____
25. *love story* _____
26. tam o shanter_____
27. globe trotter _____
28. ghana _____
29. dual purpose (ADJ)_____
30. vice-president truman _____
31. found its place_____
32. nine sixteenths _____
33. do it yourself (ADJ) _____
34. continental can company _____
35. frame up (NOUN) _____
36. long drawn out (ADJ) _____
37. main stream _____
38. italian cooking_____
39. anti feminists position _____
40. asbury park_____

B. In the exercise below, correct any errors in syllabification in the words divided into syllables; then divide the other words given into syllables. Use your dictionary as necessary.

1.	innocence	inn-o-cen-ce	1. _____
2.	round	rou-nd	2. _____
3.	coalesce	coal-es-ce	3. _____
4.	juvenile	juv-en-i-le	4. _____
5.	welterweight	wel-ter-weight	5. _____
6.	oppressive	opp-ress-ive	6. _____
7.	angularity		7. _____
8.	heroic		8. _____
9.	enlightenment		9. _____
10.	secondarily		10. _____
11.	fatuous		11. _____
12.	mononucleosis		12. _____

C. Correct each sentence, adding necessary capital letters, hyphens, and apostrophes and crossing out unnecessary ones. If you are uncertain whether an expression is hyphenated, one word, or separate words, use a dictionary.

Example On Johns tour of the *F*far *E*east, he visited his *G*grandfather in Tokyo and rode in a ~~rick sha~~ *ricksha*.

1. Edward hoppers painting *nighthawks* hangs in the art institute of chicago; john sloans work *sixth avenue elevated at third street* is in the Whitney museum.

2. Batting left handed against the right handed pitcher, Ashton lined a two base hit off the first basemans glove down the right field line.

3. My aunt Shannon has been a singing telegram deliverer, a College History Professor, and a district manager for the international finance corporation.

4. Last semester my no nonsense approach to school worked well in modern science, french 202, and african economics, as well as in my courses in english composition and european Literature.

222

5. In the late 1600s, the kings advisors suggested that the german ambassadors message meant that war was inevitable.

6. Swinging the two handed sword mightily over his head, sir brumble, the queens favorite dwarf, gave a blood-curdling yell and struck sir grubb a tremendous blow on the knee-cap.

7. the ginger-bread-man was a roly poly fellow with self composure and a well developed sense of humor.

8. After graduating from central memorial high school where she was named all around student, Risa attended Carthage University where she made the all american team in tennis, was selected for phi kappa phi honor society, and was elected president of the senior class.

9. dean hawes stated that she would not precensor the schools newspaper; never-the-less she cautioned the editor's to avoid four letter words.

10. The whig candidate for parliament, famous for her off-the-cuff speeches, easily defeated colonel blitherington, the tory incumbent.

16

ABBREVIATIONS, ACRONYMS, AND NUMBERS

16.1 Abbreviations

Few abbreviations should be used in formal writing. Abbreviations are more appropriate in technical writing, documents, reference works, footnotes, and other places where saving space is important. Use the following guidelines.

Academic degrees and courtesy titles, such as *Dr., Mr., Ms., Jr., St. (Saint),* are abbreviated when used with proper names. Other titles, such as *Professor, Judge,* and *President,* are usually written out:

>   **Mr.** John Goodwin, **Jr.**   Barbara Taylor, **Ph.D.**   **Professor** Lionel Glazer

Given names should not be abbreviated. Spell them out or use initials:

>   **T. J.** Carling *or* **Thomas J.** Carling *[not* Thom. J. Carling]

Place names and dates are written out, except for a few long place names:

>   Canada   Hawthorne Boulevard   Tuesday, October 8   Christmas *[not* Xmas]
>   **USSR**   Barbados, **B.W.I.** (British West Indies)   Washington, **D.C.**
>   Duluth, **Minn.** (*or* Duluth, **MN**)

Government agencies, organizations, technical terms, and trade names that are especially long may be abbreviated if the abbreviations are familiar:

>   **NASA**   **AM** radio (amplitude modulation)
>   **NAACP**   **DNA** (deoxyribonucleic acid)

If an abbreviation which is to be used repeatedly may not be known to every reader, explain it the first time it is used:

>   Through the Organization of American States **(OAS),** twenty-three American nations work to develop strong economic and military ties.

Units of measurement are generally written out in formal writing:

>   six pounds   three hours   several grams   two centimeters

Measurements expressed in *technical terms* are abbreviated when used with figures but not abbreviated when used without figures:

> The Phoenix is capable of **20 mpg** in city driving.
> The **miles per gallon** figures for this year's models are higher than for those of last year's models.

The designations *a.m.* and *p.m.* are always abbreviated and refer only to a specific time:

> 3:20 **a.m.**   4:00 **p.m.**   *[not* It was early in the a.m.*]*

The designations *B.C.* and *A.D.* are always abbreviated *B.C.* follows the date; *A.D.* precedes it.

> 44 B.C.   A.D. 750

Some common Latin abbreviations are used in formal writing (without italics):

> **cf.** (compare)   **e.g.** (for example)   **i.e.** (that is)   **etc.** (and so forth)

HINT: Try to avoid *etc.* by using *such as* or *and so forth* or *and the like:*

Weak	I enjoy fly fishing, bowling, and golf, **etc.**
Better	I enjoy activities **such as** fly fishing, bowling, and golf.
Still better	I enjoy **such** activities **as** fly fishing, bowling, and golf.

Capitalize abbreviations when the words they stand for are capitalized:

> **Dr.** Wilson   **AEC (A**tomic **E**nergy **C**ommission)   kgps (kilograms per second)

Use periods with abbreviations of a single word and with most other abbreviations. Some abbreviated names of two or more letters may be written either with or without periods, but be consistent:

> p.   hr.   Oct.   M.A.   c.o.d.   P.T.A. *[or* PTA*]*   U.S.N. *[or* USN*]*

16.2 Acronyms

An *acronym* is a word formed from the initial letters of the words in a phrase or name:

> radar (**ra**dio **d**etecting **a**nd **r**anging)
> scuba (**s**elf-**c**ontained **u**nderwater **b**reathing **a**pparatus)

Organizations sometimes form their popular names through the use of *acronyms:*

> MADD (**M**others **A**gainst **D**runk **D**rivers)
> NOW (**N**ational **O**rganization of **W**omen)

16.3 Numbers

Use the following general guidelines for using figures or words for numbers.

Use words (1) for numbers through one hundred, (2) for numbers that can be written in two words, and (3) to begin a sentence (except for dates):

four million   Twenty-one thousand soldiers were killed.
three thousand   1976 was our bicentennial year.
seventy

Use figures (1) for numbers that cannot be written in two words and (2) for statistics and series of numbers that are to be compared.

135   42,800   750,000
In his first try for office, he received 13,740 votes or 39.3% of the total; in his next attempt, he gathered 27,824 or 64% of those cast.

HINT: Be consistent in using figures or words. Do not shift needlessly:

Inconsistent   She caught **3** bass and **two** pickerel.
Consistent   She caught **three** bass and **two** pickerel.

Figures are conventionally used—

1. In dates (March *23, 1940;* April *17*).
2. With *a.m.* and *p.m.*, but not with *o'clock* or *noon* (*9:15* a.m.; three o'clock).
3. In mathematical and technical terms (*.45* caliber; latitude *42°14'N.*; π = *3.1417; 72%*).
4. To refer to parts of a book (p. *82;* Act *II*, scene *1*, line *28;* chapter *5*).
5. For sums of money, except round numbers (*$9.95;* seventeen thousand dollars).
6. For street numbers and zip codes (*181* Magnolia Lane, Reading, MA *01867*).

    Plurals of figures are written either with *'s* or *-s* (by *5's* or by *5s*).
    Ordinal numbers (*first, twentieth*) are usually spelled out rather than abbreviated (*1st, 22nd*). Ordinals can be either adjectives or adverbs; thus the *-ly* forms (*firstly, secondly*) are unnecessary and should be avoided.

Exercise 16 Abbreviations, Acronyms, and Numbers

A. Complete the following chart by providing abbreviations or the words abbreviated. Use a dictionary to find abbreviations with which you are unfamiliar.

Examples

Abbreviation	Word abbreviated	Abbreviation	Words abbreviated
a. M.S.	*Master of Science*	c. cg.	*centigram*
b. *B.W.I.*	British West Indies	d. *Fe*	iron

Abbreviation	Words abbreviated	Abbreviation	Words abbreviated
1. NYSE		11.	milliliter
2. Ed.D.		12. SPCC	
3. ibid.		13. dkm	
4.	registered nurse	14.	pages
5. r.p.m.		15.	horsepower
6. e.g.		16. i.e.	
7. HUD		17. gm	
8. UMW		18.	Doctor of Philosophy
9. DDT		19. GATT	
10.	miles per hour	20. Btu	

B. In each sentence correct any improper uses of abbreviations and numbers. Because there often are choices in usage, pay particular attention to the consistent use of numbers and abbreviations.

Example Professor Battles told us to read ~~3~~ *three* chapters in one book and two chapters in the other book.

1. On June 3rd, 1972, she consulted Dr. Hortense Higby for the 2nd time in 3 weeks.

2. Our 27th pres., Wm. Howard Taft, stood 5 ft. eleven inches tall and weighed three hundred and twenty-five pounds when he was in-

augurated on Mar. 4, nineteen-nine; to bathe, he had a special bathtub large enough to hold 4 people.

3. In Sweden, where the ave. life expectancy is 74.2 yrs., men have an ave. life expectancy of seventy-one point 8 years, women of seventy-six.5 yrs.

4. Between eighteen hundred and 1950, the pop. of London, Eng., increased from 865,000 to eight million, three hundred and forty-eight thou.

5. After you cross the Thos. Alton Bridge, take the 1st exit; at the end of the ramp, turn rt., drive 7 miles exactly, turn lt. onto Memorial Dr., and proceed one and one-half miles to the first traffic light.

6. Although the CIA avoids publicity, 1 Central Intelligence Agency representative, Col. Wm. Williams, has been quoted as saying that the CIA keeps files on over one hundred and forty-two thousand extremists in the U.S. and over 350,000 in Can., Cent. America, and So. America.

7. A 5-year study of the police records in two thousand four hundred U.S. cities indicates that the most probable mos. for burglaries are Dec., Jan., and Feb., that the most probable night for burlaries is Sat., and that most burglaries occur between 6 p.m. and 2:00 a.m.

8. 27 pages of material dealt with events which preceded the development of networks like NBC, the American Braodcasting Co., and etc.; one-hundred and seventy-two pgs. covered the rise of networks; and eighteen pp. suggested future trends in ultrahigh frequency broadcasting.

9. Capt. H. R. Scott, Junior, told reporters that police raided the Chas. A. Flyly warehouse on High St. at two a.m. and seized 30 gms. of cocaine, twenty-seven kilos of heroin, and nearly 1 gal. of lysergic acid diethylamide.

10. Prof. Ima Nutt reported that a survey of three-hundred and ninety-two people, taken in Nutley Pk. on Nov. twenty-first, indicated that ninety-nine% preferred to consume less than 1 gal. of beer or wine daily.

17

SPELLING

17.1 Some Principles of Spelling

The following rules deal with some specific spelling situations.

Retaining or Dropping Final *-e*. When adding suffixes to words ending in a silent *-e*—

1. Generally retain the *-e* before suffixes beginning with a consonant
    (*-ment, -some, -ful, -ly, -ness*):

    arrange, arrangement   lithe, lithesome   spite, spiteful

    Exceptions:

    argue, argument   awe, awful   due, duly   nine, ninth   true, truly

2. Generally drop the *-e* before suffixes beginning with a vowel (*-ing, -able, -ous, -ary*):

    believe, believing   desire, desirous   imagine, imaginary

    Exceptions: In a few words, the *-e* is retained to avoid confusion:

    dye, dyeing (compare *dying*)   singe, singeing (compare *singing*)

3. With words ending in *-ce* or *-ge,* retain the final *-e* before suffixes begin-
    ning with *a* or *o:*

    change, changeable   outrage, outrageous

Words with *-ie-* and *-ei-*. Remember the familiar jingle: "Write *i* before *e* except after *c*, or when sounded as *a* as in *neighbor* and *weigh*." Words with *-ie-* are more common than words with *-ei-*.

> **Words with *-ie-:*** achieve, believe, chief, field, mischief, relief, siege, view
> **Words with *-cei-:*** ceiling, conceive, deceive, perceive, receipt, receive

229

Words with *-ei-* sounded as *a:* eight, freight, neighbor, reign, vein, weigh
Other words with *-ei-:* either, leisure, neither, seize, weird, counterfeit, foreign, height, heir

Doubling the Final Consonant.
Double the final consonant before a suffix beginning with a vowel *(-able, -ed, -er, -ing)* —

1. In one-syllable words ending with a single vowel and a single consonant:

    bat, batter, batting   grip, gripped, gripping   spot, spotted, spotting

2. In other words ending with a single vowel and a single consonant, if the last syllable is accented:

    control, controllable, controlled   occur, occurred, occurring
    omit, omitted, omitting   prefer, preferred, preferring

Do *not* double the final consonant—

1. In words with two vowels before the final consonant:

    daub, daubed   keep, keeping

2. In words ending with two consonants:

    help, helping   lurk, lurked

3. When the accent of the lengthened word shifts to an earlier syllable:

    infer', in'ference   refer', ref'erence

Usage is divided about doubling the consonant in some words, but American spelling generally favors the single consonant:

    bias, biased   counsel, counseling   diagram, diagramed
    quarrel, quarreling   travel, traveler   worship, worshiped

Words with Final *-y.*
A final *-y* preceded by a consonant regularly changes to *i* before all suffixes except those beginning with *i.*

    busy, business   mercy, merciful   easy, easily   study, studious, studying

A final *-y* preceded by a vowel remains unchanged when a suffix is added:

    enjoy, enjoyable, enjoying   play, player, playful

Words that End with *-cede, -ceed, -sede.*

1. Only one word ends in *-sede: supersede.*
2. Only three words end in *-ceed: exceed, proceed,* and *succeed.*
3. All other words of this sort end in *-cede: intercede, precede, recede, secede,* and so on.

Words that End with *-able, -ible, -ance, -ence.*
Words with *-able, -ible, -ance,* and *-ence* endings are often misspelled and should be checked in a dictionary because no rules of spelling or pronunciation can be used to distinguish them. Some common words with these endings are listed on p. 231.

230

-able	-ible	-ance	-ence
acceptable	accessible	acceptance	adolescence
available	compatible	acquaintance	confidence
considerable	irresistible	appearance	dependence
irritable	plausible	ignorance	existence
noticeable	susceptible	maintenance	interference
valuable	visible	significance	occurrence

Variant Spellings. When a word has more than one spelling, use the more common form. In a dictionary, the first spelling listed is the more common and preferred form. It is generally preferable to use—

1.   The more modern form:

     draft, mold, plow [*not* draught, mould, plough]

2.   The simpler form:

     anesthetic, medieval, program [*not* anaesthetic, mediaeval, programme]

3.   The American form:

     center, labor, theater [*not* centre, labour, theatre]

HINT: When quoting directly from a source which uses variant spellings, do not change the spelling.

Source	To determine the popularity of comedy, we studied the programme at each theatre in London.
Quote	The authors indicated that they "studied the programme at each theatre in London." [not *program* and *theater*]

17.2   Spelling Troublesome Plurals

Nouns Ending in -*y*, -*o* or -*f* are made plural as follows—

1.   Nouns ending in -*y* following a vowel: Add -*s* (*buoys, keys*).
2.   Nouns ending in -*y* following a consonant: Change the *y* to *i* and add -*es* (*company, companies; library, libraries*).
3.   Nouns ending in -*o* preceded by a vowel: Usually add -*s* (*studios, tattoos*).
4.   Nouns ending in -*o* preceded by a consonant: Usually add -*es* (*heroes, echoes, tomatoes*). For a few, add only -*s* (*pianos, egos, sopranos*).
5.   A few nouns ending in -*o*: Add either -*s* or -*es* (*cargos, cargoes; hobos, hoboes; zeros, zeroes*).
6.   Nouns ending in -*f* or -*fe* often form the plural by adding -*s* (*chiefs, beliefs, fifes, reefs*). Some nouns ending in -*f* form the plural by changing -*f* to -*ves* (*knife, knives; half, halves; calf, calves*). A few nouns ending in -*f* may add either -*s* or -*ves* (*elfs, elves; hoofs, hooves; scarfs, scarves*). (Note: *roof* forms the plural by adding -*s*—*roofs*.)

Words with Foreign Plurals. Some nouns have two plural forms: a *foreign* plural and an *anglicized* plural ending in -s or -es. The foreign plural is more often used formally, particularly in scientific, technical, and academic writing. Occasionally the two plurals have two different meanings.

Singular	Formal plural (foreign)	General plural (anglicized)
antenna	antennae (zoology)	antennas (radio, TV)
appendix	appendices	appendixes
cactus	cacti	cactuses
index	indices (mathematics)	indexes (in books)
radius	radii	radiuses
vertebra	vertebrae	vertebras

Some nouns ending in -is that are derived from Greek or Latin form their plurals by changing -is to -es:

analysis, analyses   crisis, crises   neurosis, neuroses

Group Words and Compound Nouns usually form their plurals by adding -s to the last word:

baby-sitters   lieutenant colonels   cross-examinations

When the first word is the significant word (as in many hyphenated compounds), the first word is made plural:

mothers-in-law   men-of-war   passers by

Compound nouns ending in -ful are made plural by adding -s either to the end of the word (*teaspoonfuls, cupfuls, barrelfuls*) or before -ful (*teaspoonsful, cupsful, barrelsful*).

17.3 Common Spelling Errors

Errors Caused by Faulty Pronunciation. Some words are often misspelled because of the way they are pronounced (or mispronounced):

acciden**tal**ly	accompan**y**ing	ath**l**etics	dis**g**ust	environ**m**ent
labo**r**atory	mischie**vous**	**p**rescribe	privilege	temper**a**mental

Omission of Final -ed frequently causes misspellings—

1. In verb forms. Do not drop the final -ed in past tenses and past participles, especially before words beginning with t:

    He **used to** take long walks every morning. [not *use to*]
    She is **supposed to** arrive tonight. [not *suppose to*]

2. In verbal modifiers. Do not drop the final -ed (*elevated train, fractured leg*) unless the shortened form has become established (*grade school, roast beef*).

3. In modifiers from nouns. Do not drop the final -ed *(two-sided, pear-shaped)* unless the shortened form has become established *(queen-size mattress, high-heel shoes)*.

Separate Words and Combined Forms. Maintain the distinction in meaning between expressions written as one word and similar expressions written as two words.

all ready (adjective phrase)—*already* (adverb)

> The people were **all ready** for the show to start.
> He had **already** asked permission to go.

all together (adjective phrase)—*altogether* (adverb)

> The members of the team were **all together** again.
> He had eaten **altogether** too much food.

a while (noun)—*awhile* (adverb)

> He waited for **a while** before leaving.   She wanted to remain **awhile** longer.

may be (verb phrase)—*maybe* (adverb)

> She **may be** your partner on the project.   **Maybe** you will be hired soon.

Confusion of Words That Sound Alike. The following pairs of words are often confused in writing. Check your dictionary for any that you cannot distinguish.

accept—except	credible—creditable	principal—principle
access—excess	desert—dessert	quiet—quite
affect—effect	its—it's	stationary—stationery
aisle—isle	knew—new	than—then
allusion—illusion	know—no	their—there—they're
birth—berth	lead—led	to—too
capital—capitol	loose—lose	weather—whether
choose—chose	passed—past	where—were
cite—site	peace—piece	who's—whose
conscience—conscious	personal—personnel	
coarse—course	precede—proceed	

Separate Words Erroneously Combined. These expressions should always be written as separate words:

all right (not *alright* or *alrite*)

> The arrangements were **all right** with me.

a lot (not *alot*)

> It was **a lot** warmer than I expected.

threw out (not *throughout*)

> President Eisenhower **threw out** the first ball.

beck and call (not *beckon call*)

> He was at her **beck and call.**

Errors Caused by Phonetic Advertising.
Commercial products often use phonetics spelling in their brand names, on labels, and in advertising.

Kool-aid	Sta-Puff (stay puff)	Chex (checks)
Klean 'n Shine (clean and)	Neet (neat)	Bif (biff)
Finast (finest)	krisp (crisp)	quispy (crispy)
Scotch-gard (guard)	kleer (clear)	kruntchy (crunchy)

Some of these phonetic spellings appear in extremely informal language:

> luv (love)   cuz (because)   slo (slow)   thru (through)

Unless you are referring directly to a brand name (I bought some Klean 'n Shine) or quoting an advertisement directly (it was advertised as being "krispy and kruntchy" even after being covered with milk), phonetic spellings should be avoided.

Difficult or Troublesome Words.
The following one hundred words are frequently misspelled:

accommodate	dining room	knowledge	psychology
acquainted	disappearance	leisure	quantity
across	disappoint	library	receive
agreement	dormitory	lik[e]able	referring
all right			repetition
already	embarrass	maintenance	resemblance
analysis	environment	manufacturer	
appearance	equipment	misspelled	schedule
article	exaggerate	monotonous	secretary
athletics	existence	mysterious	seize
attendance	extremely	necessary	separate
believe	familiar	noticeable	similar
benefited	fascinate	occasionally	sophomore
Britain	foreign	occurrence	succeed
business	formerly	omitted	sympathize
	forty	opportunity	
changeable	grammar		temperament
choose		particularly	tendency
comparative	height	pastime	therefore
conceive	hindrance	perform	tragedy
conscience	imaginary	preceding	truly
continuous	immediately	prejudice	undoubtedly
decision	incidentally	privilege	until
definite	independent	probably	usually
dependent	intelligent	procedure	valuable
description	irresistible	pronunciation	writing
develop	judg[e]ment	proportion	

Exercise *17.1*   Some Principles of Spelling

A.   Change or complete each word as indicated.

Examples Add -*ing*:

establish   *establishing*   admit   *admitting*

Add -*ous*:

mischief   *mischievous*   parsimony   *parsimonious*

1. Add -*ment*:

    judge   _____   acknowledge   _____

    improve   _____   argue   _____

2. Add -*some*:

    awe   _____   win   _____

    whole   _____   tire   _____

3. Add -*ful*:

    force   _____   awe   _____

    mercy   _____   duty   _____

4. Add -*ly*:

    apprehensive   _____   whole   _____

    incidental   _____   body   _____

5. Add -*ness*:

    white   _____   blessed   _____

    busy   _____   hardy   _____

6. Add -*ing*:

    regret   _____   disgrace   _____

    hoe   _____   modify   _____

7. Add -*able* or -*ible*:

    forget   _____   access   _____

    notice   _____   dispense   _____

8. Add *-ous:*

grieve   _____   victory   _____

joy   _____   monotony   _____

9. Add *-ie* or *-ei:*

y____ld   perc____ve

s____ge   p____rce

w____rd   conc____t

10. Add *-ed:*

proclaim   _____   bug   _____

concur   _____   encumber   _____

11. Add *-er:*

chop   _____   quit   _____

quiet   _____   modify   _____

12. Add *-ance* or *-ence:*

excel   _____   confide   _____

ignore   _____   defy   _____

B. Select the correct spelling or the preferred spelling and write it in the space at the right. If in doubt, consult a dictionary.

Example Her knowledge of the (mediaeval, medieval) period is extensive.   *medieval*

1. Her greed (superceded, superseded) her sense of (honor, honour).   1. _____ _____

2. The next event on the (programme, program) takes place in the (center, centre) ring.   2. _____ _____

3. Nothing can (altar, alter) our plans to (seceed, secede) from the Union.   3. _____ _____

4. The Governor's (Counsel, Council) is meeting tonight.   4. _____

5. Rather than fight a (dual, duel), I will (conceed, consede, concede) that you are right.   5. _____ _____

6. (Procede, Proceed) to (plow, plough) the field.   6. _____ _____

NAME . . . .   SCORE . . . .

7. A light supper will (preceed, precede) our trip to   7. _____
    the (theater, theatre).   _____

8. Will you (acceed, accede) to my wishes?   8. _____

9. She (perchased, purchased) the (pajamas, pyjamas)   9. _____
    at Greeley's Department Store.   _____

10. Should I (intercede, intersede) on your behalf)   10. _____

11. We have (draft, draught) beer.   11. _____

12. A (catalogue, catalog) of spring (clothes, cloths)   12. _____
    came in the mail today.   _____

Exercise 17.2   Spelling Troublesome Plurals

A. Form the plural of each word. If more than one plural is acceptable, write both plural forms. If in doubt, use a dictionary.

Examples	Singular	Plural
	library	*libraries*
	half	*halves*

	Singular	Plural		Singular	Plural
1.	berry	_____	11.	court-martial	_____
2.	oasis	_____	12.	domino	_____
3.	alto	_____	13.	formula	_____
4.	roof	_____	14.	medium	_____
5.	spy	_____	15.	ellipsis	_____
6.	cuckoo	_____	16.	jack-in-the-	
7.	diagnosis	_____		pulpit	_____
8.	wolf	_____	17.	potato	_____
9.	armful	_____	18.	prophesy	_____
10.	sister-in-		19.	wharf	_____
	law	_____	20.	smokehouse	_____

B. Rewrite each sentence, changing the italicized word or words to plural. Also change any other words (such as verbs, pronouns, and articles) so that they agree in number with the nouns.

Example An *elf* was hiding behind a *leaf.*

Elves were hiding behind leaves.

1. She sang a *lullaby* to the *baby.*

2. A *convoy* of ships skirted the edge of the *reef.*

3. The *cry* of the *wolf* sent chills down his spine.

4. Her *diagnosis* was accurate.

5. For the archery tournament we bought a *sheaf* of arrows.

6. A presidential *veto* will prevent the *bill* from becoming law.

7. We fed a *mango* to the *giraffe*.

8. My *brother-in-law* is a *spy*.

9. The *governor-elect* had a favorable *prognosis* for the economy.

10. A *thief* stole my mounted *butterfly*.

11. The *lady-in-waiting* told Queen Helena that a *fairy* had brought her a *pocketful* of gold.

12. From the *wharf* the *echo* of the crash was easily heard.

Exercise *17.3*   Common Spelling Errors

A.   Select the correctly spelled word and write it in the space at the right. If you are uncertain, consult a dictionary or the list of frequently misspelled words.

Example Did I (embarass, embarrass, embarrous) you?   *embarrass*

1. She decided to study in the (liberry, libary, library).   1. _____

2. Last summer we visited Great (Britan, Britain, Britian).   2. _____

3. Experts say we must clean up our (environment, environment, envirament).   3. _____

4. Please (seperate, separate, sepirate) these coins into four equal piles.   4. _____

5. Many students participate in intercollegiate (athaletics, atheletics, athletics).   5. _____

6. That Tiffany lamp is quite (valuble, valueable, valuable).   6. _____

7. The strange (disapearence, disappearence, disappearance) of Alan worried us.   7. _____

8. You will have the (opertunity, opportunity, oportunity) to ask questions later.   8. _____

9. The appearance of a comet is an unusual (occurrance, occurrence, occurence).   9. _____

10. Why don't you two get (acquainted, aquainted, acquianted)?   10. _____

11. The (preceeding, preceding, preseding) program has been brought to you by Precious Products, Inc.   11. _____

12. I would rather be a help to you than a (hindrance, hinderance, hindrence).   12. _____

13. The (mischievious, mischievous, mischeivous) elf tickled the giant's feet with a feather.   13. _____

14. Renaissance (tradgedy, tragedy, tragady) often shows the human struggle between reason and emotion.   14. _____

240

15. Tonight's (appearence, apearance, appearance) by the Great Hodoni has been canceled.

15. _____

16. Her (pronounciation, pronunciation, pronunsiation) of German was nearly flawless.

16. _____

17. Due to the explosion, the (maintenance, maintainance, maintenence) of the airport runways was halted.

17. _____

18. He bore a striking (resembleance, resemblence, resemblance) to his brother.

18. _____

19. It is (alrite, all right, alright) with me if you go.

19. _____

20. Their anniversary was a happy (ocasion, occassion, occasion).

20. _____

21. I would be (privledged, priveleged, privileged) to introduce you at the banquet.

21. _____

22. The equator is an (imaginary, immaginary, imaginery) line dividing the earth into two hemispheres.

22. _____

23. The sponsor's name was inadvertently (ommited, omited, omitted) from the program.

23. _____

24. After considering all of the testimony, the jury reached its (desision, decition, decision).

24. _____

25. The chocolate cake was (irresistable, irresistible, iresistable).

25. _____

B. Select the correct word and write it in the space at the right. If in doubt, consult a dictionary.

Example My (coarse, course) in botany is quite exciting.   *course*

1. Mourning her dead husband, Olivia vowed to be (chased, chaste) the rest of her life.

1. _____

2. The pipe was clogged by (sediment, sentiment).

2. _____

3. On this (cite, site) will be built the largest grain elevator in the Midwest.

3. _____

4. Little Rock is the (capital, capitol) of Arkansas.

5. The bride looked radiant as she walked down the (aisle, isle).

6. Did you (lose, loose) your watch?

7. She was (conscience, conscious) of movement behind her.

8. Ned is older (than, then) Husein.

9. The lights created an (allusion, illusion) of sunset.

10. There is a hole in the (sole, soul) of my shoe.

11. The road turned at a forty-five degree (angel, angle).

12. He shaved the edge of the door with a (plain, plane).

13. She (died, dyed) the material turquoise.

14. Marigolds formed a (boarder, border) around the garden.

15. By the time they arrived, the train had (all ready, already) left.

16. Last week you (choose, chose) to ignore my instructions.

17. Will you (accept, except) a check?

18. My flu shot did not (affect, effect) me at all.

19. What are you having for (desert, dessert)?

20. The television set has blown (its, it's) picture tube.

21. We (maybe, may be) stranded here for several days.

22. She refused to compromise her (principals, principles).

23. I am not (to, too) fond of snakes.

24. The stag was (stationary, stationery) by the edge of the brook.

25. We maintained a (discreet, discrete) silence.

4. _____

5. _____

6. _____

7. _____

8. _____

9. _____

10. _____

11. _____

12. _____

13. _____

14. _____

15. _____

16. _____

17. _____

18. _____

19. _____

20. _____

21. _____

22. _____

23. _____

24. _____

25. _____

C. Write a sentence for each word to show the difference between these often confused words.

Example coarse

The shirt was made of coarse material.

course

We laid out a challenging course for the cross-country race.

1. credible

    creditable

2. access

    excess

3. accept

    except

4. awhile

    a while

5. lead

    led

6. affect

    effect

7. all together

   altogether

8. who's

   whose

9. its

   it's

10. than

    then

11. passed

    past

12. loose

    lose

13. stationary

    stationery

14. where

    were

Review Exercise 17   Spelling

Correct the following sentences, crossing out each misspelled word and writing in the correct spelling. If in doubt, consult a dictionary.

coarse
Example She was embarrassed by his ~~course~~ manners.

1. Although I initialy was a psycology major, in my sophmore year I developped an intrest in enviromental studies.

2. If you had refered to your notes (as you were suppose to), you would have been familar with the replys from the foriegn ambasadors.

3. She was acquited because the procecusion lacked tangable evidence that she had really commited a criminal act.

4. On our trip across the dessert, we escepted loafs of bread and caraffes of wine at each of the oasises we visitted.

5. When Clyde was a sargent, he was transfered from ordinence to intelligance where he suceeded brilliantly.

6. The crusador delt vengance on those who were guilty of reprehensable behaviour.

7. He had wierd fantasys about being maroned on a lonly topical aisle with only religous pamplets to read.

8. Lord Carling, a prominant politicion who had served in Parlament for all most fourty years, excaped procecusion for missapropriating funds by committing suiside.

Review Exercise *15–17*   Capitals, Hyphens, Apostrophes, Abbreviations, Numbers, and Spelling

A. Select the correct or preferred form and write it in the space at the right. If you are uncertain about some words, use a dictionary.

1. (12, Twelve) years earlier (Gen., General) Shaw had (prophesized, prophesied) that the (treaty of versailles, Treaty of Versailles) would eventually lead to another war.

    1. _____
    _____
    _____
    _____

2. Her father was a (rolly-polly, roly-poly, roly poly) (swede, Swede) (who's, whose) leisure time was devoted to studying (Aegyptian, Egyptian, egyptian) hieroglyphics and the *(Book of the Dead, Book of the dead, Book of The Dead).*

    2. _____
    _____
    _____
    _____
    _____

3. The modern (worlds, world's, worlds') conception of the universe differs from the view held in the (pre Renaissance, pre renaissance pre-Renaissance) period.

    3. _____
    _____

4. In the (1200s, 1200's, 1200s') twelve-hundreds) the (medieval, mediaeval, mediaevil) period was at its peak and (knight-hood, knighthood, knight hood) flourished.

    4. _____
    _____
    _____

5. The (pres., Pres., president, President) of (Allied Broadcasting Co., Allied Broadcasting Company, ABC,

    5. _____
    _____
    _____

A.B.C.) announced that of the

(eleven, 11) new shows aired this

season, only (2, two, too) were not

being canceled.

6. At (7 p.m., 7:00 p.m., seven p.m.,   6. _____

7 P.M.) (Sen., Senator) H. B.   _____

Gabble will deliver a (two-hour, two   _____

hour, 2 hr., 2 hour) address on the   _____

environmental protection bill cur-

rently before (Congress, congress).

7. The (A.M.A., AMA, American   7. _____

Medical Association) believes that   _____

an (all-out, allout, all out) battle   _____

looms over prospective legislation

involving (feesplitting, fee-splitting,

fee splitting) within the medical

profession.

B. Correct each passage, crossing out all errors and inconsistencies in capital letters, hyphens, apostrophes, abbreviations, numbers, and spelling, and writing in your corrections.

1. On August 10th, 1947, we embarked on our journey to So. America,

hoping to explore the lost caves of the amogoc Indians.

2. My wifes brothers wifes both demonstrated against the burning of toxic

wastes in their communities.

3. Although duke charles usually prefered to be lenient, he adpated a

nononsence attitude toward the thieves who absconded with the royal

treasury.

4. Old uncle Eph said, "Back in 98 I was servin aboard a man of war in a Battle with the Spanish when I received my first wound."

5. I may have exagerated when I claimed that the surgeon I caught in Lake Erie was 11 feet long and weighed over two hundred lbs.

6. The three-hundred and twenty-seven bag-pipes were preceded by 3 doz. Scottish dancers.

7. Adrenocorticotrophic hormone, which is produced in the anterior part of the pituitary gland, simulates the adrenal cortex.

18

USING A DICTIONARY

18.1 Selecting a Good Dictionary

Dictionaries vary in size and purpose. The following are best for general use:

Unabridged dictionaries, found in college libraries and public libraries, offer the most complete descriptions of contemporary English.

> *New Standard Dictionary of the English Language* (Funk & Wagnalls)
> *The Random House Dictionary of the English Language* (Random House)
> *Webster's Third New International Dictionary* (G. & C. Merriam) [the most complete dictionary available]

College dictionaries are the most practical kind to own for everyday use.

> *American Heritage Dictionary* (American Heritage and Houghton-Mifflin)
> *Random House Dictionary,* College Edition (Random House)
> *Webster's New World Dictionary of the American Language* (Collin & World Publishing Company)
> *Webster's Ninth New Collegiate Dictionary* (G. & C. Merriam)

There are also many special dictionaries that have more specific purposes.

Historical dictionaries trace the forms and meanings of words from the time of their first appearance to the present.

> *The Oxford English Dictionary* (twelve volumes and a *Supplement,* 1888–1928) traces the history of British English up to 1928. A multi-volume *Supplement* to bring the history to modern times is being issued.
> *The Dictionary of American English* (four volumes) gives the history of American English from 1620 to 1900.
> *A Dictionary of Americanisms* (two volumes) brings the history of American English to 1944.
> *Harper's Dictionary of Contemporary Usage* (1975) reviews contemporary word use and discusses new uses and questionable word choices.

Dictionaries in special subjects are available in several fields. The following list represents the range of such texts:

Ballentine, J. A., *Law Dictionary*
Clark, D. T., and B. A. Gottfried, *Dictionary of Business and Finance*
Dorland, W. A. N., *American Illustrated Medical Dictionary*
English, H. B., *A Student's Dictionary of Psychological Terms*
Good, C. V., *Dictionary of Education*
Hackh, I. W. D., *Chemical Dictionary*
Rice, C. M., *Dictionary of Geological Terms*
Wentworth, H., and S. B. Flexner, *Dictionary of American Slang*

18.2 Learning to Use Your Dictionary

Before you use a new dictionary, examine it carefully. Read the front matter, examine a page of entries, test the pronunciation guide, and look over the table of contents to see what sections the dictionary contains.

Most dictionaries contain the following kinds of information:

1. **Spelling.** Dictionaries give not only the spelling of the base form of a word but also the spelling of other forms—principal parts of verbs, plurals of nouns, degrees of adjectives and adverbs—when these forms are in any way irregular (*invariable, invariability, invariably*). Dictionaries also may give variant spellings (*theater, theatre*).

2. **Word division.** Dictionaries divide words into units which are usually the same as spoken syllables (*com•mis•sion•er, man•i•fes•ta•tion*). In writing, divide a word at the end of a line only where your dictionary shows a division.

3. **Pronunciation.** Dictionaries use special symbols to indicate how words are pronounced (*indecency* [in dē's'n sē]), and often given variant pronunciations (*Caribbean* [kar'ə bē'ən, kə rib'ē ən]).

4. **Meaning.** Dictionaries begin each definition, or group of definitions, by indicating the part of speech of the word as it is being defined (*fate* [fāt] n. [noun]). The definitions follow.

    In using dictionary definitions, remember that a dictionary does not require or forbid a particular meaning; it only records the ways in which a word has been used. Also, dictionary definitions are a record of the *denotations,* or specific meanings, of words; they can, at best, only suggest the *connotations,* or implied meanings.

5. **Areas of usage and special labels.** Some words are labeled as *obsolete* (no longer used), *archaic* (seldom used anymore), *foreign, dialectal* (used in a particular geographical area), *colloquial, slang,* and the like. Words may also be identified with a particular field, such as law, medicine, or sports, to suggest areas of usage.

    Most dictionaries include words and expressions from foreign languages, usually labeling them (It.), (Gr.), and such. (See 14.3 for the use of italics with foreign words.)

6. **Synonyms and antonyms.** Most dictionaries list *synonyms* (words of similar meaning—*fearless* and *valiant* are synonyms for *brave*). Some list *antonyms* (words of opposite meaning—*cowardly* and *craven* are antonyms for *brave*).

Several volumes contain lists of related words:

Fernald's *Standard Handbook of Synonyms, Antonyms, and Prepositions*
Roget's *Thesaurus* (synonyms, some antonyms)
Soule's *A Dictionary of English Synonyms*
Webster's *Dictionary of Synonyms*
Webster's *New World Thesaurus*

7. **Etymology.** Dictionaries also give the *etymology*, or origin, of words.

8. **Other information.** Most dictionaries contain comments on grammar, mechanics, punctuation, language, spelling, and etymology. Dictionaries may also contain some or all of the following:

Abbreviations	Lists of signs and symbols
Biographical and place names	Vocabulary of rhymes
Forms of address	Proofreader's marks
Notes on manuscript form	Lists of colleges and universities
Tables of weights and measures	

Sample dictionary entry:

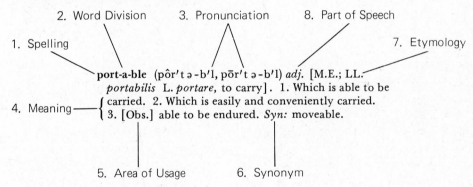

2. Word Division   3. Pronunciation   8. Part of Speech

1. Spelling   7. Etymology

port-a-ble (pôr′t ə -b′l, pōr′t ə -b′l) *adj.* [M.E.; LL. *portabilis* L. *portare*, to carry]. 1. Which is able to be carried. 2. Which is easily and conveniently carried. 3. [Obs.] able to be endured. *Syn:* moveable.

4. Meaning

5. Area of Usage   6. Synonym

Exercise 18   Using a Dictionary

A. Use your dictionary to divide each word into syllables and indicate the correct pronunciation. Then use each word in a short sentence to illustrate that you understand the meaning of the word.

Example	Syllables	Pronunciation
comet	_com·et_	_köm′ət_

A comet follows an elliptical or parabolic orbit around the sun.

1. elaborate _____ _____

2. audacious _____ _____

3. reciprocity _____ _____

4. heterogeneous _____ _____

5. verisimilitude _____ _____

6. brandish _____ _____

7. equivocal _____ _____

8. precedence _____ _____

9. felicitous _____ _____

10. banal _____ _____

B. Using your dictionary, indicate the part(s) of speech and usage label of each word. (If your dictionary does not provide a usage label for a word, use the label *general.*) Then use the word correctly in a short sentence.

Examples	Part(s) of Speech	Usage Label
kooky	*adj.*	*slang*

a kooky person is one who is eccentric or silly.

| pseudonym | *n.* | *general* |

Francois Marie Arouet's pseudonym is Voltaire.

1. kaput

2. drabbet

3. fey

4. incumbent

5. fess

6. whop

7. gunk

8. buzz

9. hold

10. flapdoodle

254

C.   Use your dictionary to give the etymology of each word below.

Example   **Etymology**
island < *ig*, *ieg* (*isle*) < *M.E. iland* < *O.E. igland, iegland, and ealand*

1.   holocaust _____

2.   moccasin _____

3.   fiasco _____

4.   brandy _____

5.   cosmetic _____

6.   armadillo _____

7.   goop _____

8.   kowtow _____

9.   jeopardy _____

10. sandwich _____

D.   Use your dictionary to answer the following questions.

Example What is a warlock?
a male who practices witchcraft and magic.

1.   Where is Principia College located?

2.   How long is a cubit?

3.   On what gulf is the city of Marseilles, France?

4.   How is *Caribbean* pronounced?

5.   For what is coriander used?

6.   What is a *lusus naturae*?

7. What is the etymology of *paradise?*

8. When did Charles James Fox live?

9. How many square miles has Liechtenstein?

10. What does *q.v.* mean in a physician's prescription?

11. What profession might use the word *proptosis?*

12. Distinguish between *Ob, ob-, OB,* and *ob.*

13. If you had an obol, a rupiah, a forint, and a real, what would you have?

14. What kind of medical assistance should be sought for someone suffering from lycanthropy?

15. If you received a letter in which the words *lustre* and *frowsty* were used, what could you guess about the letter writer?

16. Where in the Bible would you find the golden rule?

17. What are three synonyms of *mutiny?*

18. What is the speaker in the following quotation suggesting? "Hey, big boy, want to come over to my place and *paginate* with me?"

19. What is the relationship between Conrad Dibble and Theola Thapper, his *amanuensis?*

20. Who was *von Steuben?* When did he live? What city is named after him? Where is it located? How large is it?

NAME . . . .   SCORE . . . .

Further Practice Exercise 2
Punctuation and Other Conventions (Chapters 10–18)

A. Complete the following form. Be sure to use punctuation marks, italics, capital letters, abbreviations, and numbers correctly and to spell all words correctly. Use information about yourself. When you are done, you will have a start toward developing your own résumé.

Name _____
              (first)   (middle)   (last)

Address _____
                   (number)   (street)

_____
         (city)   (state)   (zip)

Telephone _____
              (area code)   (number)

Social Security number _____

Job objective:_____

_____

_____

_____

Education

_____ I will graduate in _____ from _____
   (date of grad.)   (name of college)

_____ with a _____ degree.
                      (name of degree)

Major: _____ Minor: _____

Honors: _____

Activities: _____

_____

_____

_____ _____
  (date of grad.)   (name of high school or preparatory school)

Honors: _____

Activities: _____

_____

Work Experience

_____   _____

(date)   (name and address of place worked)

_____

(duties)

_____

_____

_____   _____

(date)   _____

_____

_____

_____

_____   _____

(date)   _____

_____

_____

Interests:

_____

_____

References

Name _____   _____

Title _____   _____

Address _____   _____

_____   _____

Telephone_____   _____

258

B. Correct each passage, providing punctuation marks, italics, and capital letters as needed; using abbreviations and numbers correctly and consistently; and correcting all misspelled words.

1. *ARIES* Forego such off beat places as zooes and aquaria perticularly if you have resently read the naked Ape and Jaws to remain persistant in your persuit of intellectuel things you should decide weather or not you really want to hold discusions about vegtables aboard a yaucht.

2. *TAURUS* Your day to day activitys should centre on 3 things assembling alunimum trysycles for elfs dying sheep red orange and hiting flys on cielings you have an artistik temprament and can exspect a long life however your mottos are both latin ones cave canem and ars longa, vita brevis

3. *GEMINI* You will suffer embarasment if you sieze sophmores in librarys you will be noticed if you devower mangoes in bowling allies your mischiefous personality and a most mischeifous personality it is indeed may cause you to start kidnaping playwrites and if you are not careful politisians as well.

4. *MOON CHILDREN* Look out if you participate in a house raising carry a self adressed stamped envelop in an acessable place because your personnel affects will have to be mailed home pospone until mañana your curiosty about financialy independant norweigians be true to yourselfs

5. *LEO* Have you lead a valuble existance have you heeded the words of Sen. Claudia Carnivale who said when you are knee deep in quick sand

you genarally do not have to fear being struck by litening if so you may prophet from the haitian credo joie de vivre in saecula saeculorum incidently mixing french and latin.

6. *VIRGO* On Jan 4th researve 3 mins for meditation, four mins for contempletion, and 6 hrs. for surgary try to read all of the novels of Ant. Trollope, especialy Barchester Towers you would be wise to suround yourself with grandmother Farquars jacks in the pullpits yeild the theatre shedule to rebelious butterflys

C. Write the sentences described.

1. a sentence with two main clauses showing the difference between *allusion* and *illusion*

2. a sentence using *however* and the plural form of *hobo*

3. a sentence using a question mark, italics, and either *choose* or *chose*

4. a sentence containing a quotation and the word *creditable*

5. a sentence containing a subordinate clause, a main clause, a dash, and the word *prefer* + *-ed*

D. Use your dictionary to provide the information requested about each of the words in this exercise. Then use each word correctly in a short sentence.

260

NAME SCORE

Example

Word	Division into Syllables	Pronunciation	Part of Speech
adage	ad-age	ad'ij	noun

  meaning: a proverb or maxim

  sentence: He began his talk by citing the popular adage, "Too many cooks spoil the broth."

1. *eternal*
  meaning:

  sentence:

2. *brougham*
  meaning:

  sentence:

3. *folksy*
  meaning:

  sentence:

4. *rankle*
  meaning:

  sentence:

5. *kinetic*
  meaning:

  sentence:

19

THE PROCESS OF WRITING: PURPOSE AND AUDIENCE

Writing usually depends upon its *purpose* (what it is supposed to do) and its *audience* (to whom it is supposed to communicate).

19.1 Defining and Understanding Your Purpose

Writing expresses the relationship among the writer, the subject matter, and the audience. If the written work centers on the writer, it is termed *expressive writing;* if it is primarily concerned with the subject, it is called *informative writing;* and if it is mostly concerned with the audience, it is labeled *persuasive writing.*

Expressive Writing. Expressive writing provides individuals and groups the opportunity to present their ideas, opinions, feelings, or beliefs. Such types of private writing as personal letters, diaries, journals, autobiographies, greeting cards, meditations, and some forms of essays are usually expressive in nature. Consider this entry in the journal of an American soldier in Vietnam:

> January 18, 1964
>
> We have still not been relieved by fresh troops. After four months in the line without enough food and very little shelter, I'm beginning to feel forgotten. I've never been this hungry, cold, or lonely.

Expressive writing can also be public, allowing a group to express its beliefs, opinions, or goals. The platforms of political parties, sermons, declarations, manifestos, credos, cheers, banners, and eulogies are all examples of public expressive writing.

> In the area of foreign policy, the Bull Elephant Party stands firmly behind the twin protective shields of political isolation and high tariffs. —from a party platform

While the *subject matter* for expressive writing is limitless, the *audience* may range from quite narrow (a friend to whom one writes a personal letter) to quite broad (the world to whom a political group addresses a manifesto). The *style* is generally informal, although public expressive writing is often formal.

Informative Writing. Informative writing centers on the clear presentation of a subject, either through an exposition of facts, an examination of proofs, or an exploration of alternatives. It tends to make both the writer and the audience impersonal. Examples of informative writing are numerous: reference books, manuals, laboratory reports, office memos, business letters, legal briefs, scientific and professional articles, newspaper articles, recipes, travel books, catalogues, classified ads, biographies, and textbooks.

The *subject matter* for informative writing is varied; it ranges from highly technical data in some reports to pieces of pure speculation. Much informative writing, however, is concerned with facts, observations, objects, numbers, and statistics. Informative writing must be organized, accurate, and objective, and it usually answers questions beginning with *who, what, where, when, why,* and *how.*

The *audience* for informative writing may be general (that served by a good dictionary), less general (that served by a juvenile dictionary), or specific (that served by a dictionary of chemical terms). The *style* of informative writing tends to be formal and plain.

Persuasive Writing. Persuasive writing focuses on an audience with the intention of convincing the members of that audience to think or act in a particular way. Persuasive writing permeates our culture. Persuasion is employed in legal and legislative areas (the argument of a defense attorney; a senator's call for support of a particular bill), as well as in ceremonial (a union leader's Labor Day speech), religious (a minister's sermon), political (a candidate's appeal for votes), business (an advertisement for a particular product), and other contexts. Persuasion often takes the form of speeches, advertisements, pamphlets, editorials, essays, and newsletters.

Because the purpose of persuasive writing is to move the audience, writers who use persuasion carefully choose and use types of appeal that can reach those audiences. Appeals are generally classified as logical, emotional, or ethical. They may be used separately or together.

The *logical appeal* relies upon facts, figures, evidence, common sense, deduction, and induction to build its case, as in this report from a college committee on graduation requirements:

> In 1938, a survey of eighty public and private colleges in New England indicated that fifty (62.5%) required their students to complete a course in public speaking in order to graduate. A survey of the same eighty institutions in 1980 revealed that only two (2.5%) still had the same requirement. This significant change suggests that the faculties at nearly all colleges in New England no longer believe a course in public speaking to be a necessary part of an undergraduate degree pro-

gram. Therefore, we recommend that the present requirement in public speaking at Northern State be abolished.

The *emotional appeal* engages the feelings and sensitivities of an audience either to make them feel favorably about something the writer favors, or to make them angry about something the writer does not like, or both. Consider this mock advertisement that uses an emotional appeal:

> Discriminating and cultured individuals of exquisite taste serve Old Rotgut to their wide circle of friends. It spreads a warm glow of companionship over any social occasion. Old Rotgut—Because you deserve the very best.

Using an *ethical appeal,* the writer presents a person's character so as to move an audience to trust or distrust the individual. This attack on a political rival, though exaggerated and perhaps tongue-in-cheek, nonetheless illustrates the use of an ethical appeal:

> It is widely rumored that my worthy opponent, whose divorce became final only ten years ago and who once ran over a small dog, was an active member of a subversive organization during his college days. And just as I am sure that such loyal Americans as you agree with me that our great country has had enough of those who seek to undermine its foundations from within, I am sure that I can count on your support in the election.

19.2 Recognizing the Needs of Your Audience

Each occasion for writing involves a relationship between the writer and a particular audience. Most of the time you will probably be addressing a "general" audience—that is, an audience of reasonably literate, relatively neutral, and generally sympathetic people who will be interested in what you have to say. But audiences can also be classified according to distance and size, specialization, beliefs and group identity, attitude, age, and other such characteristics.

HINT: Although there is no easy way to learn how to address specific audiences, there are things you can do to help:

1. Identify your audience and learn all that you can about that audience.
2. Try to view the subject from the perspective and point of view of the audience.
3. Acknowledge opposing points of view, work to understand them, and credit them when they are valid.
4. Attempt to find common ground which you and the audience share, moving from that common ground to less common material.

Distance. The *distance* between the writer and the audience is determined by the writer's actual relationship with the audience and by how close to or distant from the audience the writer wants to be.

In writing a personal letter to a friend, the writer may wish to maintain the actual close personal relationship shared; on the other hand, the writer may want to create distance and be less personal if the purpose of the letter is to admonish the friend. Similarly, in addressing an audience of strangers, a writer may wish to maintain a formal distance in order to present information objectively, or the writer may want to establish a more personal relationship in order to persuade the audience.

Size. The *size* of the audience a writer addresses may be one individual, a small group, a large group, or an abstract general audience of thousands or millions. Usually, the smaller the audience is, the more personal and informal the writing is. Conversely, the larger the audience, the more impersonal and formal the writing. However, it is possible and often necessary to be more formal and impersonal with a small audience the writer does not know (the personnel director of a business to which the writer is applying for a job), or to be less formal and more personal with a larger audience the writer knows fairly well (the members of a club to whom the writer is addressing a report). In dealing with larger groups particularly, writers often attempt to identify common interests and concerns of the group as a means of bridging the gap between the writer and the audience.

The abstract general audience, which can be defined as all reasonable people within a specific area (city, state, country, or continent, or the entire world), is the largest group a writer can address. Most writers approach such an audience in an impersonal, formal, and neutral way.

Specialization. A writer must also consider the degree of *specialization* or expertise of an audience. A specialist in crime prevention who is writing on that topic will approach the subject differently if the audience consists of other experts in the field of crime prevention than if the audience has only a general knowledge of the topic. With the first group, for example, the writer can use technical language knowing that it will be understood and can assume that basic concepts need not be expressed. With the less knowledge-able audience, the writer will employ a more general language and may need to explain some basic matters. A writer who is dealing with specialized subject matter in one field (energy conservation, for instance) and is addressing an audience whose expertise lies in another field (crime prevention, for example), will treat that specialized audience as a general one.

A more difficult problem exists, however, when the writer is less of an expert in a field than is the audience being addressed. (Students are often confronted with this situation when they take essay examinations or write research papers. Although they must display a reasonable degree of knowledge, they should avoid trying to sound like too much of an expert. And they should remember that their audience does not expect them to have totally mastered the subject.)

Beliefs and Group Identifications. Large groups and general audiences can often be regarded as special interest groups based upon categories such as these—

1. *beliefs:* Protestant, Roman Catholic, Jewish, Atheist, Marxist
2. *racial or ethnic heritage:* black, white, Hispanic, American Indian
3. *nationality:* Greek, Russian, Bolivian, Liberian, American
4. *political party or inclination:* Republican, Democrat, liberal, conservative, anarchist
5. *sex or sexual preference:* female, male, gay, lesbian, straight
6. *economic condition:* poor, middle class, wealthy, blue-collar worker
7. *hobbies and interests:* coin collecting, photography, cats

Such audiences tend to share certain beliefs, likes and dislikes, backgrounds, interests, and vocabularies which can help a writer reach the audience, but which may also make it difficult for the writer to speak with authority.

Attitude. Writers must identify and deal with their audience's *attitude* toward the subject matter and, occasionally, toward the writer. They must determine whether the audience will react favorably, unfavorably, or neutrally toward the message and the messenger. Then they must devise ways to handle those anticipated attitudes. The best writers, however, neither grovel before hostile audiences, assume that friendly audiences will remain friendly no matter what they say, nor underestimate neutral audiences.

Age. The *age* of an audience is an important consideration, for it can reveal the level of development of a group (children, adolescents, adults) as well as the experiences, ideas, social conventions and fads, and historical events a group has in common.

Exercise **19.1**   **Defining and Understanding Your Purpose**

A. For each of the following items, use the audience, subject, and type of writing indicated and write a brief paragraph.

Example
Audience: general
Subject: what you did last night
Type: expressive / diary
Paragraph:

April 6, 1984

I finally got a chance to see Brenda's cousin about that summer job last night. After history class (during which I probably flunked *another* quiz), I went over to the Pizza Palace and saw Bob. You'd think I was applying to be a Supreme Court Justice, I was that nervous. And, really, the job isn't that great. It's just so important to me to find work here—and an apartment—so that I don't have to return to "Hicksville" for the summer. Mom and Dad are coming around; they seem resigned to the fact that I'm nineteen now and no kid any more. And if I work full-time on weekends and four nights during the week, I may be able to get a great tan *and* get in that course in computer science I couldn't take this term. Jobs are so hard to get around here. Too many college bums like me wanting to leave home, I guess.

1.   Audience: your great-aunt Maybelle
     Subject: the book on beekeeping she gave you for your birthday
     Type: expressive / thank you note
     Paragraph:

2.   a. Audience: general
       Subject: the arrival of Hips Hendleman, rock star, at the airport
       Type: informative / newspaper article
       Paragraph:

b. Audience: your best friend
   Subject: the arrival of Hips Hendleman, rock star, at the airport
   Type: expressive / letter
   Paragraph:

3. Audience: a friend of the opposite sex
    Subject: birthday greetings
    Type: expressive / greeting card

Front of Card	**Inside Card**	**Your Written Message**

4. Audience: general
    Subject: a piece of furniture you want to sell
    Type: informative / classified ad
    Paragraph:

B. Use the audience, subject, and type of writing given to write a short persuasive paragraph designed to meet the purpose stated. Remember to use a logical, emotional, or ethical appeal (or any combination of appeals) that is appropriate to the subject and the audience.

Example Audience: a relative or friend
Subject: your financial situation
Type: persuasive / letter
Purpose: to obtain a loan
Paragraph:

Dear Aunt Sue,

As you know, Mom's birthday is only three weeks away. Because I can't be with her this year, I'd like to send her a special gift to show her how much she means to me. I've found just the right thing, a mother's ring with three birthstones representing Tom, Patti, and me. Although I've saved most of what the ring costs, I'm short by $25. If you could please lend me that amount, I'll be able to pay you back when I get the first check from my summer job.

1. Audience: general
Subject: Belly Beer
Type: persuasive / advertisement
Purpose: to get the audience to purchase Belly Beer
Paragraph:

2. Audience: a group of voters
   Subject: your suitability for office
   Type: persuasive / campaign pamphlet
   Purpose: to get the audience to vote for you
   Paragraph:

3. a. Audience: the state legislature in general
      Subject: drinking age
      Type: persuasive / essay
      Purpose: to convince the audience to support raising the legal drinking age to twenty-one (or keeping it at twenty-one if it already is that age)
      Paragraph:

   b. Audience: young people aged eighteen to twenty
      Subject, Type, Purpose: same as in 3a
      Paragraph:

Exercise *19.2*   Writing for an Audience

A. Define as fully as possible a different audience for each of the following subjects. Pay particular attention to *distance, size, specialization, beliefs and group identity, attitude,* and *age.* Note that you must determine the audience for which you would be writing.

Example
Subject: dormitories
Audience:

A group of thirty new freshmen; both male and female in about equal numbers; most are eighteen or nineteen years old; all will be living in a dormitory for the first time; all are excited by the prospect of dorm life; many are a bit afraid; nearly all have never had a roommate before now; some are away from home for the first time; all wonder what regulations there are; most have heard myths about dorm life.

1.   Subject: sexual harassment
Audience:

2.   Subject: a critical review of a new ballet
Audience:

3. Subject: the virtues of the free enterprise system
   Audience:

4. Subject: personal computers
   Audience:

5. Subject: the contributions of black and Hispanic scientists
   Audience:

B. Create different audiences for the same subjects as in A.

1. Subject: sexual harassment
   Audience:

2.   Subject: a critical review of a new ballet
      Audience:

3.   Subject: the virtues of the free enterprise system
      Audience:

4.   Subject: personal computers
      Audience:

5.   Subject: the contributions of black and Hispanic scientists
      Audience:

C. Select three of the topics and audiences in A and B above and write a paragraph for each subject to the audience you have defined.

1. Subject:
    Audience:
    Paragraph:

2. Subject:
    Audience:
    Paragraph:

3. Subject:
    Audience:
    Paragraph:

NAME . . . . SCORE . . . .

D. For each of the following subjects, determine the characteristics of the audience and write a short expressive, informative, or persuasive paragraph directed to the specific audience. Then rewrite the paragraph to direct it to the other audience given.

1. Subject: rock music
    a. Audience: young people aged sixteen to twenty
    Paragraph:

    b. Audience: people over sixty
    Paragraph:

2. Subject: a sunrise or sunset
    a. Audience: a group of blind children
    Paragraph:

    b. Audience: a group of blind adults
    Paragraph:

3.   Subject: equality in educational opportunity
    a. Audience: a mixed group of school committee members
       Paragraph:

    b. Audience: a group of black parents
       Paragraph:

4.   Subject: the advantages of being seventy years old
    a. Audience: a group of people below forty years of age
       Paragraph:

    b. Audience: a group of seventy-year-olds
       Paragraph:

20

DISCOVERING WHAT
YOU HAVE TO SAY

Before you can write, you must have something about which to write. Sometimes a topic will be assigned to you; other times you will have to develop a topic yourself. In either case, *you* must determine what to say.

20.1 Techniques for Generating Ideas

There are several techniques you can use to help you develop your own topic or find something to say about a topic assigned to you.

Collecting Impressions

1. *Keep a journal* in which you make regular entries recording your ideas and beliefs, registering your impressions and feelings and reactions, and expressing yourself on both important and trivial things.
2. *Practice making abstractions concrete* by writing sentences and phrases that make generalizations specific. For example, you might make *wealthy* specific by writing "able to buy an automobile without considering the price."

Seeing Patterns and Connections

1. *Freewriting.* Try writing nonstop for a certain period of time—fifteen minutes or more. Write down everything that occurs to you; don't worry about spelling, grammar, or punctuation. Some of the ideas that appear in your freewriting may suggest patterns to you, or give you some subjects worth exploring further.
2. *Observing and Questioning.* Look for patterns and connections in your ideas and experiences. Here are some questions to ask yourself that may lead to some ideas to look at more closely and develop further:

a. Do any actions, attitudes, or emotional reactions seem to recur in your experience?
b. What do you focus on when you look at something? Try to shift your focus from a "close-up" to a "long-shot." Can you see individual members of a whole, and then the whole itself?
c. How do your experiences differ from those of others? How varied are your experiences? What is their significance for you?
d. What can you learn about a subject by examining its parts? By looking at the relationships among the parts? By considering it as part of a larger context?
e. What about your experiences can be shared with others? How can you connect the experiences of others to you and your subject?

20.2 Exploring Your Subject

Once you have a subject, you still may need to examine it further to decide what to say about it and to determine what you still might need to learn about it. Here are some techniques that will help you explore your topic further.

Brainstorming. For a certain period of time—say five or ten minutes—make a list of everything you can think of that you know about the subject. Your list can then become a catalogue of ideas that you can categorize, link together, and rank in order of importance.

Asking the Journalist's Questions. When your writing is informative, you may examine your subject by asking six key questions (not every one of which is relevant to every topic):

1. *Who?* is involved, deserves credit or blame, is affected?
2. *What?* is involved, happened, are the results?
3. *Where?* did it happen, and why did it happen there rather than somewhere else?
4. *How?* did it happen, does it work, did it succeed or fail; what made it possible, probable, or inevitable?
5. *When?* did it occur; what was the sequence of events; does it fit into a larger time frame; why was it so slow or so long or so fast or so short?
6. *Why?* did it occur; what motivated the action; what caused the event? [*Why?* is the most abstract and difficult of the six questions to answer.]

Exploring Patterns and Relationships. There are a number of observations you may make to help you see patterns and relationships in your topic. These observations include—

1. *Description:* What does something look like or consist of? What are its colors, shapes, dimensions, weights, properties, features? What are its distinguishing characteristics?

2. *Narration:* What is the sequence of events? What event is central or pivotal? Can the sequence be narrated in another way (flashback, reversed order, association)?

3. *Process:* How does something work, function, or operate? Are there subsystems within a major process? What can cause something to begin or cease to function?

4. *Cause and Effect:* What are the reasons that something has occurred or failed to occur? Which causes are direct? Indirect? What are the effects? Who or what is responsible?

5. *Classification:* How is something similar to and different from other things? How is it similar to like objects? What helps you identify an object or idea with one group rather than with another?

6. *Division:* Can the subject be divided into parts? Which parts are more important than others? Can the parts be rearranged for clarity?

7. *Comparison and Contrast:* How is the subject similar to related objects or ideas? How is the subject unlike related objects or ideas? What are the advantages and disadvantages, or strengths and weaknesses, of the subject?

8. *Definition:* How can you distinguish one object from all others? What is its group or class? What are its identifying characteristics?

9. *Evaluation:* What is the purpose or function of an object? What goals are indicated by an idea, concept, or proposal?

Drawing on Personal Resources. Your own experiences will provide ideas and materials for essays: the people you know, the places you have been, the groups and clubs to which you belong, your hobbies and interests, the jobs you have had, the opinions and beliefs you hold, your years in school, the places you have lived, embarrassing moments you have had, your experiences as a consumer, your attempts to repair things, and the like. Interesting and informative essays can be written on such topics as "How to Establish a Pet-Grooming Business," "My Most Embarrassing Moment," "How to Beat the Lines at the Bookstore," or "The Trials and Tribulations of Buying a Stereo."

20.3 Limiting Your Subject

Once you have a topic, it is often necessary to limit that topic to one that can be developed fully in the length allowed. Topics such as "Sports," "College Life," and "The Civil War" are far too broad for most writing assignments. Narrowing such topics to "Football," "Freshman Week," and "Major Battles of the Civil War" will help somewhat; but these topics are still too broad for most assignments. Further narrowing will yield such workable topics as "Defensive Line Play," "Registration Day," and "The Battle of Chancellorsville."

HINT: One topic (a snack bar) can lead to many different specific subjects for writing (the food, the help, the decor, the customers, the atmosphere). Unless a specific topic is assigned, there is no one right or correct subject for a paper.

20.4 Locating a Thesis

Once you have a good idea of what you are writing about, it is usually helpful to create a *thesis statement*. The thesis statement (usually a sentence with only one main clause) specifically states the central point of your paper. The thesis statement should answer the question "What is the main idea you are trying to present?"

Here is a sample thesis statement for a specific topic:

Topic	Registration Day
Thesis statement	Although Freshman Week is a bewildering time, no part of it is as confusing and discouraging as Registration Day.

HINT: It is usually possible to write several different thesis statements for any topic. For one thing, different types of writing (exposition, argumentation, description, narration—see Chapter 19, The Process of Writing: Purpose and Audience) call for different kinds of thesis statements. For another thing, each perspective on a topic calls for a different thesis statement. These thesis statements, for example, all relate to the subject "customers at a snack bar":

Customers at a snack bar can be divided into two groups, the regulars and the drop-ins.
Customers at a snack bar reveal much about themselves by the way in which they drink their coffee.
Being a customer at a snack bar is an eye-opening experience.
Customers at a snack bar do not give enough credit to their waitresses.
Waitresses see snack bar customers differently from the way cooks see them.

Questions that may help you think about a subject:

The Journalist's Questions

1.	Who?	4.	When?
2.	What?	5.	How?
3.	Where?	6.	Why?

Questions of Status

1. What happened? (describe and narrate)
2. What is its nature? (classify and define)
3. What is its quality? (evaluate)

Exercise 20.1   Techniques for Generating Ideas

A.   Assume that you have been assigned to write a paper but have been
given no specific topic. List four broad topics on which you could write
a paper using your own experiences for details. For each topic, write a
brief journal entry in which you try to make at least part of the topic
concrete.

Example   Topic: *kindness*

Entry: *letting the smallest kid on the block
play too... not treating him/her differently...
choosing him/her first or second, rather
than last, for your side.*

1.   Topic:

Entry:

2.   Topic:

Entry:

3.   Topic:

Entry:

4.   Topic:

Entry:

B. For each item, examine the subject by answering each of the six questions given which are relevant to the subject.

Example   Topic: kindness to the smallest kid on the block

Who: *the smallest kid on the block*

What: *kindness*

Where: *everywhere – at school or at home*

How: *by treating him/her the same as everyone else.*

When: *all the time*

Why: *so he/she won't feel different or left out.*

1. Topic: the armed robbery of a liquor store

    Who:

    What:

    Where:

    How:

    When:

    Why:

2. Topic: an embarrassing moment

    Who:

    What:

    Where:

    How:

    When:

    Why:

3. Topic: (Select a topic that you used in Exercise 20.1 A.)

    Who:

    What:

    Where:

    How:

    When:

    Why:

NAME . . . . SCORE . . . .

C. For each subject, write notes using the type of observation given.

Example Topic: kindness
Observation: classification
Notes: *a nice way of relating to other people
you can be kind to someone who is not a friend
an act of kindness is done out of sympathy for others
and for their feelings, not out of necessity and
not for a reward*

1. Topic: an embarrassing moment
   a. Observation: narration
      Notes:

   b. Observation: cause and effect
      Notes:

2. Topic: a rainbow
   a. Observation: description
      Notes:

   b. Observation: process
      Notes:

3. Topic: "Thou shalt not kill."

   a. Observation: classification
      Notes:

   b. Observation: evaluation
      Notes:

4. Topic: (Select a topic you used in 20.1 A.)
   a. Observation: (select one)

   b. Observation: (select one)

Exercise *20.2/20.3* Limiting a Subject / Locating a Thesis

A. For each item, choose one of the general topics given. Then limit each general topic to two or three topics specific enough for a short paper. For the last five, supply your own general topics.

Example Topic: *kindness*

    a. *The smallest kid on the block*

    b. *a modern Good Samaritan*

    c. *Be kind to your spouse*

1. Topic: television *or* radio

    a.

    b.

    c.

2. Topic: autumn *or* spring

    a.

    b.

    c.

3. Topic: college *or* high school

    a.

    b.

    c.

4. Topic: friends *or* foes

    a.

    b.

    c.

5. Topic: embarrassment *or* elation

    a.

    b.

    c.

6. Topic:

    a.

    b.

    c.

7. Topic:

    a.

    b.

    c.

8. Topic:

    a.

    b.

    c.

C. For each subject, write notes using the type of observation given.

Example   Topic: kindness
Observation: classification
Notes: *a nice way of relating to other people*
you can be kind to someone who is not a friend
an act of kindness is done out of sympathy for others
and for their feelings, not out of necessity and
not for a reward

1. Topic: an embarrassing moment
   a. Observation: narration
   Notes:

   b. Observation: cause and effect
   Notes:

2. Topic: a rainbow
   a. Observation: description
   Notes:

   b. Observation: process
   Notes:

3. Topic: "Thou shalt not kill."

   a. Observation: classification
   Notes:

   b. Observation: evaluation
   Notes:

4. Topic: (Select a topic you used in 20.1 A.)
   a. Observation: (select one)

   b. Observation: (select one)

Exercise *20.2/20.3*   Limiting a Subject/Locating a Thesis

A.   For each item, choose one of the general topics given. Then limit each general topic to two or three topics specific enough for a short paper. For the last five, supply your own general topics.

Example   Topic: *kindness*

a. *The smallest kid on the block*
b. *A modern Good Samaritan*
c. *Be kind to your spouse*

1. Topic: television *or* radio

   a.

   b.

   c.

2. Topic: autumn *or* spring

   a.

   b.

   c.

3. Topic: college *or* high school

   a.

   b.

   c.

4. Topic: friends *or* foes

   a.

   b.

   c.

5. Topic: embarrassment *or* elation

   a.

   b.

   c.

6. Topic:

   a.

   b.

   c.

7. Topic:

   a.

   b.

   c.

8. Topic:

   a.

   b.

   c.

NAME . . . .   SCORE . . . .

9. Topic: **10.** Topic:

    a.   a.

    b.   b.

    c.   c.

B. For each of the following topics a thesis statement is given. If the thesis statement is weak, cross it out and write a better one. If the thesis statement is acceptable, write a second, different thesis statement on the same topic.

Example Topic: movies

    Thesis: I enjoy movies which use symbolism effectively.

The use of symbols makes movies more enjoyable.

1. Topic: dragons

    Thesis: Dragons are frightening creatures.

2. Topic: a club or organization

    Thesis: The members of the Cloud Club are dedicated to providing a social life for themselves and service to others.

3. Topic: summer

    Thesis: Summer is fun.

4. Topic: waiting in line

    Thesis: You can tell a lot about people by watching them as they wait in a long line.

5. Topic: wheelchairs

Thesis: Seldom do wheelchairs get the respect they deserve for transporting some of the most courageous people alive.

C. For each of the following general topics, first narrow the topic to a more specific one, then write a thesis sentence for the specific topic. Remember that the thesis sentence should present the main point or central idea of a paper.

Example   Topic: kindness

Specific topic: *kindness toward the smallest kid on the block.*

Thesis: *Kindness is treating the smallest kid on the block just as you treat everyone else.*

1. Topic: witches

   Specific topic:

   Thesis:

2. Topic: autumn

   Specific topic:

   Thesis:

3. Topic: voting

   Specific topic:

   Thesis:

4. Topic: computers

   Specific topic:

   Thesis:

5. Topic: leisure time

   Specific topic:

   Thesis:

6. Topic: the suburbs

   Specific topic:

   Thesis:

7. Topic: the kitchen

   Specific topic:

   Thesis:

8. Topic: happiness

   Specific topic:

   Thesis:

21

DEVELOPING AND ARRANGING
YOUR MATERIAL

Most writing depends at least in part on one or more of the traditional methods for developing and arranging material: _description, narration, process, exposition, cause and effect,_ and so on.

21.1 Patterns of Development

Description. The purpose of description is to enable an audience to see an object, person, or scene as the writer has seen or imagined it. In description you must see a subject clearly in all of its concrete, sensory details and describe precisely what you see:

Weak	The creature's face was horrible to look at.
Better	The creature's face, deformed and scarred by flames and dominated by fierce red eyes, was terrifying.

Although descriptive writing is precise, it is also selective. Too many adjectives and adverbs will detract from rather than add to description:

Weak	The warm beach with its cool, damp, white sand and its very sparkling, clear, cold blue water was magnificently inviting.
Better	The cool white sand and clear blue water made the beach inviting.

HINT: Both description and narration provide concreteness and substance to support exposition and argumentation.

Narration. The purpose of narration is to re-create an experience or event, usually without expository comment. Like description, narration depends upon specifics; but unlike description (which moves through space), narration moves through time. Most narrative writing is presented from the point of view either of a first-person observer or participant, or of a third-person observer. In pacing a narrative include enough details to make the narrative interesting and understandable, yet be selective, eliminate irrelevant and unimportant details.

Process. A process essay relates steps in sequence (painting a house, dissecting a frog). To write an effective process paper, be sure to list the steps in a simple, clear order. Explain in plain English any special terms that your readers might not understand.

Exposition. The purpose of exposition is to inform your audience about your subject. Document your information with specific details and examples from private and public resources:

> In the six summers I have worked as a lifeguard, I have observed that carelessness causes more drownings and near-drownings than anything else. [private resources]
> Herman Wolfe, in his classic study *Legends of Werewolves,* reported: "No firm evidence has yet been found to substantiate any legend about the existence of werewolves" (p. 18). [public resources]

Cause and Effect. A cause and effect paper either starts with an analysis of causes and concludes with the effect, or starts with the effect and then analyzes the causes. A paper on the high cost of medical care, for instance, might begin by presenting those costs—the effect—and then consider the reasons for those costs—the cause.

Classification and Division. When using the pattern of development called classification and division, a writer explains a term either by assigning it to a class and then examining the characteristics of the class, or by dividing the subject in order to consider each of its parts.

Definition. Definition involves explaining a term by assigning it to a class and then distinguishing it from other members of the class, or by discussing what something is or is not, or by stating what something does or does not do. (For example, a *novella* is a work of prose fiction longer than a short story but shorter than a novel.)

Comparison and Contrast. An essay of this type involves the comparing and contrasting of the major points of two ideas, situations, events, and the like, ending with a conclusion about the two (the 1927 New York Yankees and the 1976 Cincinnati Reds; city life and country life).

Analogy. Using the pattern of development termed *analogy,* a writer explains a new or difficult idea in terms of another idea or concept the readers are more likely to be familiar with (the activity in a beehive defined in terms of the crowds in Times Square, for instance).

Support and Illustration. Support and illustration starts with a general statement and then supports it with specific details, examples, reasons (the value of a liberal education; the dangers of nuclear power).

21.2 Strategies of Argumentation

The purpose of argumentation is to *convince* your audience. While the various patterns of development *present* information, argumentation *uses* information to support or test a belief. An argumentative paper proposes a particular action or a particular point of view which should be carefully stated in a thesis statement:

> To provide relief for low- and middle-income families, tax credit must be given for money spent on a college education.

Support your opinions and generalizations, and state your facts specifically:

Weak	One leading biologist said that genetic research was dangerous but necessary.
Better	In an article in *Scientific Research* in 1973, Lydia Swartly, T. D. Lysenko Professor of Genetics at Corinth University, wrote: "Genetic research, particularly that branch dealing with modifications of genes, is dangerous, but it is also absolutely necessary for the future of humanity."

Argumentation has a number of general characteristics:

1. An argumentative paper *proposes* something; it centers on a proposition that the writer must be prepared to prove.
2. An argumentative paper uses *facts, evidence,* and *resources* to prove the proposition.
3. An argumentative paper may use *induction* or *deduction.*
    a. *Induction* involves arguing from specifics to arrive at a generalization (after observing the specific phenomenon of the sun rising in the east for many mornings, one can generalize that the sun rises in the east every morning).
    b. *Deduction* involves arguing from generalizations or *premises* already existing to conclusions about a specific case or cases. Deductive arguments may be stated in a *syllogism:*

Major premise	All humans are mortal. [a generalization arrived at through induction]
Minor premise	Clyde is a human.
Conclusion	Clyde is mortal.

HINT: Deductive arguments require careful attention to the premises, for if you can prove the premises, the conclusion must follow. Or, if you can disprove an opponent's premise, you will disprove your opponent's conclusion.

4. An argumentative paper may use any number of traditional kinds of logical argument.
    a. *Argument from nature:* arguing that a male cannot run for Homecoming Queen because a queen is, by nature, a female;

b. *Argument from analogy:* arguing for urban renewal by comparing an urban slum area to a malignant growth that must be removed;

c. *Argument from consequence:* arguing that something should or should not be because of the desirable or undesirable effects of it;

d. *Argument from authority:* arguing that because respected authorities believe something, then everyone should.

Testing the Argument. Examine your argument (or that of someone else) for these common flaws in reasoning.

1. **Hasty generalizations.** Few statements can accurately use such absolute terms as *all, always, everyone, nobody, never, none, only,* and *most.*

2. **False analogy** occurs when an attempt is made to compare two things which lack a basic similarity. Arguing that education should operate as an assembly line would probably not be effective because, unlike videosets produced on an assembly line, students are not identical to each other.

3. *Post hoc, ergo propter hoc* ("after this, therefore because of this") assumes that because two events or things are related chronologically they are also related causally. If you break your arm after eating eggs for breakfast, you probably cannot argue that eating eggs caused the injury.

4. *Non sequitur* ("it does not follow") refers to a conclusion which does not follow from the evidence presented. It is not valid to base an argument that a new Ice Age is coming only upon the statement that winters seem colder lately than they used to.

5. **Begging the question** is assuming the truth of something that needs to be proved. Educators who argue "Because our curriculum is weak, we must change it" are begging the question unless they first prove that the curriculum is weak.

6. **Ignoring the question** is a broad term which applies to all irrelevant arguments. When politicians argue that they deserve to be elected because they have families, they are ignoring the question. The following are two specific ways of ignoring the question:

    a. *Argumentum ad hominem* ("argument against the man") involves attacking the integrity of one's opponents rather than their arguments.

    b. **Glittering generalities** are the use of high-sounding words which ignore the question. ("Vote for me because I am for peace and freedom.")

7. **Either/or fallacy** involves assuming that one has the choice of only two alternatives, rather than several or both alternatives. Someone who argues that a car will not start either because the battery is low or because the car is out of gas has not exhausted all the possibilities. The alternator may be broken, for example, or the battery may be low *and* the car may be out of gas.

Exercise 21   Developing and Arranging Your Material

A. Indicate the kind of writing displayed in each passage by writing *exposition*, *argumentation*, *description*, or *narration* in the space at the right.

Example Cholera, a severe epidemic disease, is fatal to   *exposition*
about half of the people who contract it.

1. Blast gasoline with new, improved cyclomate is   1. _____
    better for your car. Buy Blast!
2. It was a dark, foggy evening. The only thing pene-   2. _____
    trating the thick mist was the shrill foghorn.
3. Roasting chickens are usually full-grown males that   3. _____
    are fed special diets.
4. My concern has always been for you, my constitu-   4. _____
    ents. Reelect me and I will continue to serve you
    well.
5. We must limit the spread of nuclear weapons be-   5. _____
    fore the earth erupts in an atomic cloud.
6. The altar was draped with a black cloth. On the   6. _____
    right sat a large silver statue of a goat. On the left
    lay a silver dagger next to a silver chalice.
7. After hours of continuous bombardment, the artil-   7. _____
    lery stopped suddenly. The command to charge
    sounded. We spurred our horses and began our
    ride into hell.
8. The Roundheads, supporters of the parliamentary   8. _____
    party in the English Civil War during the seven-
    teenth century, obtained their name from the
    Puritan custom of wearing hair cut close to the
    head.
9. No home should be without the Grinder Gadget. It   9. _____
    dices, it slices, it peels, it chops, and it grinds.
10. Two old men were lazily playing checkers. Their   10. _____
    gnarled fingers, stiffened by arthritis, had difficulty
    picking up the smooth red and black disks.
11. We parachuted into the dense jungle while it was   11. _____
    still dark. At the first sign of light we began chop-
    ping our way through the dense underbrush.
12. Doc Smedley stretches, checks the runner at first,
    and pitches. Howard swings and misses.
13. January is named for Janus, the Roman god of be-   13. _____
    ginnings and endings, entrances and doorways.

14. He stood at the door dripping wet. Water ran down   14. _____
his arms and legs and off the bottom of his coat.
15. Zax, a tool used to trim roofing slates, is an ex-   15. _____
cellent word to use in such games as Scrabble.

B. From newspapers and magazines, clip out, label, and turn in at least
two examples each of exposition, argumentation, description, and narration.

C. Select one topic from each pair and circle it. Then write four sentences
on the topic, one each of exposition, argumentation, description, and
narration.

Example TOPICS: dormitory life *or* registration

(exposition) *Registration will begin Tuesday, September 14, at 9:00 a.m. in the gymnasium*

(argumentation) *Because the registration procedure is unnecessarily time-consuming, it should be changed.*

(description) *At registration, long lines of bored and frustrated students followed rope mazes set up in front of the tables which circled the gymnasium.*

(narration) *After a thirty-minute wait, during which I chatted with the person in line behind me, I registered for French and moved to the end of the line waiting to register for history.*

1. TOPICS: a movie *or* a television program

(exposition)

(argumentation)

(description)

(narration)

2. TOPICS: public transportation *or* private transportation

(exposition)

(argumentation)

292

(description)

(narration)

3.   TOPICS: sounds in the day *or* sounds at night
      (exposition)

      (argumentation)

      (description)

      (narration)

4.   TOPICS: energy *or* the environment
      (exposition)

      (argumentation)

      (description)

      (narration)

5.   TOPICS: a sport *or* a hobby
      (exposition)

      (argumentation)

      (description)

      (narration)

D. Write one paragraph of each type of writing in the space provided. Select a general topic for each paragraph from the following list and narrow the topic to something specific. (See Chapter 20, Discovering What You Have to Say.)

a dream	an event in your life
the color orange	something to be changed
a popular rock group	driving in traffic
repairing something	smoking

1.   (narration)   Topic _____

2.   (exposition)   Topic _____

3.   (description)   Topic _____

4.   (argumentation)   Topic _____

E. For each topic, indicate the most appropriate type of development:

Description	Cause and effect
Process	Analogy
Support and illustration	Classification and division
Narration	Definition
Comparison and contrast	

Examples Topic	Type of Development
Building a model railroad	*process*
Bill 1099 must be defeated	*cause and effect*

1. A cure for urban blight   1. _____

2. The advantages of being left-handed   2. _____

3. The ABC and NBC weather reports   3. _____

4. How inflation developed   4. _____

5. The history of motors   5. _____

6. Art and music should be required
    subjects   6. _____

7. Why handguns should be registered   7. _____

8. Why Napoleon lost at Waterloo   8. _____

9. The whales must be saved   9. _____

10. Group dynamics in a discussion
    course   10. _____

11. Report on Biology Laboratory #12   11. _____

12. The differences between capitalism
    and communism   12. _____

13. The latest recording by a pop singer   13. _____

14. Types of students   14. _____

15. The resources of the North and
    South in 1860   15. _____

16. The formation of the Rocky Moun-
    tains   16. _____

17. The creation of a consumer protec-
    tion agency   17. _____

18. The dangers of untreated mental
    illnesses   18. _____

19. The operas of Puccini and Verdi   19. _____

20. Hyde Park, London   20. _____

21. The education of Elizabeth Blackwell   21. _____

295

22. Why government bureaucracy grew complex   22. _____

23. Vincent van Gogh's painting *Starry Night*   23. _____

24. Learning to ski   24. _____

25. A review of the book *Knights of Old*   25. _____

26. A study of philately   26. _____

27. Stages in human evolution   27. _____

28. The development of penicillin   28. _____

F. For each of the topics below, write a short paragraph using the type of development indicated.

	Topic	**Type of development**
1.	studying	Process
2.	a room	Description
3.	two people	Comparison and contrast
4.	oversleeping	Cause and effect

NAME .... SCORE ....

5. the value of exercise   Analogy

G. For each type of development indicated, choose a subject and then write a paragraph using that type of development.

1. Type of development: Narration

Subject:

Paragraph:

2. Type of development: Classification and division

Subject:

Paragraph:

3. Type of development: Definition

Subject:

Paragraph:

4. Type of development: Support and illustration

Subject:

Paragraph:

H. Each passage below is weak either because it is too specific or because it is too general. Indicate the problem by writing either *too specific* or *too general* in the space at the right.

Example She does not know anything.   *too general*

1. She looked old from head to foot.   1. _____
2. The brilliant, orange-red, fiery sun shines brightly and warmly down upon my ancient, old, but well-preserved domicile and birthplace in the grand and glorious state of Kentucky.   2. _____
3. The scene was ugly.   3. _____
4. I waited. At 5:00 he hadn't come. At 5:35 he hadn't come. At 5:59 he still hadn't come. At 6:00 he arrived.   4. _____
5. When they buy shoes people reveal a lot about themselves.   5. _____
6. Leading citizens have spoken in favor of a ban on nonreturnable bottles and cans.   6. _____

I. Each passage below is weak because it contains a flaw in reasoning. Indicate the problem by writing one of the following terms in the space at the right:

hasty generalization	false analogy	*non sequitur*
begging the question	*post hoc*	either/or
ignoring the question	*ad hominem*	glittering generality

Example All witches are evil.   *hasty generalization*

1. Intercollegiate athletics do not help students academically; therefore, they should be abolished.   1. _____

2. Beef Burger Rancho is proud to be serving Americans, proud to be in America, proud to fly the flag of our great nation outside each and every one of its Ranchos from coast to coast.

2. _____

3. No loyal American could possibly object to taking a loyalty oath as a condition of employment.

3. _____

4. Professor Appleton's continental drift theory is pure poppycock. Just ask the woman who divorced him last year. Ask the dean who fired him from his first job. Ask his psychiatrist.

4. _____

5. Either you get to your room and study or you will fail the test tomorrow.

5. _____

6. Obtaining a college education is as easy as getting on a train at one station and getting off at the end of the line.

6. _____

7. Because creatures from outer space want to destroy humanity, we must kill them on sight.

7. _____

8. I knew we would have an earthquake today. I heard an owl hooting last night.

8. _____

9. Parents do not understand their children.

9. _____

10. All Americans have impeccably bad taste.

10. _____

11. My opponent for the office of senator is a man of three colors—pink, lavender, and yellow.

11. _____

12. I got caught because someone ratted on me or because I had rotten luck.

12. _____

22

USING AN OUTLINE

Once you have a topic and have discovered what to say about it, an outline will probably help you order your material. Remember that an outline is not an end in itself; it is a tool to help you organize and develop your material and give unity and coherence to your paper.

22.1 Types of Outlines

Four kinds of outlines are widely used: the scratch outline, the thesis statement outline, the topic outline, and the sentence outline.

Scratch Outlines. A scratch outline is a series of notes—single words or phrases—scratched down to guide you when you write. A scratch outline is particularly useful when you are writing papers or essay examinations in class. Because a scratch outline is brief, the order is usually not important.

Scratch outline on the topic "The Territorial Growth of the United States":

Original territory in 1783	1846 Oregon territory
Louisiana purchased from France (1803)	Mexican Cession in 1848
1818—part of No. Dakota from Britain	Gadsden Purchase
Spain cedes Florida 1821	Alaska bought from Russia (1867)
Annexation of Texas in 1845–48	Hawaii annexed 1898

Thesis Statement Outlines. It is possible to outline your paper within the thesis statement. A thesis statement outline is useful for in-class writing assignments and for short out-of-class assignments.

Thesis statement outline on the topic "Suburban Developments":

Although some suburban housing developments **are varied** and refreshingly different, most are characterized by a sameness of **layout, design,** and **landscaping** that makes suburbia **unimaginative and depressing.**

As an outline, this thesis statement suggests paragraphs on the varied settings, on layout, on design, on landscaping, and on the unimaginative and depressing quality of suburbia.

Topic Outlines. Topic outlines, the type of formal outlines used most often, are helpful in writing papers of nearly any length. These outlines consist of words and phrases arranged to show the order and relative importance of ideas.

Topic outline on the subject "Two Types of Musicians":

THESIS: A string quartet and a rock group set different moods through their modes of dress, their styles of performance, and their music.

I. Modes of dress
  A. String quartet
    1. Formal attire
      a. Men
      b. Women
    2. Customary dress, varies little
    3. Few accessories
  B. Rock group
    1. Casual attire
    2. Much variety in style
    3. Many accessories

[Parts II and III of this outline go on to discuss styles of performance and music.]

Sentence Outlines. Sentence outlines are created in the same way as topic outlines, but each heading is expressed as a complete sentence. These are particularly valuable for such long assignments as a research paper.

Part of a sentence outline on the subject "Two Types of Musicians":

I. The modes of dress of a string quartet and a rock group contribute to a feeling of formality or informality at a concert.
  A. The attire of a string quartet sets a formal tone.
    1. Dress is traditional and formal.
      a. Men wear full-dress coats, tuxedos, or suits.
      b. Women wear black floor-length dresses or skirts.

22.2 Standard Outline Form

Outlines follow certain conventions regarding numbering, indentation, punctuation, and capitalization. The standard form is this:

THESIS: _____[sentence statement]
I. _____ [roman numeral for main head]
  A. _____ [capital letter for subhead]
    1. _____[arabic numeral for second subhead]
    2. _____
      a. _____ [lowercase letter for third subhead]
      b. _____

Avoid elaborate systems. You will seldom have to go beyond a third subhead. In a topic outline, capitalize only the first word of the heading (and all proper nouns); do not punctuate the end of the entry. In a sentence outline, capitalize and punctuate each heading as you would any other sentence.

Headings should be *specific* rather than general (avoid such terms as "Conclusion" and "Results"). Headings should also be (1) accurately divided, (2) mutually exclusive, (3) equally important, and (4) parallel in form.

Inaccurate division
1. *Paradise Lost*
   A. Written by John Milton
      1. An Englishman

Accurate division
1. *Paradise Lost*
   A. Written by John Milton, an Englishman

Overlapping
Methods of travel
   I. Water
   II. Land
   III. Trains

Mutually exclusive
Methods of travel
   I. Ships
   II. Motor vehicles
   III. Trains

Unequally important
Human relationships
   I. With oneself
   II. With family and friends
   III. With your boss
   IV. With a supreme being

Equally important
Human relationships
   I. Personal
   II. Social
   III. Religious

Not parallel in form
Batting
   I. Stance
   II. Holding the bat
   III. Eyes
   IV. How to swing
   V. Follow-through is important

Parallel in form
Batting
   I. The stance
   II. The grip
   III. The eyes
   IV. The swing
   V. The follow-through

Exercise 22   Using an Outline

A. Select two of the following topics. Narrow each general topic to one specific enough for a 500-word paper. Then develop a scratch outline for each specific topic.

General topics: Religion   Modern villains   Magazines
                   Snow   Popular music   Vacations
                   Money   Student concerns   Teachers
                   Drugs   Gender gap   Meditation

1.   General topic: Specific topic:

Scratch outline:

2.   General topic: Specific topic:

Scratch outline:

B. Develop two topic outlines and one sentence outline using three of the following topics (or other topics you select). Narrow each general topic to a topic specific enough for a 500–1000-word paper. Be sure to use standard outline form.

General Topics:
   Astrology   Detective fiction   How to do something
   Salespeople   American cities   The value of something
   Newspapers   Individualism   A description of something
   Power   Law enforcement   A policy for something

1.   General topic: Specific topic:

Topic outline:

2. General topic: Specific topic:

      Topic outline:

3. General topic: Specific topic:

      Sentence outline:

C. Select one unit from the topic outline in B.1 and write a paragraph based on the outline.

D. Select one unit from the sentence outline in B.3 and write a paragraph based on the outline.

Review Exercise 19–22   Composition

A.   Prepare to write a short paper by completing in order the steps below. Choose one of the following general topics or supply your own general topic.

A personal experience from which you learned a lesson
A way to spend leisure time
Education one hundred years from now
A sport one hundred years from now
Clothing styles one hundred years from now
Transportation one hundred years from now
Medicine one hundred years from now
A strange dream
The month of August
The color purple

1.   General topic:

2.   As quickly as possible, jot down several specific ideas about your topic. Do not be concerned about narrowing the topic at this point.

3.   Review the ideas you have jotted down, then narrow your topic to a specific one that you can handle in 250–350 words.

Specific topic:

4.   Define the audience for whom you will be writing; list some of its characteristics.

Audience:

305

5. Determine whether your paper will be expressive, informative, or persuasive.

   Type:

6. Explore your topic for ideas by answering all of the following questions which relate to your topic.

   Who?   When?

   What?   How?

   Where?   Why?

   What happened? (describe and narrate)

   What is its nature? (classify and define)

   What is its quality? (evaluate)

   What examples, narratives, episodes, incidents, and such could be *included?*

   What *sequences* occur in your subject?

7. After reviewing what you have written so far, create three thesis statements expressing the main idea or central point of your paper. Select one for your paper.
   Thesis statements:

   (1)

   (2)

   (3)

   Selected thesis:

8. What method(s) of development will you use?
   Method(s) of development:

9. Using the material you have written, develop a topic outline.
   Outline:

B. Write the first draft of the paper you prepared for in A. Concentrate on ideas, organization, development, and continuity. Be sure that your paragraphs are related in sequence. Begin at any point in your paper (not necessarily at the beginning). Use your outline as a guide, but do not be afraid to deviate from it if necessary. Write rapidly, without worrying about correctness, mechanics, and spelling (which can be corrected in revision). Try to write the first draft in one sitting. Use your own paper for this first draft.

C. After completing the first draft (B above), read Chapter 23, Drafting, Revising, and Editing. Then revise your first draft carefully. Use your own paper for the final draft.

D. Select a topic from the list provided in A above. Follow the steps outlined in A, B, and C to produce a final paper of 500–750 words. Use your own paper for this exercise.

23

DRAFTING, REVISING, AND EDITING

23.1 Framing a Title

A title should be specific, accurate, and clear. It should also be short.

For a paper on seven images in Melville's *Moby Dick*, avoid such titles as "Melville" (inaccurate), "A Consideration of Seven Different Types of Images Found in Herman Melville's Novel *Moby Dick*" (too long), "Foam, Wind, and the Rainbow" (unclear), and "Imagery in Melville" (too general). Rather, use a clear, direct title such as "Seven Images in *Moby Dick*."

23.2 Revising

After you have finished writing the first draft of a paper, put it aside for as long as possible—a week or two, a day or two, or several hours at the least—before attempting to revise it. The longer the period of time the better, for time away from the paper will increase your critical perception.

When you revise your paper, do *not* simply read it through once or twice to see if anything seems wrong with it. Rather, approach the first draft systematically; go through it several times, looking for specific problems each time.

(The number following each item below refers to the section of the *Workbook* to be consulted for discussion of the problem and help in revising.)

1. **First reading:** Check the frame of your paper.
    Thesis statement (20.4)
    Do you have one? Is it clear? Is it adequate for your topic?
    Introduction (25.5)
    Is it effective? Is it weak?
    Transitions between paragraphs (25.4)
    Are the paragraphs effectively linked together?
    Are the major divisions of the paper clearly delineated?
    Conclusion (25.6)

Is it effective? Does it tie the end to the beginning?
Title (23.1)
Is it clear and direct? Is it appropriate?

2.   **Second reading:** Check the individual paragraphs.
Unity (25.2, 25.3)
Does the content of the paragraph fit the topic of the paper? Does the paragraph have a topic sentence? Does it need a topic sentence? Does the paragraph center on one topic? Are there extraneous materials?
Development (25.1)
Is the paragraph fully developed? Are there general statements that are not supported? Are more examples, details, or illustrations needed? Is the paragraph clear?
Continuity (25.4)
Are the sentences linked together? Is the material presented in the most effective order?

3.   **Third reading:** Check the sentences carefully.
Are there any *comma splices, run-on sentences,* or *fragments?* (4)
Is *subordination* used effectively? Do important ideas stand out from less important ideas? (2, 26.3)
Is *parallelism* used for effect? Are there errors in parallel structure? (26.4)
Is there *variety* in the sentence structure? (1.4, 1.5, 27.1)
Are there any errors in *modification?* (3, 9)
Are there ineffective *passives?* (6.3)
Are there *uneconomical* sentences? (28)

4.   **Fourth reading:** Check grammatical problems.
Verbs
   Do the *subjects and verbs agree?* (5)
   Are *verb tenses and forms* correct? (6.1, 6.2)
   Are verbs used *idiomatically?* (6.5)
Nouns and pronouns
   Do *pronouns agree with their antecedents?* (8.2)
   Is *pronoun reference* clear? (8.1)
   Is *pronoun case and form* correct? (8.3)
   Are *possessives* used correctly? (7.2, 8.3)
Adjectives and adverbs
   Are *forms and degrees* of adjectives and adverbs correct? (9.2, 9.4)
   Are there any *double negatives?* (9.6)

5.   **Fifth reading:** Check mechanical problems.
Is *punctuation* used correctly? (10–16)
Are there any *spelling* errors? (17)

6.   **Sixth reading:** Check diction.
Are words used *appropriately* and *effectively?* (29, 30)

7.   **Seventh reading:** Check for clarity, unity, and emphasis by reading your paper aloud at an easy, natural tempo. Also check for *awkwardness* in structure, phrasing, or wording.

8.   **Eighth reading:** Check very carefully for those types of errors which you know you have made frequently in your writing. Also be sure that in the process of correcting one error, you have not introduced a different error.

HINT: As you gain practice in revising papers, you can combine these readings together slowly.

After you have made your revisions, you are ready to type or copy over the revised draft of the paper for submission. When you have completed the final draft, check it over very carefully for omissions, typographical errors (if it is typed), spelling mistakes, and the like. Make any necessary corrections, additions, or deletions as neatly as possible.

HINT: When you proofread, read slowly and carefully. Try to see what is really said, not what you thought you said. If at all possible, let at least a day pass between your draft and your proofreading.

Exercise *23.1*   Framing a Title

Create an effective title for each paper described below. Be sure to capitalize your titles correctly. (See 15.1, Capital Letters.)

Example Paper: On cats as pets, stressing their independence
   Title: *Feline Independence*

1. Paper: A study of the causes of the Great Depression of 1929
    Title:

2. Paper: On three types of abnormal behavior
    Title:

3. Paper: A biographical sketch of Alexander the Great, who conquered most of the world before he died at thirty-three
    Title:

4. Paper: On movie melodramas
    Title:

5. Paper: An argument in favor of changing the zoning laws to permit a grand shopping center to be built in a quiet residential area
    Title:

6. Paper: An explanation of Max Planck's quantum theory which stated that energy was emitted in little packets rather than continuously
    Title:

7. Paper: On future trends in electronic media
    Title:

8. Paper: A description of the geometrics in Leonardo da Vinci's *The Last Supper*
    Title:

9. Paper: A study of the kinds of articles published in Victorian magazines
    Title:

10. Paper: Recollections of Charles de Gaulle by his private secretary
    Title:

Exercise 23.2   Drafting, Revising, and Editing

A. The following paper is a first draft. After reviewing this chapter (23), use scratch paper to revise and correct the draft. Then write out the final draft on your own paper. Be sure to check the final draft carefully.

Meditation

Meditation is a popular subject in our modern world of today.

From coast to coast millions of people are studying with a guru, books on meditation are being bought in record numbers, and taking courses in yoga and mind control. Because of the fast paced world in which we live now, individuals seek escaping from the hustle bustle existence they led into the world within himself or herself. A world of tranquility and peacefulness.

The brain emits electrical waves continually in living human beings these waves range from .5 cycles per second (for a person unconscious) to over fourteen (14) cycles per second (for a person fully awake). Within this range there are four distinct levels of brain awareness. These levels are Alpha, Beta, Delta, and Theta. At Beta level, when the person is fully awake, your brain rhythm is fourteen or more c.p.s..

At this level, the level of outer consciousness, individuals are fully aware of the physical world around us—the sights, sounds, also the smells, etc. Between 7 and fourteen cycles p.s., the brain is at Alpha level; and between four and 7 c.p. sec., it is at Theta. These are the levels at which people think, daydream, and sleep. They are the inner conscious levels.

It is empty timewise and spacewise. The brain is at Delta level when the brain rhythmn is .1 to four cycles per sec. This is the unconscious level, people unconscious or in a comma usually have brain rhythms in this area. Meditation comes in many flavors and all of the flavors seem to fit, although some individuals like the feel of one flavor more than another.

All types of meditation really involve the same things. Bringing the brain waves consciously down from Beta level to Alpha level while remaining awake. The methods used to do this vary. Some involve chanting a mantra or secret magical word over and over and over. Others rely on focusing the mind on a single non-controversial object, such as a candle flame or colored light bulb.

Any color will do, but blue or violet is perfered. Although each school of meditation has it's own method. And some insist that only their method will work. Anyone can meditate using a very simple method that can be used anywhere—with a little practice that is. Begin by sitting in a comfortable chair with your legs not crossed. Close your eyes. (This is not necessary once you have gotten the hang of it.) In your mind's eye visualize a bright white totality.

Everything is white. Beginning to count backwards from ten slowly your body should begin to relax. Forget about everything and concentrate on the white totality. When one reaches eight in the count, the white totality should turn pink. (You will have to make it pink yourself at first.) At seven, bright red. Concentrate on the red—savoring its warmth and passion. At six orange totality should take over. At five it will be yellow. Green at four. Remember to count slowly. Concentrate on the light blue at 3.

Then on indigo at 2. At one (1) deep purple falls all over and you are (or should be once youve practiced enough) in a state of mediation and totally relaxed. Then very very slow count backwards again from ten, slowly fading the purple to total black. Concentrate on the blackness for a few minutes but not longer than five. Then reverse the process. Count upwards from 1 to ten, at ten deep purple should prevail. Then count from 1 to 10 again, moving through the color spectrum from deep purple, through indigo, blue, green, yellow, orange, red, to pink and white.

Opening your eyes your body will be refreshed and relaxed, you mind will be rested and alert. And you will feel rejuvenated and ready for what ever tasks lay ahead. With practice you are able to meditate anywhere and can keep your eyes open while you do it. In the middle of a lecture, between questions on an examination, before batting in a game, before meeting your future inlaws, at other moments of crisis and tension. And you will then know why meditation has become so popular nowadays and why so many people are meditating in so many ways.

B.   Select two papers you have already written. They may be the papers written for Review Exercise 19–22 or other papers your instructor has graded and returned. Be sure to select papers you have not worked on for at least two weeks. Using scratch paper, thoroughly revise and correct the papers. Then write out the revised versions in finished form on your own paper. Be sure to check the final drafts carefully after you have completed them.

25

PARAGRAPHS

25.1 Paragraph Length and Development

In a fully developed paragraph the central idea is clear and complete.

Appropriate Paragraph Length. Paragraphs are units of separation, indicating to the reader that one part of the topic has been discussed and that another is about to begin. A paragraph that tries to cover more than one part of the topic should be divided:

Faulty	We spent three weeks in Greece exploring points of interest [discussion of those points of interest follows]. . . . We also visited Turkey [discussion]. . . .
Correct	We spent three weeks in Greece exploring points of interest [discussion. . . .] We also visited Turkey [discussion]. . . .

Related statements belong in the same paragraph, not in separate paragraphs.

Faulty	We spent three weeks in Greece exploring points of interest [discussion of points of interest]. . . . We also visited the remains of the Temple of Zeus in Athens. . . .
Correct	We spent three weeks in Greece exploring points of interest. . . . We also visited the remains of the Temple of Zeus in Athens. . . .

Generally, single-sentence paragraphs are an indication that paragraph division and development are faulty. However, single-sentence paragraphs may act as transitions between two sections of a long paper. (See 25.4, Paragraph Coherence and Cohesion.)

Underdeveloped Paragraphs are paragraphs that are too brief to convey an idea adequately or that raise questions that the paragraph does not answer:

Underdeveloped	The reorganization plan appears to be solid, but it is, in fact, faulty. The advantages offered are outweighed by the disadvantages. Therefore, the plan needs further work.

How does the plan appear solid? How is it faulty? What advantages? What disadvantages? What type of further work? The paragraph leaves these questions unanswered.

HINT: You can usually avoid underdeveloped paragraphs if you put down as many ideas as possible in the first draft. It is much easier in revision to trim a paragraph than to add to it.

Typical Content of Paragraphs. No rules definitively state what paragraphs must do or have, but most fully developed paragraphs contain three kinds of statements: general statements, specific statements, and details.

1. **General statements** may range from opinions (Senator Snort is the better candidate) to broad generalizations (advertisements are a form of propaganda). General statements also serve as *restatements*, which express ideas in different words; *summary statements*, which bring ideas together; and *conclusions*, which arrive at judgments based upon material already presented.

2. **Specific statements** are usually subtopics of general statements. (Senator Snort has consistently voted for projects that benefit his constituents; advertisements generally present only part of the story). Specific statements are often employed for one of these purposes:
   a) *to expand* a general idea expressed previously;
   b) *to define* the meaning of a word or words in another sentence;
   c) *to qualify* a general statement already presented;
   d) *to concede* facts or ideas in opposition to an earlier statement;
   e) *to refute* a statement made earlier;
   f) *to evaluate* a statement already expressed;
   g) *to identify a cause or result* of an event mentioned in a prior sentence.

3. **Details** are specific statements of particular observations and facts (Senator Snort voted in favor of awarding a defense contract to Rubberband Aircraft Corporation; The Guzzle gasoline advertisement which stresses "better mileage with our secret ingredient" does not demonstrate that Guzzle gasoline will provide better mileage than any other gasoline). Details are used for several purposes:
   a) *to particularize* by specifying facts or details implied in a more general statement.
   b) *to exemplify* by illustrating what is meant by a previous sentence;
   c) *to describe* by giving details of a particular object, person, or scene;
   d) *to narrate* by presenting actions or events particularizing an earlier statement;
   e) *to support* by offering evidence for an earlier idea;
   f) *to compare* and *contrast* something already stated with something else.

HINT: Effective writing uses significant numbers of details to support generalizations and specific statements. Often a paragraph moves from a general statement, to a specific one, to several details, to a second specific statement and its supporting details. Such a paragraph can be outlined as follows:

II. General statement
    A. Specific statement [supports II]
        1. Detail [supports A]
        2. Detail [supports A]
        3. Detail [supports A]
    B. Specific statement [supports II]
        1. Detail [supports B]
        2. Detail [supports B]

25.2 Topic Sentences

The main idea of a paragraph is usually expressed in a *topic sentence,* which is to a paragraph what a thesis statement is to a paper (Section 20.3). A topic sentence helps the *writer* focus on the one main idea to which everything else in the paragraph relates; it also clarifies for the *reader* what the paragraph is about.

Although the topic sentence may appear anywhere in the paragraph, it usually comes at the beginning or at the end.

At beginning   **Gasoline advertisements also use propagandistic techniques.** They present truth in some form, but not in a complete form. A Guzzle gasoline advertisement, for example, truthfully states that better mileage results from Guzzle gasoline's secret ingredient. But the advertisement does not admit that all gasolines contain the same ingredient. . . .

At end   On Monday evening, between 8:00 and 11:00 p.m., there occurred fourteen murders, eleven armed robberies, thirty-three assaults, and two rapes. Tuesday evening the murder rate declined slightly to twelve, while armed robberies . . . . **And all of these crimes were (or at least could have been) carefully and closely observed by children watching the television programs in which they occurred.**

25.3 Paragraph Unity

Unified paragraphs have their general statements and details arranged in sequences that move toward a single point; extraneous material is absent.

Some Patterns of Development. Paragraphs may be arranged in several patterns of development which serve to organize the materials in a sequence.

Deductive and Inductive Development are the two basic patterns of development. *Inductive development* (or *climax*) is moving toward a main point at the end of the paragraph. *Deductive development* (or *support*) is supporting a main point made at the beginning of the paragraph. Deductive development is the more common.

Inductive　　　　　　　During World War I, Woodrow Wilson, a Democrat, was President. . . . Franklin D. Roosevelt, another Democrat, presided over World War II. . . . Harry Truman, a third Democrat, involved us in the Korean police action. . . . John F. Kennedy and Lyndon B. Johnson, also Democrats, brought us the Vietnam conflict. . . . **Therefore, at the beginning of each of the four major military engagements of this century, a Democrat was in the White House.**

Deductive　　　　　　**At the beginning of each of the four major military engagements of this century, a Democrat was in the White House.** During World War I, Woodrow Wilson was President. . . .

Other patterns of development include the following:

1. *Illustration:* developing a general statement by illustrative detail.
2. *Definition:* explaining a term by logical definition (assigning the term to a species or class and distinguishing it from other members of that class).
3. *Comparison and analogy:* explaining a subject by pointing out its similarities to another subject, usually one that is better known or more easily understood.
4. *Contrast:* explaining a subject by showing how it differs from another subject.
5. *Cause-effect:* arranging material from a cause to the effects, or from an effect to the causes.
6. *Classification and division:* developing a subject either by putting it into a class and then examining the characteristics of the class or by dividing the subject in order to consider its individual parts.
7. *Chronological order:* arranging events in temporal order.
8. *Spatial order:* presenting descriptions according to their arrangement in space (near to far, high to low, left to right, and so on).

Paragraphs may, and often do, employ more than one type of development.

Eliminating Irrelevant Ideas.
Irrelevant and unrelated ideas damage the unity of paragraphs.

Contains irrelevant ideas　　Another member of the hound family is the Borzoi, or Russian wolfhound. **Russia, the world's largest country, covers one-sixth of the earth's land surface.** Originally bred to hunt wolves, the Borzoi has been relegated to the roles of show dog and pet. **Dogs make excellent pets.** . . .

This paragraph would be unified if the irrelevant ideas (in boldface) were eliminated.

25.4 Paragraph Coherence and Cohesion

Because a paragraph is a series of statements which are somewhat related, writers must make the relationships clear to the reader.

Ways of Achieving Coherence Within Paragraphs. You can make a paragraph coherent—that is, you can make the relationships within the paragraph understandable to your reader—in several ways.

1. *Repetition* of a key word or idea from a previous sentence:

   City life can be exciting. People who **live** in a **city** have a wide variety of cultural, athletic, social, and educational opportunities. . . .

2. Use of *synonyms* for key words:

   City life can be exciting. People who **dwell** in **urban** areas. . . .

3. Use of *pronouns* to refer to key words or ideas:

   The **city** is an exciting place. *It* offers a variety of opportunities. . . .

4. Use of a *connecting word or phrase* (adverbs or conjunctions) to point out the relationship between statements of ideas:

   The city can be an exciting place. **Nevertheless,** each year thousands of people leave for suburban areas. . . .

   HINT: Common connecting words include: *afterward, although, and, and then, before, but, consequently, for, hence, however, in addition to, in summation, moreover, nevertheless, on the contrary, since, therefore, when, while, until, yet.*

5. Use of *parallel structures, sentences, or phrases* that repeat a particular grammatical form:

   The city can be **an exciting place.** It can also be **a dangerous place.** . . . [Note that this example uses parallel structure, repetition of key words *(can be, place)*, a connecting word *(also)*, and a pronoun *(it,* referring to *city).]*

6. Use of *chronology* to indicate sequence or time:

   The city appeared quiet **just before dawn. As the sun rose,** the city began to waken and stretch. **A short time later,** it began to move slowly. . . .

As the following paragraphs demonstrate, the use of these techniques to provide coherence clarifies the relationships between ideas:

Lacks coherence	Many suburban homeowners have become slaves to lawns. The amount of time and money spent on lawns is ridiculous. Weekends and evenings, which could be used for such other things as hiking, reading, or canoeing, are devoted to mowing, raking, trimming, watering, weeding, and feeding. Most curse their lawns. Most continue to slave over them.
Has coherence	Many **suburban homeowners** have become **slaves** to their **lawns. They** spend a ridiculous amount of time and money on their **yards.** Weekends and evenings, which **suburbanites** could use for such activities as hiking, reading, or canoeing, **they** devote to mowing, raking, trimming, watering, weeding, and feeding their **green monsters. Although** most **property owners** curse their **lawns, they slavishly** continue to care for the **grass.**

Achieving Coherence Between Paragraphs.
Just as the sentences within a paragraph need to have coherence, the paragraphs within a paper need to be related in sequence, linked together, and connected to the thesis statement of the paper. In general, the same methods used to provide coherence within a paragraph are used to obtain cohesion between paragraphs.

1. *Repetition* of key words, synonyms, and pronouns to link paragraphs:

   The **Ptolemaic** and **Copernican universes** were significantly different. The system conceived by **Ptolemy** was **geocentric. He** placed the **earth** at the **center** and had the **sun,** moon, stars, and planets revolving around it. . . .
   The **Copernican universe,** on the other hand, was **heliocentric. Copernicus,** unlike **Ptolemy,** saw the **sun** as the **central,** fixed body. . . .

2. Use of *transitional words, phrases, and sentences* to link paragraphs:

First paragraph	The North had far greater natural and industrial resources than the South. . . .
Second paragraph	**In addition,** the North had superior manpower. . . .
Third paragraph	**Therefore,** the North began the war with certain advantages. . . .
Fourth paragraph	**However, although the South did not have the resources and manpower of the North,** they did have superior officers. . . .

3. Use of *transitional paragraphs* to make major transitions from one main section of a long paper to another.

   [First section of paper deals with the disadvantages of being an only child.]

Transitional paragraph   An only child, then, can be at a disadvantage when there is work to be done, when something is mysteriously broken, or when each parent tries to mold the child in his or her image. However, being an only child does have certain advantages which outweight the limitations. [Next section of paper discusses the advantages of being an only child.]

25.5 Opening Paragraphs

Effective Openings. The beginning of your paper should catch the readers' interest and get them into the subject. You can catch your readers' interest by opening your paper with—

1.   A statement of purpose or point of view:

When I was growing up, like most children I dreamed of being a cowhand, a professional athlete, and a neurosurgeon. Entering college I had a vague notion of becoming a lawyer or business executive. But after two years of course work and much thought, I have decided for several reasons to become a commercial artist.

HINT: Avoid such beginnings as "In this paper I will discuss. . . ." and "This paper is about. . . ."

2.   A definition (particularly if your subject has several possible meanings):

A vocation is more than just a job. While a job begins and ends as work, a vocation starts as work and ends as pleasure. A vocation. . . .

HINT: Avoid such beginnings as "According to Webster a vocation is. . . ." and "The dictionary defines *vocation* as. . . ." It is better to define in your own words to show how you are looking at the term in your paper.

3.   An important fact:

Witchcraft is usually thought of as something out of the past, as something prevalent in the Dark and Middle Ages, as something based on ignorant superstitions. However, at this moment there are approximately two million persons in the United States practicing witchcraft in some form—more than there were in the Dark and Middle Ages combined.

4.   A reference to personal experience:

Four years ago, after a series of unpleasant medical tests, I learned that I had diabetes mellitus. After the initial shock, I set out to learn all I could about my affliction, and I soon discovered that diabetes is usually not the terrifying disease that most people think it is.

5.   A lively detail, anecdote, or illustration:

On May 2, 1949, a warm spring morning, Joseph Walters, Ralph Carlson, and Sean McTyghe set off from Key Largo in a twenty-two-foot fishing boat, the *Dragon*. Sailing northeastward, they radioed their position to the Coast Guard station in Miami Beach early in the afternoon. Then, at 4:42 p.m., the Coast Guard received a garbled message: "Mayday . . . can't get bearings . . . water . . . *Dragon*." On a clear day in calm seas, the *Dragon* and its crew had disappeared without a trace—the fourth small vessel lost that year in the area known as the Bermuda Triangle.

6. A question:

    Do fast foods have any nutritional value? According to a recent issue of *Consumer Reports*. . . .

Openings to Avoid. These common mistakes make ineffective beginnings:

1. Beginning too far back. There is, for example, no need to begin a paper on Robert E. Lee's military strategy with an account of his birth, childhood, and education.
2. An apology or a complaint. Avoid such openings as "Because I'm not an expert, I do not. . . ." and "Although I could find only a little material on. . . ."
3. Too broad a generalization. Avoid generalizations too large for the size of your paper. "The field of medicine has advanced more in the past one hundred years than it had in the thousands of years earlier" is far too large. Whenever possible, begin with a specific statement: "Knee surgery has become routinely effective in the past decade." (See also Chapter 20 on Limiting a Subject.)
4. A self-evident statement. Avoid the obvious ("A number of sports are available whatever the season") and the commonplace ("It has been said that growing up is difficult").

25.6 Closing Paragraphs

The end of your paper should be definite and emphatic, if possible. It should tie together the ideas you have developed in your paper and restate in some way the main idea of the paper—thus linking the conclusion to the introduction.

Effective Conclusions:

1. A climax. Make the final paragraph the culmination of the paper:

    [concluding a paper on advertising]
    The advertisements of the Parnassus Company are filled with inaccuracies, appeal primarily to the emotional side of people, and depict life in an unrealistic way. They are also effective enough to help the Parnassus Company gross over two billion dollars each year.

2.   A suggestion for action:

[at the end of a paper discussing the rising crime rate]
     This rise in crime will continue as long as our court system is antiquated, as long as our laws protect the criminal rather than the victim, and as long as our prisons are incapable of rehabilitating inmates. What society needs is a complete revision of our judicial, legal, and penal systems—to protect the innocent, to punish the guilty, and to rehabilitate the wayward.

3.   A summary statement (most useful with long rather than short papers):

[completing a long paper on Shakespeare]
     Shakespeare stands as the most universal of dramatists. His language is the language of all people of every time; his imagery strikes at the collective unconscious of all humans in all countries. His characters, both sympathetic and unsympathetic, have walked in Nero's Rome, Arthur's England, Napoleon's France, Lorca's Spain, and Carter's America. His themes express the eternal concerns of men and women. Shakespeare was, as Ben Johnson stated, "not of an age, but for all time!"

Endings to Avoid:

1.   An apology. Avoid such endings as "Although I'm not sure my point is clear. . . ." and "A full discussion of this topic is impossible. . . ."
2.   A qualifying remark. Stay clear of conclusions which qualify or detract from the point you are trying to make. ("Although I have presented only the case for capital punishment, there is a case against it that is also arguable.")
3.   Minor details or afterthoughts. Do not, for example, conclude a paper on mass transit as a way to help conserve energy by stating: "Of course, there are other ways of conserving energy which are as effective as mass transit."
4.   Repetition of opening. Avoid a conclusion which repeats, rather than summarizes, the introduction.

Exercise 25.1/25.2/25.3/25.4   Paragraph Length/Topic Sentences / Unity / Coherence and Cohesion

A. Rewrite each paragraph. First provide a topic sentence if one is needed. Next eliminate any irrelevant material to provide unity. Then develop the paragraph and give it coherence.

1. The store went out of business. It did not attract enough customers. It had a good location, but its merchandise was overpriced. Its salespeople were not helpful.

2. Swans are said to sing extraordinarily beautiful songs just prior to their death. According to Greek legend, swans learned from Apollo, the god of music, of the peace and joy of life after death. The expression "swan song" is used to refer to the last act or work of a person before death. Swans live a relatively long time and are faithful to their mates. A single swan is supposed to foretell death. The swan's graceful appearance in the water provided the model for Viking ships and for Italian gondolas.

3. The room was delightfully different. Unusual colors dominated the visual effect. The furnishings were quite distinct. Plants and other things gave the room much of its appeal.

4. Crossing the uncharted swamp proved hazardous to the expedition and fatal to some of its members. Several dangers presented themselves. Four people were killed, and several were injured.

5. Of all of the twelve months of the year, June is the most popular for weddings. Weddings, of course, do take place in all twelve months. The month of June is named after Juno, Jupiter's queen (Jupiter was king of the Roman gods and goddesses) and the goddess of women. Juno was supposed to bless weddings that took place during June, her month. Also, the month of May was in Roman times not a popular one for weddings. It was named after Maia, the goddess of old people. June is also a month between planting and harvest, so people would have time to get married without worrying a great deal about crops. The weather is usually pleasant in June. Today school often ends so that June is a good month to marry.

6. My memory has dimmed over the years. I can still remember some of my childhood. I enjoyed being a child, as I think everyone does. My favorite toy was a very small black and white panda bear. I named the black and white panda bear Pandy. Pandas are an endangered species. Pandy shared my minor triumphs and tragedies when I was three years old.

7. Some animals have horns. Automobiles and other things have horns. Orchestras have horns. Horns are used for several things, like protection.

B. Write a paragraph for each type of development given. Select a topic that suits the particular type of development (one of the suggested topics or one of your own). Next, create a topic sentence narrow enough for a paragraph. Then, using the method of development given, write a unified, developed, and coherent paragraph which includes the topic sentence. (You may use your own paper for the paragraph.)

Suggested Topics:

a superstition	a sound
a color	a number
a favorite spot in nature	the negative effects of a habit
the positive effects of sports on observers	two kinds of breakfast cereal
	an exciting event
a social problem about which you feel strongly	a friendly person you know
	two types of bosses

1.   Type of development: Spatial

     Topic:

     Topic sentence:

     Paragraph:

2.   Type of development: Chronological

     Topic:

     Topic sentence:

     Paragraph:

3.   Type of development: Comparison *or* Contrast

     Topic:

     Topic sentence:

     Paragraph:

4. Type of development: Cause-effect

   Topic:

   Topic sentence:

   Paragraph:

5. Type of development: Inductive *or* Deductive

   Topic:

   Topic sentence:

   Paragraph:

6. Type of development: Definition

   Topic:

   Topic sentence:

   Paragraph:

7. Type of development: Illustration

   Topic:

   Topic sentence:

   Paragraph:

C. For each item, narrow the general topic given to a specific topic. Then state briefly two ideas that might be discussed in a paper on that specific topic. Then write a short transitional paragraph that would effectively link the two parts of the paper dealing with those two ideas.

1.   General topic: childhood   Specific topic:
                   (or adolescence)

     First idea:

     Second idea:

     Transitional paragraph:

2.   General topic: dormitory living   Specific topic:
                   (or commuting
                   to school)

     First idea:

     Second idea:

     Transitional paragraph:

Exercise *25.5/25.6*   Opening and Closing Paragraphs

A.   For each item, narrow the general topic given to a specific topic. Then write the kind of paragraph called for on that specific topic. (Review 25.5 and 25.6 which discuss effective opening and closing paragraphs.)

1.   General topic: fears   Specific topic:

Opening paragraph:

2.   General topic: smells   Specific topic:

Opening paragraph:

3.   General topic: crowds   Specific topic:

Closing paragraph:

4.   General topic: advertisements   Specific topic:

Closing paragraph:

B.   Write an opening paragraph on the topic indicated. Then add a second paragraph on the same topic. Be sure that your paragraphs are effectively linked together. (Review 25.3, which discusses achieving coherence between paragraphs.) You might find it helpful to jot down a brief outline of your paragraph before you write.

1.   Topic: outer space

Opening paragraph:

Second paragraph:

2. Topic: the non-academic side of college

    Opening paragraph:

    Second paragraph:

C. Write the final two paragraphs of a paper on the topic indicated. Be sure that your paragraphs are effectively linked together. You may find it helpful to jot down a brief outline and a thesis to provide a context for the paragraphs.

1. Topic: a comparison and contrast of two television shows (or two books, or two movies)

    Next to last paragraph:

    Closing paragraph:

2. Topic: contemporary pop music (or modern classical music)

    Next to last paragraph:

    Closing paragraph:

26

SENTENCE DEVELOPMENT

Because effective sentences depend in part upon appropriate sentence grammar, you may want to review the following sections in the workbook:

1.3	Phrases and Clauses
1.4/1.5	Sentences Classified by Clause Structure and Purpose
3.3/3.4/3.5	Misplaced, Dangling, and Absolute Modifiers
4.1/4.2/4.3	Sentence Fragments, Comma Splices, Run-on Sentences
6.3	Active and Passive Voice

26.1 Combining Related Sentences and Ideas

The length of your sentences may vary depending upon your purpose, your own manner of expression, and your material. Longer sentences generally appear in somewhat formal writing, shorter sentences in informal writing; more complicated material is often expressed in shorter sentences, less complicated in longer sentences. Sentence length alone is seldom as important as variety and appropriateness.

There are, however, instances when you may be able to improve your writing by combining sentences. You should consider combining sentences when what you have written contains—

1. a series of sentences with identical or similar (pronouns, synonyms) words as subjects:

Not combined   The **soccer team** plays on Saturday. **It** plays against Northern State.

Combined   The soccer team plays Northern State on Saturday.

2. a series of sentences in which the last item of one sentence is the same as the first item of the next sentence:

Not combined   On Saturday the soccer team plays **Northern State.** *Northern State* won the league championship last year.

Combined   On Saturday the soccer team plays Northern State, last year's league champion.

330

3. a series of sentences which use some form of *to be* as the main verb:

Not combined	The next soccer game **is** Saturday. The soccer team **is** playing Northern State. Northern State **was** the league champion last year.
Combined	On Saturday the soccer team plays Northern State, last year's league champion.

By combining ideas and adding details to your sentences, you can make your ideas more specific and more understandable.

There are a number of ways to add material to basic sentences.

1. Make the subject, the verb, or the complement compound:

Compound subject	**Both San Francisco and New Orleans** have excellent restaurants.
Compound verb	New Orleans **has** excellent restaurants and **enjoys** warm weather during the winter months.
Compound complement	New Orleans has **excellent restaurants** and several **professional athletic teams.**

2. Insert appositives into the subject-verb-object structure:

Appositive	San Francisco, **a city of cable cars and hills,** has some of the best restaurants in the world.

3. Use verbals or verbal phrases:

Verbal	**Visiting California,** we spent nearly a week in San Francisco.

4. Use noun clauses for the subject or the complement:

Noun clause	We left San Francisco convinced **that its restaurants ranked among the best in the world.**

5. Use adjective clauses to modify the subject or complement:

Adjective clause	We planned to spend two weeks in San Francisco **which we believed to be an exciting city.**

6. Use adverb clauses to modify the verb:

Adverb clause	**Although we had heard that San Francisco was a fine place to visit,** we were surprised at how exciting a city it is.

7. Add adjectives, adverbs, or prepositional phrases:

We **gladly** [adverb] visited an **exciting** [adjective] restaurant **in the evening** [prepositional phrase].

You can also combine sentences by using coordination, subordination, and parallelism.

26.2 Effective Coordination

Coordinate sentence structures link independent clauses that are roughly equal in importance. Coordinating conjunctions *(and, but, or, for, nor, yet, either . . . or)* and conjunctive adverbs *(however, therefore, thus, moreover, nevertheless)* link independent clauses:

> She turned, **but** he had gone.
> She turned; **however,** he had gone.

Coordinate constructions are used—

1. to indicate that independent clauses are related:

    > She turned, **and** she called to him.

2. to emphasize contrasts:

    > She turned, **but** she could not see him.

3. to express alternatives:

    > **Either** she agrees **or** he leaves.

26.3 Effective Subordination

Subordinating conjunctions *(because, although, since, when, while, until, after)* and **relative pronouns** *(who, which, that)* link dependent clauses to main or independent clauses.

> I revisited my old high school **while** I was home.
> I saw the woman **who** gave me my first job.

Showing the Relative Importance of Ideas.
Subordinate clauses may be used to show the relative importance of ideas and the precise relationship between statements. Main ideas should be expressed in independent clauses; related but less important ideas should appear in subordinate clauses. If only main clauses are used, all ideas are given equal emphasis:

Weak   The U.S.S. *Maine* was the first United States battleship [main clause]. It sank after an explosion in Havana Harbor [main clause]. The date was February 15, 1898 [main clause]. Two hundred and fifty men were killed [main clause].

To show the relative importance of ideas, place main ideas in independent clauses; place less important ideas in subordinate clauses or modifying phrases.

Revised   The U.S.S. *Maine*, which was the first United States battleship [subordinate clause], sank after an explosion in Havana Harbor [main clause] on February 15, 1898 [prepositional phrase], killing 250 men [verbal phrase].

In the revised sentence, the idea expressed in the main clause is the most important, the concept presented in the subordinate clause is less important, and the facts stated in the two phrases are the least important elements.

Using Exact Connectives. Because subordinating connectives are more specific in meaning than coordinating conjunctions, subordinating connectives more effectively show the exact relationship between two ideas:

Inexact	*Hamlet* is one of Shakespeare's best-known plays **and** it has been translated into many languages.
More exact	*Hamlet,* **which** is one of Shakespeare's best-known plays, has been translated into many languages.
Inexact	We had some sherry **and** she told me of her trip to London.
More exact	**While** we had some sherry, she told me of her trip to London.

As and *so* in particular can usually be replaced by more exact connectives, such as *while, when, since,* or *because:*

Inexact	The cards had already been shuffled, **so** he dealt them.
More exact	**Since** the cards had already been shuffled, he dealt them.
Inexact	He decided to go **as** he enjoyed soccer.
More exact	He decided to go **because** he enjoyed soccer.

Faulty Subordination.
Subordination is faulty when it is *tandem* and when it is *inverted.*

Tandem Subordination. *Tandem subordination* is excessive subordination; it occurs when a series of subordinate clauses are strung together. Revise such passages by changing some subordinate clauses to modifying words or phrases. Some ideas could be placed in a separate sentence.

Tandem	We thanked the people **who** helped pick the strawberries **which** we served **when** we had the party **that** celebrated the anniversary **which** we shared.
Revised	We thanked the people who helped pick the strawberries we served at our anniversary party.

Inverted Subordination. *Inverted subordination* occurs when the main idea of a sentence is placed in a subordinate clause. Revise such passages by putting the main idea in a main clause.

Inverted	She was in high school **when she decided to become a lawyer** which meant **that she had many years of college and law school to complete.**
Revised	When she was in high school, **she decided to become a lawyer.** As a result, **she had many years of college and law school to complete.**

26.4 Parallelism

Ideas of equal value can be made parallel by expressing them all in the same grammatical form (such as words, phrases, or clauses).

1. Elements in a series should be all words, all phrases, or all clauses:

Not parallel	We visited **France, Germany, toured Spain,** and **went also to Austria.**
Parallel	We visited **France, Germany, Spain,** and **Austria.**

When necessary for clarity, a preposition or a conjunction should be repeated with each item of a series (*for* lawyers, *for* accountants, and *for* corporations).

2. Elements being compared or contrasted by the use of such conjunctions as *either . . . or, neither . . . nor, not only . . . but (also),* should be parallel:

Not parallel	We enjoyed Montana *not only* **because of its scenic beauty** *but also* **we enjoyed its tranquillity.** [phrase and main clause]
Parallel	We enjoyed Montana *not only* **because of its scenic beauty** *but also* **because of its tranquillity.** [both phrases]

3. Elements in a list should usually be parallel:

Not parallel	1. Put Tab A into Slot A.
	2. Next you should fold Side B over to Side C.
	3. Placing Tab B into Slot B is the next thing.
Parallel	1. Put Tab A into Slot A.
	2. Fold Side B over to Side C.
	3. Place Tab B into Slot B.

4. Balanced sentences contain clauses equal in length and similar in movement:

Hitler attacked the Soviet Union in the winter and was defeated, just as a century earlier Napoleon drove into Russia during the winter and was routed.

5. Antithetical sentences place contrasting clauses in parallel constructions:

In high school I put myself before others, but in college I considered others first.

Exercise *26.1*   Combining Related Sentences and Ideas

A.   Combine the following series of short sentences into one or two longer sentences. After you have completed all ten series, go back and combine each one in a different way.

Example We stood on the platform. We were waiting for the train. The train was late.

> a. *We stood on the platform waiting for the train, which was late.*
>
> b. *We stood on the platform and waited because the train was late.*

1.   *The Mousetrap* is a mystery play. It was written by Agatha Christie. She wrote it for Queen Mary. It was originally titled *Three Blind Mice.*

   a.

   b.

2.   *The Mousetrap* holds a world's record. It holds the record for the longest running play. It made its debut on November 25. The year was 1952. It is still running over thirty years later.

   a.

   b.

3.   The year 1564 was important. It was the year in which Michelangelo died. It was the year Galileo was born. It was the year in which Shakespeare was born also.

   a.

   b.

4. Islam is one of the great religions of the world. At the heart of the Islamic faith is a simple sentence. That sentence is this. "There is no god but God, and Mohammed is his Prophet." Islam has a holy book. That book is called the Koran.

   a.

   b.

5. There is a name for those who practice the Islamic faith. That name is Mohammedan. There are over 525 million Mohammedans in the world. They live in many countries.

   a.

   b.

6. Mohammedan pilgrims visit the Kaaba. They come from all over the world. The Kaaba is an ancient shrine. It is located in Mecca. Mecca is a city in Saudi Arabia. Mecca is the center of the Islamic faith. It has been since A.D. 630.

   a.

   b.

7. Cats like catnip. Catnip belongs to the mint family. It stands two to three feet tall. It has heart-shaped leaves. It contains a juice. The juice gives energy to cats. It makes them feel like frisky kittens.

   a.

   b.

8. Forest fires are caused by two things. Lightning causes one out of every ten forest fires. People cause nine out of every ten forest fires. People cannot prevent all forest fires. They can only prevent 90 percent of them.

   a.

b.

9. Smokey the Bear is a real bear. The original Smokey retired. He did so in the spring of 1975. He had served for twenty-five years. He was a fire prevention symbol. The second Smokey lives in a zoo. The zoo is in Washington, D.C.

a.

b.

10. The soldier huddled for warmth. He was in a shallow hole. Mortar shells burst. They burst all around him. He was hungry. He was cold. He was lonely. He was afraid.

a.

b.

B. Rewrite the following paragraph, combining sentences together where appropriate and effective.

Charles Lindbergh was the first person to fly the Atlantic Ocean alone. He made his flight on May 20 and 21, 1927. He flew a Ryan monoplane. The plane was called *The Spirit of St. Louis.* He flew from Roosevelt Field, New York, to Le Bourget Air Field, Paris. His flight took thirty-three hours and thirty minutes. He left New York at 7:52 a.m. He arrived in Paris at 5:24 p.m. He had two nicknames. One was "Slim." The other was "Lucky Lindy." He was awarded the Medal of Honor. A dance was named in his honor. It was called the Lindy Hop. He won a Pulitzer Prize. The year was 1954. He won it for his autobiography. The autobiography was titled *The Spirit of St. Louis.*

Exercise *26.2/26.3* Effective Coordination and Subordination

A. To each of the following sentences, add a main clause, linking the two clauses together by using the coordinating word in italics.

Example He waited impatiently, *but* *no one opened the door.*

1. *Either* the rain must end soon, *or*

2. She reviewed her calculations; *however,*

3. The instructor stressed the importance of accuracy, *for*

4. The bell did not ring; *therefore*

5. The drapes were a pale blue, *and*

B. Select a topic from those given and write sentences using the coordinating words in brackets.

Example Topics: governments, garages, grease

    a. [but] *Garages are useful additions to houses; but they have several disadvantages.*

    b. [nevertheless] *Garages have several disadvantages; nevertheless they are useful additions to houses.*

1. Topics: apples, arguments, acrobats

    a. [and]

    b. [however]

2. Topics: nightmares, numbers, neighborhoods

   a. [therefore]

   b. [for]

3. Topics: clouds, candles, clothing

   a. [either . . . or]

   b. [nevertheless]

4. Topics: rockets, roses, robots

   a. [yet]

   b. [thus]

5. Topics: laws, lemons, lions

   a. [moreover]

   b. [but]

C. Make each of the following subordinate clauses into a complete sentence by adding a main clause and any other necessary materials.

Example whoever seeks help

He will assist whoever seeks his help.

1. which they kept in a large cage

2. as if she were Sandra Day O'Connor

3. in whatever costume you can find

4. because it was extremely fragile

5. provided that you can obtain tickets

6. that unemployment rose for the third successive month

7. since we moved to Detroit

8. while the tiger crept closer

9. until the bats return to the cave

10. after Brad and Heddy got married

D. Rewrite each of the following sentences, adding one or more subordinate clauses.

Example She won the match.

When her opponent missed the return, she won the match.

1. The shutters banged against the side of the house.

2. The cereal flew all over the room.

3. Ricardo told us about his trip to Burundi.

4. It refused to start.

5. The jungle was unusually quiet.

6. You should consider yourself fortunate.

7. The line of people stretched two blocks.

8. The lights went out.

9. Maestro Mephistof raised his baton.

10. Paula spoke persuasively.

E. Revise the following passages, using subordination to combine sentences together and to control and clarify meaning.

Example We went to South Dakota. We visited the Black Hills.

When we went to South Dakota, we visited the Black Hills.

1. It was a Saturday in late June. We went to the carnival. We rode the Ferris Wheel and the Caterpillar.

2. The Blocked Duck is a new country and western group. The group's first album was called "Is That Fair?" It sold over three million copies.

3. The first manned balloon flight took place in 1783. It happened on November 21 of that year. It occurred near Paris. The flight lasted twenty minutes.

4. One of the most popular series on television was M*A*S*H. It had several character changes over the years. It dealt with an army field hospital unit in the Korean Conflict.

5. She entered the room. She saw two red eyes. They glared at her in the dark. She was frightened.

6. Pope John Paul II visited the United States. He came in the fall of 1979. He appeared in such places as Boston, Harlem, and Des Moines. Huge crowds greeted him wherever he went.

7. Representative Walker rose to speak. She argued that the administration's proposal would not solve the problem. She stressed the need for long-range planning. Short-term efforts, she said, would not be effective.

8. Gwendolyn Brooks is one of America's finest poets. She writes often of the black experience. She presents a perceptive and sensitive view of human existence. Her poetry is technically excellent as well.

9. Bonnie Parker and Clyde Barrow were bank robbers. They murdered fourteen people. A movie was made about them in 1967. It starred Warren Beatty and Faye Dunaway.

10. Andrew Johnson was impeached by the House of Representatives. It took place on March 4, 1868. He was acquitted by the Senate. The Senate failed by one vote to reach the two-thirds majority needed for conviction. Andrew Johnson is buried with a copy of the United States Constitution.

F. Combine the following pairs of sentences, first using coordination (CO) and then using subordination (SUB).

Example We rushed to the window. The geese had gone.

> a. CO: *We rushed to the window, but the geese had gone.*
>
> b. SUB: *although we rushed to the window, the geese had gone.*

1. Peter was late. We started without him.

   a. CO:

   b. SUB:

2. She swung the bat with power and grace. She missed the ball.

   a. CO:

   b. SUB:

3. Lasers can be used for beneficial purposes. They can be used for destructive purposes.

   a. CO:

   b. SUB:

4. He frantically twisted the radio dial. He pounded his fist on the table in frustration.

344

  a. CO:

  b. SUB:

5.   Erica mowed the lawn. Gerdes planted the garden.

  a. CO:

  b. SUB:

G.   Rewrite the passages below, changing some main clauses to subordinate
     clauses to show the relative importance of ideas. In some passages, you
     will need to decide which ideas you want to emphasize.

Example The spring floods came; however, the dam burst. It had been weakened by
     an earth tremor.

*When the spring floods came, the dam burst
because it had been weakened by an earth
tremor.*

1.   Monrovia is the capital of Liberia; it was named for James Monroe.

2.   Pablo Picasso was born in 1881. He painted *Guernica* to protest the wan-
     ton destruction of a small Spanish town by Hitler's bombers.

3.   Harlem is the best-known black community in America. It has over
     500,000 inhabitants.

4.   Hollywood producers take liberties with their material. Therefore, the
     film *The Natural* has a more upbeat ending than does the novel.

5. A tardigrade is a microorganism. It is also known as a water bear. It lives in waterdrops on plants.

6. The transmission was broken. He had to pay for the repairs himself; the warranty had expired.

7. Elizabeth I was a great queen. She put the welfare of England ahead of her own comfort. She ruled forty-five years.

H. In each sentence circle the word (or words) used to connect the clauses. If the connective expresses an inexact relationship between the clauses, rewrite the sentence using a more exact connective. If the connective is already exact, do not rewrite the sentence.

Example The accelerator jammed   and   the car careened out of control.
Because the accelerator jammed, the car careened out of control.

1. As it was midnight, they decided to leave.

2. We were running through the park and a dog jumped at us.

3. As the river was nearly dried up, we were able to cross easily.

4. We went on a safari in Kenya and so we saw a herd of wild elephants.

5. I do not experiment with hard drugs as they could affect my brain.

346

6. Wilhelm C. Roentgen, who discovered X rays, was awarded the first Nobel Prize in physics.

7. Polio is a crippling disease and it attacks the nervous system.

8. Francisco Pizarro wanted gold, so he destroyed the Incan civilization.

9. They cooked our lunch as we waited.

10. Susan was angry and she forgot to lock the door as she slammed it.

11. Alan and Betty walked along the beach as lovers had done for generations.

12. She turned the knob, and the door refused to open.

I. Rewrite each sentence to correct all tandem and inverted subordination.

Example He was a young child when he was abandoned on the steps of a hospital which sent him to an orphanage where he spent the next sixteen years.

When he was a young child, he was abandoned on the steps of a hospital. He was sent to an orphanage where he spent the next sixteen years.

1. Her luggage did not arrive, causing her to borrow clothes from a friend.

2. While we were marching to the front, we sang patriotic songs while we tramped along the dusty road.

3. It was Senator Wilson who spoke in behalf of the bill which Senator Minzner filed that would require all states to lower the speed limit.

4. Doug thought he was prepared although he failed the examination which meant that he had to repeat the course before he could graduate.

5. The volumes that I had the library order are research tools which are needed by anyone who is studying literature of the Middle Ages which was written in England.

J. The following paragraph suffers from excessive and faulty subordination. Rewrite the paragraph so that (1) important ideas are in main clauses and minor ideas are in subordinate clauses; and (2) the relationships between main and subordinate clauses are clear and exact.

(1) I was six years old when I went to the circus for the first time. (2) The aerialists and clowns who performed were interesting, although I was totally captivated by the lion tamer. (3) A huge cage with thick bars was in the center ring into which a dozen ferocious lions ran. (4) As my spine tingled, the lion tamer cracked his whip causing the lions to spring onto the stools. (5) He then had the lions jump from stool to stool making them move faster and faster so I got dizzy watching them. (6) But the lion tamer was not yet done because he made the meanest lion which I had ever seen lie down. (7) When the lion was ready he forced him to open his mouth which was filled with sharp teeth and into which he carefully lowered his head. (8) I thought my heart which was beating rapidly would burst as the trainer slowly removed his head which he did without being bitten. (9) That is why I remember my first circus.

K. Revise the following passages so that (1) main ideas are in main clauses and minor ideas are in subordinate clauses; (2) the relationships between main and subordinate clauses are exact; and (3) tandem subordination is eliminated.

1. The *Titanic* was supposedly unsinkable; it hit an iceberg. Then it sank.

2. When Phil slid into third base, he was upset when the umpire called him out.

3. As the garden yielded very little, insects attacked the young plants.

4. That the forest fire would spread was possible, so all people living nearby were evacuated.

5. She was attempting to cross the street when the car that appeared suddenly from around the corner and which was speeding struck her which knocked her to the pavement.

6. The cardinal is a vivid red bird and which often remains north when other birds such as the robin go south for the winter.

7. The Babington Plot was a conspiracy. It was the work of Anthony Babington and John Ballard. It took place in 1586. It was a plan to murder Queen Elizabeth I. It was an attempt to place Mary, Queen of Scots, on the English throne.

8. It was a book that explored the artistic progress which humanity had made since the first group of people discovered that art was a means by which they could express themselves.

9. William Faulkner was a famous writer. He was American. He wrote fiction. He won a Nobel Prize. He also won a Pulitzer Prize. Some of his novels are *The Sound and the Fury, As I Lay Dying,* and *Sanctuary.*

10. A solution is made of at least two substances—solids, liquids, and gases. The substances combine completely. One seems to disappear into the other. This one is said to dissolve in the other. It is called the *solute.* The other substance does the dissolving. It is called the *solvent.*

Exercise 26.4   Parallelism

A.   Revise each passage, correcting all unparallel structures and adding
parallel structures where appropriate.

Example We ate dinner, dressed hurriedly, and then we rushed to the theater.

*We ate dinner, dressed hurriedly, and rushed to the
theater.*

1.   Because she enjoyed his company, he was attractive, and also they were
in love, she asked him to marry her.

2.   Not only did we study the stories of Jesse Cornplanter, Lee Yu-Hwa,
and also those of Andrew Garcia, and we also read poetry by James
Weldon Johnson, Ted Berrigan, and some written by David Harnandez.

3.   We spent the afternoon at Maudlin Museum where we saw a number of
exhibits including an Oriental torture chamber, and an examining room
of the Spanish Inquisition, and we viewed such devices as a rack, electric chair, and guillotine.

4.   If I maintain my position, I am a person who is guided by principles; for
you to hold to your position means that you are stubborn.

5. To finance your college education, either you may win a scholarship, a government or bank loan can be taken out, working after school to earn money, your parents could underwrite the cost, or some combination.

6. The hypothalamus, a small but extremely significant part of the brain, controls body metabolism and temperature, the activities of the organs are regulated here, the sexual drive is controlled by the hypothalamus, and such sensations as hunger and fear originate here.

7. Whoever seeks respect must first earn it, but if someone wants friendship he or she has to offer it first.

8. Neither the poetry of George Gascoigne nor the plays of William Dunlap are often studied today.

9. His horoscope warned him about speculative business ventures, to be careful when he was in motion, and that he should accept an offer of friendship.

10. When we could not find the cat we searched in all of the closets, underneath all of the beds, and behind the bushes until we found her curled up on top of the refrigerator.

B. Write the sentences described, employing parallel structure effectively.

1. a sentence containing a series of three sounds

2. a sentence containing two balanced clauses that compare the ways in which two people smile

3. a sentence following the pattern *Either* (main clause) *or* (main clause)

4. a sentence containing three subordinate clauses stating three reasons for working during summer vacation

5. a sentence including three places, each of which appears in a phrase

6. a sentence containing a series of four smells

7. an antithetical sentence with two main clauses linked by *but*

8. a sentence containing a series of three main clauses about transportation

9. a sentence discussing something supernatural and following the pattern (subordinate clause), (main clause); (subordinate clause), (main clause).

27

SENTENCE VARIETY
AND EMPHASIS

27.1 Sentence Variety

Variety in sentence structure may be obtained in the following ways—

1. Vary sentence beginnings by using a modifying word, phrase, or clause:

Lacks variety

Israel is one of the youngest nations in the world. . . . **Its people** were dispersed throughout the world. . . . **Its national language** was revived. . . . **It is** one of the world's smallest nations. . . .

Revised

Israel is one of the youngest nations. . . . **In ancient times** its people were dispersed. . . . **Revived from ancient religious writings,** its national language. . . . **Although it is one of the world's smallest nations.** . . .

2. Varying S-V-O order (the usual order of subject-verb-object). Varying S-V-O order adds variety, but should be used only when the words put first deserve the emphasis:

Typical order   The top members in each class were receiving awards.
Inverted   Receiving awards were the top members in each class.

3. Use cumulative and periodic sentences to vary sentences. In a *cumulative sentence* the main statement comes first, followed by subordinate modifying elements. In a *periodic sentence,* the main statement appears at or near the end of the sentence.

Cumulative

They walked to the library holding hands, chattering about their date that evening, and making plans for spring vacation.

Periodic

In the distance, standing atop a hill and gazing over the plain **was an Indian.**

4. Vary kinds of sentences (*simple, compound, complex, compound-complex* and *statements, questions, commands, exclamations*) to provide variety, but use this method only if appropriate.

HINT: Different sentence patterns and types of sentences should not be used only for the sake of variety. They must also serve legitimate writing purposes.

27.2 Sentence Emphasis

Sentence emphasis helps the reader determine the relative importance of the ideas expressed in the sentence. Use the following methods to give appropriate and effective emphasis to your ideas:

1. Emphasis by position in the sentence. In longer statements the most emphatic position is usually at the end, the next most emphatic position at the beginning. Sentences should end strongly, not with a weak qualifying idea.

Weak	You will enjoy the performance of Mozart's *Don Giovanni,* probably.
Improved	You will probably enjoy the performance of Mozart's *Don Giovanni.*

Periodic sentences are usually more emphatic than loose sentences. *There is/ There are* statements are usually both unemphatic and wordy.

2. Emphasis by separation. Setting material off with semicolons, colons, or dashes gives greater emphasis to those ideas:

   We can send our children to school; we cannot force them to learn.

3. Emphasis by repeating key words or phrases:

   Believe what you like, but be able to support your **beliefs.**

NOTE: Emphasis by mechanical devices (underlining or capitalizing words, using quotation marks and exclamation marks) is ineffective and should be avoided.

Sentence Length and Meaning. Appropriate sentence length is usually determined by what a sentence contributes to the total meaning of a paragraph. Avoid the following types of sentences—

1. Choppy (too short) sentences which give writing a jerky effect:

Choppy	I owned my first car when I was seventeen. It was a Buick. It was ten years old.
Improved	I owned my first car, a ten-year-old Buick, when I was seventeen.

2. Stringy sentences (strung together with expressions like *and, but, so, and then):*

Stringy	We spread our blankets on the sand **and then** went for a swim **but** the water was cold **so** we only stayed in a short time.
Improved	After we spread our blankets on the sand, we went for a swim. However, because the water was cold we only stayed in a short time.

3.   Sentences containing unrelated ideas:

Unrelated   Boston contains many historic sites, and some sports fans consider the Boston Celtics of 1956–69 the greatest basketball team ever.

Improved   Besides its many historic sites, Boston is the home of the Celtics whose basketball team of 1956–69 is considered the greatest ever.

Exercise 27.1   **Sentence Variety**

Diversify the following sentences as indicated by varying the beginnings, by changing subject-verb-object order, by constructing loose or periodic sentences, or by using different kinds of sentences. You may add material to the sentences as needed.

Example He raised the flag.

(vary beginning) *To signal victory, he raised the flag.*

(change S-V-O order) *The flag he raised at dawn.*

(periodic) *After the battle as a signal of victory he raised the flag.*

(different kind) *Raise the flag.*

1.   Cesar cashed the check.

(vary beginning)

(periodic)

(loose)

(vary beginning)

2.   The robot destroyed the laboratory.

(vary beginning)

(periodic)

(loose)

(vary S-V-O order)

3.   The crowd tried to assault the referee.

(loose)

(periodic)

(vary beginning)

(vary beginning)

4.   You should not provoke the bull.

(different kind)

(vary beginning)

(loose)

(periodic)

5.   The mission was dangerous.

(loose)

(vary S-V-O order)

(vary beginning)

(periodic)

Exercise 27.2   Sentence Emphasis

A. Rewrite each sentence so that one idea is appropriately and effectively emphasized. To place emphasis, use subordination, position, separation, or repetition.

Example The vote had already been taken. Whether or not we intended to support the bill was irrelevant.

Because the vote had already been taken, whether or not he intended to support the bill was irrelevant.

1. She placed the glass to her lips. She had finished offering a toast.

2. Washington Irving's stories are excellent, at least some of them.

3. Galileo increased humanity's understanding of the universe. He was compelled by the Inquisition to deny his findings. The Inquisition considered his ideas to be heretical.

4. If you are interested in ECONOMY, if you are after QUALITY, if you like good STYLE, you should visit your European Motors dealer today and test-drive the new five-cylinder AARDVARK.

5. There are many tales which I have heard about werewolves, but those tales are untrue, most likely.

6. A great earthquake struck Alaska. It occurred on Good Friday, March 27, 1964. It was the most powerful earthquake ever recorded in North America. It registered 8.5 on the Richter scale.

7. It is your *intelligence*, not your good will, that I question.

8. He drove toward the finish line. Crossing the line he realized that he had won despite his injury!!

B. Rewrite each sentence, shifting the emphasis to a different idea from the one presently emphasized.

Example Darkness fell before we reached the cabin.

After darkness fell we reached the cabin.

1. Before she left the office, she made sure that the vault was closed and locked.

2. You have planned your time well if you can both study and play.

3. When the engine exploded, we were forty miles from port.

4. Picasso, who is one of the outstanding painters of this century, has had an incalculable effect on the direction of modern art.

5. The emerald ring which she had lost had sentimental value because it belonged to her grandmother.

6. While chained to a post awaiting execution, he thought back to the day when he was captured.

7. The desk clerk indicated that when she was on duty yesterday no one answering the suspect's description registered.

8. Although he was elected President himself in 1924, Calvin Coolidge became the nation's chief executive in 1923 when Warren G. Harding died in office.

C. Revise each passage to eliminate obvious statements, choppy sentences, and stringy sentences, and to relate ideas clearly.

Example John saw a speck on the horizon so he took out his binoculars and looked through them and as the speck drew closer he saw that it was a boat.

When John saw a speck on the horizon, he looked through the binoculars. As the speck drew closer, he saw that it was a boat.

1. Louis Braille went blind at the age of three. He accidentally thrust an awl into his eye. It was his left eye. He later developed a way for blind persons to read.

2. Many people are born every day. They are born into a world that is overpopulated already.

3. The mayor spoke on St. Patrick's Day and listed the accomplishments of Irish immigrants but he forgot to include the effects of the Irish upon our cultural life.

4. The evolution of life may be traced through fossils found in stratified rocks, and the field of archaeology is becoming a popular one.

5. Alligator purses, shoes, and luggage continue to be popular; alligators are an endangered species.

6. We were warned that a hurricane was approaching so we took the proper precautions and waited but shortly before it was supposed to strike the hurricane changed direction and went out to sea.

7. The color red does not affect bulls one way or another. Bulls are color-blind. A moving object can arouse bulls.

8. Rosamond Lehman was born in London in 1903. She was educated at Cambridge University. Her autobiography is entitled *The Swan in the Evening.* She was a novelist.

9. Attending movies is one of my hobbies. I enjoy watching such movies as *This Is Spinal Tap* and *The Rocky Horror Picture Show.* Science fantasy movies are among my favorites. I am also fond of adventure movies. I liked *Return of the Jedi* and *Gremlins.* I also liked *Romancing the Stone* and *Indiana Jones and the Temple of Doom.*

28

SENTENCE ECONOMY

Sentence economy means wording your sentences carefully so that their meaning is delivered in an intelligible and concise way. Sentence economy does not depend upon the length of a sentence, but upon stating ideas as accurately and directly as possible. You can practice sentence economy by avoiding wordiness, by removing deadwood, and by eliminating careless and unnecessary repetition.

28.1 Avoiding Wordiness

Wordiness, using more words than necessary, detracts from your writing. You can minimize wordiness in the following ways—

1. Reduce a sentence or clause to a phrase or word:

Wordy   He heard the applause. It delighted him.
Revised   The applause he heard delighted him.
               The applause delighted him.

2. Eliminate unnecessary verbs and their modifiers:

Wordy   He **stood on the stage** listening for the applause **which would mean that he was appreciated.**

Revised   He listened for the appreciative applause.

3. Eliminate unnecessary passive verb constructions:

Wordy   A chain **was dragged** across the floor by the ghost.
Revised   The ghost dragged a chain across the floor.

4. Eliminate forms of the verb *to be* and *to have* when possible:

Wordy   Some of the students who **were** serious about studying **would go** to the library where they **would have** uninterrupted quiet.

Revised   Some serious students utilized the uninterrupted quiet of the library.

5. Eliminate such constructions as *there is, there are, it was,* and *it seems:*

| *Wordy* | **There are** three subjects that I enjoy. |
| *Revised* | I enjoy three subjects. |

6.   Eliminate *that, which,* and *who* whenever possible:

| *Wordy* | The boy **that** I saw took the book **which** you left on the table. |
| *Revised* | The boy I saw took the book you left on the table. |

28.2   Removing Deadwood

Deadwood refers to words and phrases that clutter up a sentence without adding anything to the meaning:

| *Deadwood* | **Due to the fact that** Mr. Johnson failed **to get in touch with me, I was not able to** complete the dossier. |
| *Revised* | **Because** Mr. Johnson failed **to call me, I could not** complete the dossier. |

Some common expressions are wordy ways of saying what could be said more directly:

at the same time that	*means*	while
It seems that he arrived.	*means*	He arrived.
a dirty **type of** work	*means*	dirty work
in this day and age	*means*	today
due to the fact that	*means*	because
get in touch with	*means*	call
in a clever manner	*means*	cleverly
a fun-loving **type of** guy	*means*	a fun-loving guy

28.3   Avoiding Careless Repetition

Unless repeated for a specific purpose, a word, phrase, idea, or sound should not be used frequently in the same passage.

1.   Useless repetition of words:

The **difficulty** of finding **one's** suitable place in life is **one** of nearly every**one's** greatest **difficulties.**

Avoid repeating the same word using two different meanings of the word:

He **trained** to repair **trains.**

2.   Unnecessary repetition of meaning:

in the present world today   rectangular **in shape**

3.   Unnecessary repetition of sounds:

The document **meant** the banish**ment** of the old establish**ment.**
She saw slimy snakes slithering in the **sand.**

Exercise *28.1/28.2/28.3*   Sentence Economy

A.   Revise each sentence to eliminate wordiness, deadwood, and unnecessary repetition.

Example I was late for the game due to the fact that my car would not start and I had
to take a taxi.

> *I was late for the game because I had to
> take a taxi when my car refused to start.*

1.   It seems that at this point in time we should seek financial assistance
from the government.

2.   The careless king crashed his Cadillac into a creek.

3.   The moon is a natural satellite of the earth and it affects the ocean tides.

4.   Because of the fact that the social conditions which exist in society are
detrimental to people often, he decided to enter the field of sociology.

5.   His study of the pyramids was an interesting type of study.

6.   Due to the fact that the house was large in size, freshly painted brown
in color, and had roomy rooms, they bought it.

7. Although her motivations were of a sufficient nature, she could not have committed the crime due to the fact that she was out of town at the same time that the criminal committed the crime.

8. Many of the townspeople who were frightened kept to their cottages in the evening where they would be protected from the danger lurking outside.

9. It seems that the verdict was reached by the jury only after considerable debate.

10. In the fall leaves turn bright colors and then fall from the trees.

B. Revise each passage so that the main points are made as economically as possible.

Example The natural satellite of the earth has reached that point in its monthly cycle where it forms a complete circle visible in the heavens on clear evenings.

The moon is full.

1. In most instances when the circulation of air diminishes, water-going vessels which depend upon capturing breezes in their sails for mobility are incapable of continuing on their journeys.

2. Although the landmass west of Europe was discovered by Vikings at least as early as the year *anno Domini* 1000, credit is received by Columbus for the discovery.

3. Members of the finny tribe often move about from place to place by traveling in groups composed of many members of the same species.

4. It seems that socio-politico-economic conditions in which individuals are raised are important factors in the ultimate determination of the future existence of those individuals.

5. Due to the fact that Clyde was of a stubborn and unyielding character, he absolutely refused to believe that in some instances he could be wrong.

Review Exercise 25–28   Sentences and Paragraphs

A.   Revise the following passages to correct all problems in sentence variety, subordination, parallelism, and emphasis.

1.   We went to the exhibit. It was held at the Randolph Museum of Fine Arts. We saw paintings by Botticelli and Monet. We also saw works by Renoir. We also saw *The Judgment of Paris* by Rubens. It was on loan from the National Gallery of Art in London.

2.   Margaret Mitchell wrote *Gone with the Wind* over a ten-year period. It was published in 1936. She received the Pulitzer Prize for fiction in 1937. It was made into a major motion picture. The motion picture set box office records in theaters across the country. It has also been shown on television. It was seen by millions of people. *Gone with the Wind* has sold over twelve million copies. It has been translated into at least thirty languages.

3.   Alexander Hamilton was killed in a duel. He was shot by Aaron Burr. Burr was Vice-President of the United States at that time. Hamilton was forty-nine years old. The duel took place in 1804. Burr's career was ruined.

4. Tarzan has had a long career. It has also been a distinguished career. Tarzan was created in 1914. His creator was Edgar Rice Burroughs. Tarzan first appeared in the novel *Tarzan of the Apes.* Many other novels and stories followed. Tarzan also appeared in a comic strip. The strip was drawn by Harold Foster. The year was 1929. Tarzan has had a long career in films. It began in 1918. He has been featured in both silent films and "talkies." There was a radio drama about Tarzan. There has also been a Broadway play about him.

B. Revise the following paragraphs. Provide development and continuity as needed, and correct all problems in sentence variety, economy, subordination, parallelism, and emphasis.

1. One of the most ancient and colorful holiday celebrations is that of the Chinese New Year. It starts on the first new moon between January 21 and February 19, and the festivities last several days. The Chinese do not distinguish between B.C. and A.D. To find out what Chinese year it is, simply add 2698 to the present year. For example, 1978 plus 2698 equals Chinese year 4676. It is a time of public merriment and private worship. It is highlighted by a great parade. Because of the fact that the parade is supposed to drive away all of the evil spirits which have collected during the year, it is effective noisewise and colorwise. There are symbols, gongs, drums, and also there are other instruments sounded continually, and bright lights are present with firecrackers going off. Costumes in bright colors are on parade. The parade is dominated by the image of a Golden Dragon. It is a huge, flamboyant creature made of silk, velvet, colored lights, and held together by wires. Traditionally the Golden Dragon has the head of a camel, a deer's horns, its neck is that of a snake, hawk's claws, a belly like a frog, and its scales are like those on a fish.

2. In this day and age there is one subject all students should study in college whatever their respective majors are. It helps along academic lines and also along personal lines. It could well be the most important subject a student ever studies. The effects it can have on a student are many.

3. It is a fact that in the middle of the fourteenth century bubonic plague swept across Europe. It was introduced into Italy by rats which escaped from ships which had arrived from the East. Fleas on those rats of a diseased nature transmitted the disease to humans. It seems that the lack of simple sanitary precautions was an important factor in helping to spread the disease also. Quick as a wink the infected person would in most cases suffer from headaches, a sore throat, and also from dizziness. Painful black lumps or buboes (from which it seems the disease gets its name) would appear in the groin and under the arms, among other places. There would be fever, nausea, people would get delirious and comas would result. Its victims either died or, in some cases, recovered. The mortality rate was nearly ninety percent. From Italy the Black Death, as it was also called, moved northward. It killed between one-quarter and one-half of the population of Europe, or thereabouts.

4. The game was over. We had won. It was the most exciting game I had ever been in. And I helped contribute to our victory. I was very happy. But I was also sad remembering what had happened.

Further Practice Exercise **3** Practices in Composition (Chapters 19–28)

Follow the directions from start to finish to create a paper of about 500 words. Select one of the following general topics or supply your own general topic.

science fiction	dreams	jazz
truth in packaging	super heroes	phobias
mass transportation	competition	shyness

1. General Topic:

2. Narrow the general topic to a specific topic.
    Specific Topic:

3. Using one of the methods discussed in chapter 19, jot down as many ideas as possible about the subject you have chosen.
    Ideas:

4. Develop a thesis statement for the paper.
   Thesis Statement:

5. Organize your material into a topic outline, indicating what methods of
   development you will use for each section of the paper.
   Outline:

6. Give your paper an appropriate title.
   Title:

7. Write the first draft, using your outline as a guide. Concentrate on
   careful word choice, sentence effectiveness, paragraph development,
   and continuity both within and between paragraphs. Use your own
   paper for this first draft.

29

THE MEANING OF WORDS

29.1 Words in Context and Situation

The meaning of words comes partly from the *context,* or the words around them, and partly from the *situation* in which they are used. Note how the meaning of *beat* changes in these sentences:

He **beat** the drum slowly.   They **beat** a path through the underbrush.
The Tigers **beat** the Indians.   His heart**beat** was irregular.
I am **beat.**   Office Soule walked his **beat** daily.
If that doesn't **beat** all.   Ginsberg was a voice of the **beat** generation.

Denotation. The *denotation* of a word is its specific meaning. Depending upon their meanings, words can be classified into three groups:

1. **Concrete words** name specific people, places, or things and are the most exact in meaning *(Sherlock Holmes, the hospital, alligator, Chicago).*
2. **Relative words** describe qualities and are less definite than concrete words *(cold, evil, happy, tall).*
3. **Abstract words** refer to general concepts and are the least definite, and thus the most difficult to use *(love, education, goals, culture).*

Connotation. The *connotation* of a word involves the associations and suggestions which the word has acquired through use. The words *janitor* and *custodian* both refer to an individual who cleans up, but *janitor* has a more demeaning connotation than *custodian.* Writers must pay attention to the connotative value of words in order to gain the proper effect.

29.2 Fair Words and Slanted Words

Writers should present their material fairly and avoid using slanted words. Writers can use the connotative values of words honestly and fairly to represent their subjects precisely and show their attitudes toward their material:

Deciding whether or not to drive down a highway at eighty miles per hour is deciding whether to act responsibly or to risk indiscriminate slaughter.

Words such as *act, responsibly, risk, indiscriminate,* and *slaughter* are used fairly to present the author's opinion rather than unfairly to deceive.

Writers may use words, intentionally or unintentionally, to deceive or to tilt meanings. Slanting occurs when writers (1) use intense words in statements presented as fact; (2) assume they are the only reliable resource and expect readers to accept their opinions without thinking; (3) fail to consider more than one possibility or position; (4) intentionally slant words, particularly in writing about political or social problems:

> All science fiction writing is designed for adolescents.
> All intelligent citizens are outraged over the despicable and irresponsible statements of a misguided and uninformed Senator Brown.
> Only an ignoramus could disagree with the brilliant, clear, thoughtful, and correct opinion of Senator Brown.

29.3 Choosing the Right Word

Words of Similar Spelling should be carefully distinguished. (See also 17.3.)

adapt – adopt	detract – distract	precede – proceed
complement – compliment	formally – formerly	respectful – respective

Words of Similar Meaning (synonyms) should be carefully chosen. Although synonyms refer to the same general idea or object, they usually differ somewhat in denotation or connotation. Note how the meaning and tone of a sentence changes when various words denoting anger are used:

She was **enraged**.	She was **displeased**.	She was **irascible**.
She was **irritated**.	She was **hostile**.	She was **choleric**.

Words of Opposite Meanings (antonyms) are sometimes confused:

condemn – condone	former – latter	subjective – objective
explicit – implicit	inductive – deductive	temerity – timidity

Exercise *29.1*   Words in Context and Situation

A.   Select five of the following words. Use your dictionary to find four different meanings for each word. Then write four sentences for each word to illustrate those different meanings. (See 29.1 for examples using *beat.*)

ground	drag	crank	ray	odd
time	thick	shot	period	read
draft	manner	hot	lie	service
move	puff	plant	return	job

1.   Word:

    a.

    b.

    c.

    d.

2.   Word:

    a.

    b.

    c.

    d.

3.   Word:

    a.

    b.

    c.

    d.

4. Word:

    a.

    b.

    c.

    d.

5. Word:

    a.

    b.

    c.

    d.

B. For each group of words below, give a *denotative* meaning that all three words have in common. Then write a sentence for each word to illustrate the different *connotative* meanings of the words. If you do not understand the meaning of a word, look it up in your dictionary.

Example a. ask   **b.** demand   **c.** request

    Denotation: *seek to obtain*

    Connotation: **a.** *He asked for help in preparing the financial report.*

        b. *The union leaders demanded more medical benefits and longer vacations.*

        c. *The village board requested that all citizens conserve water.*

1. **a.** police officer   **b.** cop   **c.** pig

    Denotation:

    Connotation: a.

              b.

              c.

2. **a.** statesman   **b.** politician   **c.** politico

Denotation:

Connotation: a.

   b.

   c.

3. **a.** refuse   **b.** scorn   **c.** regret

Denotation:

Connotation: a.

   b.

   c.

4. **a.** sympathetic   **b.** condescending   **c.** considerate

Denotation:

Connotation: a.

   b.

   c.

5. **a.** practical   **b.** unimaginative   **c.** realistic

Denotation:

Connotation: a.

   b.

   c.

Exercise 29.2   Fair Words and Slanted Words

Indicate whether the use of words in each passage is *fair* or *slanted*. If you do not understand the meaning of a word, look it up in your dictionary.

Example College students are troublemakers.   *slanted*

1. The belly-aching of so-called environmentalists is dangerous because it drowns out those voices of reason and intellect that support this vital project.   1. _____

2. Although Mr. Thermapopolis has a long and well-known history of contributing to charitable organizations, he also appears to have an equally long but not as well-known record of controlling the numbers game in this city.   2. _____

3. Surrounded by her usual group of hangers-on, Ms. Rosen swept regally through the airport waiting room ignoring those dedicated and loyal fans who had waited for hours to welcome her.   3. _____

4. The IRS hires only mean, cruel, and petty people.   4. _____

5. A large increase in the tax on gasoline will not hurt the wealthy owners of large, gas-guzzling cars because they can afford to pay such a tax; it will, rather, work a hardship on those individuals of low and middle incomes who already drive economy cars because they have to make every cent count.   5. _____

6. If you do not support our efforts to bring a badly needed oil refinery to this area, you are short-sighted, unresponsive to the needs of your neighbors and friends, and selfish.   6. _____

7. When you have a financial problem, go to your neighborhood Accessible Loan Company where one of our friendly counselors will help you solve your problem. Remember, quick as a flash we give you the cash.   7. _____

8. I find the ideas of contemporary youth to be shallow.   8. _____

9. Competition has both positive and negative effects upon children.   9. _____

10. Some children's cartoon shows have a level of violence which may be unhealthy for young viewers.   10. _____

Exercise 29.3   Choosing the Right Word

A. Select the exact word needed in each sentence and write it in the space at the right. If you do not understand the meaning of a word, look it up in your dictionary.

Example The physician (prescribed, proscribed) an antibiotic.   *prescribed*

1. His careful work showed that he was (conscientious, conscious).   1. _____
2. Winston Churchill was a (famous, notorious) Englishman.   2. _____
3. Did you (know, no) him well?   3. _____
4. The district attorney (persecuted, prosecuted) the criminal.   4. _____
5. If a species does not learn to (adopt, adapt) to its surroundings, it perishes.   5. _____
6. A strand of pearls (complimented, complemented) her black dress.   6. _____
7. I will not (condemn, condone) lawlessness.   7. _____
8. I do not understand you; please be more (explicit, implicit).   8. _____
9. Are you (implying, inferring) that I am wrong?   9. _____
10. Cocktails will (precede, proceed) dinner.   10. _____
11. Before joining our firm, he was (formally, formerly) employed at the Kimberly Company.   11. _____
12. She based her (subjective, objective) decision on facts.   12. _____
13. Poor acting will (detract, distract) from the performance.   13. _____
14. Although his body was sound, he had serious (psychological, physiological) problems.   14. _____
15. Mr. Krinkle was known as a (cheep, cheap) person.   15. _____

B. Write a sentence for each word to show clearly the distinction between these frequently confused words. Use your dictionary as necessary.

Example profit *I do not expect to profit from this venture.*

prophet *Most religions revere at least one great prophet.*

1. concave

   convex

2. inductive

   deductive

3. respectful

   respective

4. covert

   overt

5. former

   latter

6. conscientious

   conscious

7. morale

   moral

8. emigrate

   immigrate

9. sensual

   sensuous

10. imminent

    eminent

NAME . . . . SCORE . . . .

C. Indicate whether each word is *concrete* (specific) or *abstract* (general). Use your dictionary as necessary.

Examples food   *abstract*

          apple   *concrete*

1.	jewel		16.	inconvenience	
2.	ox		17.	function	
3.	thought		18.	tree	
4.	plant		19.	athlete	
5.	oak		20.	bullet	
6.	game		21.	gargoyle	
7.	element		22.	mistletoe	
8.	stetson		23.	intellect	
9.	art		24.	question	
10.	zodiac		25.	hydrogen	
11.	Arthur Fiedler		26.	ruby	
12.	semicolon		27.	Cairo	
13.	courtesy		28.	pelican	
14.	basketball		29.	disadvantage	
15.	clarification		30.	place	

D. Indicate whether each passage is *concrete* (specific) or *abstract* (general). Then rewrite the abstract passages to make them more concrete.

Example One teacher taught us an important lesson.   *abstract*

Dr. Stipp taught us that business leaders exert great influence on government in the United States.

1. A scientist at a leading educational institution supported the President's plans for the economy.

          1. _____

2. The room was tastefully decorated.

2. _____

3. We served a chocolate cake topped with red, white, and blue frosting and a miniature American flag.

3. _____

4. One day last week we worked in the yard for a while.

4. _____

5. The contest ended in controversy.

5. _____

6. A large, furry paw crept over the windowsill behind her unsuspecting head.

6. _____

7. Our product is better, more economical, and safer than our competitors'.

7. _____

8. My strange childhood helped mold me into what I am today.

8. _____

9. Someone was hurt in the accident.

9. _____

10. Professor Robert Carlson received the Fuchs Award of $1000 as Carthage College's Teacher of the Year.

10. _____

30

THE EFFECT OF WORDS

To make your word choice more effective, carefully select words that suit the situation and words that are direct and vivid.

30.1 Formal Words

Word choice is _formal_ if it goes much beyond the basic spoken vocabulary to such specialized words as _brecciate, dulcet, impedimenta,_ and _physicality._ Use formal words when they are appropriate and necessary. Do not use them to impress or to translate ordinary matter into "big words." When writers use words that are too formal for the situation, the result is _stilted language:_

Stilted	It is necessary to distinguish between the subjective and objective responses of subjects to visual and verbal stimuli of a dyslogistic nature.
Improved	A distinction can be made between people's emotional and rational responses to visual and verbal insults.

Technical words and unfamiliar terms not made clear by the context should be defined or explained for a general audience. These include scientific terms (_cysticercoid, dolichocranial_), terms from specialized activities (_allegretto, microfiche_), common words used in special ways (_justify_ type, _fleet_ a rope), and foreign words not widely used (_chaussure, estancia_).

Abstract and Concrete Words. _Concrete_ (or specific words) should be used in discussing situations, incidents, and processes that are based upon personal experience or direct observation. _Abstract_ (or general) words are necessary and proper in discussing general ideas, summarizing facts, stating opinions, and analyzing theoretical problems. However, most writing (and most generalizations) gains force through the use of specific words.

Abstract (general)	drink, scientist, institution, work
Concrete (specific)	coffee, Enrico Fermi, Boston Public Library, chopping wood

Excessive Use of Abstract Words results in writing that lacks focus and specificity.

Too abstract	In one interesting course, I learned how to broaden my horizons.
Improved	In one humanities course, I learned how to view human existence through the eyes of an artist, composer, or writer.

30.2 Informal Words

Informal words include those labeled *colloquial* in dictionaries and most of those labeled *slang.* Informal words are appropriate in informal situations, such as discussions of sports and humorous material. Occasionally they may be used in discussions of more serious topics:

The Bruins **stole a page from the** Maple Leafs' **book** when they built up a two-goal **edge** and **sat on it** by continually icing the puck.

The Internal Revenue Service **cracked down** on tax delinquents last year, collecting millions of overdue dollars for the coffers of **Uncle Sam.**

In general, however, informal words do not belong in formal writing:

Weak	The Indian representative withdrew from the disarmament talks because she thought that her country was not **getting an even break.**
Better	The Indian representative withdrew from the disarmament talks because she thought that her country was not **being treated fairly.**

30.3 Lively Words VS. Tired Expressions

Use words and phrases that are fresh and direct. Vogue words, trite expressions, and euphemisms represent ineffective language which makes writing lifeless and boring.

1. **Vogue words** are those which have currently come into popular use and begin to be used everywhere, usually with little or no meaning. Such words as *relevant, charisma,* words with *-in, (sit-in),* and words with *-wise (energywise)* are vogue words.

2. **Trite expressions** (or clichés) are words and phrases that have been used so often they have become lifeless and, often, meaningless:

    according to Webster   history tells us   last but not least   the rat race
    tall as a tree   the root of all evil   all the world's a stage   as pretty as a picture
    through thick and thin   as strong as an ox   lie like a rug

3. **Euphemisms** are polite and often affected expressions used in place of more common (and often more specific) terms which the user considers offensive:

Euphemistic expression	**Direct expression**
a previously owned automobile	a used car
preferred customer	customer who pays bills regularly
zero-defect system	perfection

30.4 Figures of Speech

When used correctly (and sparingly), figurative language can be effective. The following types of figurative language are the most common—

Hyperbole: deliberate exaggeration (*the most beautiful girl in the world*).
Irony: use of a word to signify the reverse of its literal meaning (*a brilliant* [stupid] remark).
Metaphor: implied comparison between unlike things (*reality is an elusive cloud*).
Personification: attributing human qualities to nonhuman or abstract things (spiders *playing their harps in deadly concert*).
Simile: stated comparison between two unlike things, usually using *like* or *as* (through the fog the castle appeared *like a mirage*).

Figures of speech must be both accurate and consistent to be effective. Mixed metaphors particularly should be avoided.

Ineffective	The Berlin Airlift was a feather in the warbonnet of the airplane.
Mixed metaphor	His courage was a **rock** which **blossomed** in times of danger.

Exercise *30.1/30.2*   Formal and Informal Words

A.   Label each word or expression as either *formal* or *informal*. Use your dictionary as necessary.

Examples abominate   *formal*

foul up   *informal*

1.	have it in for you	_____	**6.**	kickback	_____
2.	impalpable	_____	**7.**	rat race	_____
3.	in the pink	_____	**8.**	fair and square	_____
4.	cordial	_____	**9.**	quixotic	_____
5.	belligerency	_____	**10.**	shyster	_____

B.   Provide formal synonyms for the following informal words and expressions. Use your dictionary as necessary.

Example drunk   *intoxicated*

inebriated

1.	boondocks	_____	**6.**	whoop it up	_____
		_____			_____
2.	fire (from a job)	_____	**7.**	spiel	_____
		_____			_____
3.	VIP (Very	_____	**8.**	cop (on the beat)	_____
	Important Person)	_____			_____
4.	off the cuff	_____	**9.**	state pen	_____
		_____			_____
5.	bull session	_____	**10.**	lay down the law	_____
		_____			_____

C. For each sentence, indicate whether the use of formal words is *appropriate* or *inappropriate*. If a sentence uses words inappropriately, revise it. Use your dictionary as necessary.

Example She made the grade as a lawyer.   *inappropriate*

   She succeeded as a lawyer.

1. He knew that if he did not shape up, the powers   1. _____
   that be would have him erased.

2. The customs agent accepted the tourist's explana-   2. _____
   tion hook, line, and sinker.

3. Automation and unionization have fractionalized   3. _____
   interpersonal relationships businesswise.

4. The mayor's crash program to revitalize the city   4. _____
   has put the squeeze on owners of older buildings.

5. The actualization of many complex finalizations has   5. _____
   concluded in a zero-defect system of postal service.

6. Radiosonde readings from the ionosphere indicate that the annual mean temperature of the outer atmosphere has decreased insignificantly in the past decade.

6. _____

7. The firm's treasurer took a powder because he knew that the independent audit would show that the company was on the rocks.

7. _____

8. Van Gogh sliced off part of an ear at a time when he was off his rocker.

8. _____

9. Attempting to beef up the forward wall, the Grizzlies snared All-Pro tackle Claude Cupcake who has been a rock on defense for the past five seasons.

9. _____

10. Senator Snood relaxed over the weekend by kicking up his heels in a family softball game.

10. _____

Exercise *30.3/30.4*   Lively Words VS. Tired
Expressions / Figures of Speech

A.   Complete each of the following comparisons—first with a trite expression, then with an original expression.

	Trite	Original
Example as strong as	*an ox*	*spun gold*
1. as soft as		
2. as smooth as		
3. as sly as		
4. as flat as		
5. as pretty as		
6. as quiet as		
7. drink like a		
8. lie like a		
9. sing like a		
10. as dead as		

B.   Translate each of the following euphemisms into common, direct language.

Example passed away   *died*

1. substandard housing		9. sanitation worker	
2. the john		10. in the family way	
3. the departed		11. mortal remains	
4. the oldest profession		12. maintenance engineer	
5. incarcerated		13. senior citizens	
6. imbibe		14. moral victory	
7. under the weather		15. unmentionables	
8. sexually assaulted		16. misrepresent the facts	

C. Revise each sentence that contains vogue words, trite expressions, ineffective euphemisms, ineffective figures of speech, and mixed metaphors.

Example Dr. Hazelton's new book is relevant to all who wish to be as fit as a fiddle.

Dr. Hazelton's new book appeals to all who wish to be physically fit.

1. The proposed youth center will result in relevant and meaningful social interaction.

2. Dante stood with one foot in the Middle Ages and with the other became the father of the Renaissance.

3. History tells us that the downfall of a civilization follows moral corruption.

4. It was a virgin wilderness where nothing had set foot except the hand of God.

5. In this modern day and age, we must order our priorities economywise.

6. As a preferred customer, you have the opportunity to attend our anniversary sale and select outfits from our selection of recycled apparel.

7. Her eyes were as blue as the sky, her lips as red as wine.

8. Let's wind it up, set it on the tracks, and see who salutes it.

9. During the social hour, Henry consumed alcohol rather heavily and got a little high.

10. Because the workers were as mad as hornets, they staged a sick-in, hoping to receive a raise that would buy them the finer things in life and expand their horizons.

Further Practice Exercise 4   Words (Chapters 29–30)

A. Revise the following passages to correct all inappropriate and erroneous uses of words and figurative language. If a passage is correct, do not revise it.

1. Like ships passing in the night, they flew on their separate roads, never converging.

2. The judge asked both mouthpieces to see her in her chambers.

3. One of the functions of imagery in writing is to present livid descriptions.

4. People who dress informally think unclearly.

5. A famous writer once described something quite well.

6. History informs us that during the Rain of Terror the guillotine spoke elegantly for the revolutionaries.

7. Our sunglasses are worn by both famous and infamous people.

8. Once I have all the facts, I attempt to arrive at a subjective opinion.

9. Although he has a charismatic affect on people, he is really as sly as a fox.

10. The principle called Harold into his office to discuss the protective reaction episode on the playground.

11. The executive, who had been missing for four days, explained that he had been holed up in a small hotel while he attempted to finalize the plan without the input of his staff.

12. He was dressed in an unusual way.

13. My grandparents emigrated to the United States to be as free as the breeze.

14. After the web was spun, he sprang the trap on his victim.

15. Maximization of substandard housing units attenuates the social responsibility of slumlords.

B. Write the sentences described.

1. a sentence using a simile

2. a sentence using a euphemism for *stupid*

3. three sentences showing the difference between *revenge, reprisal,* and *repayment*

    a.

    b.

    c.

4. two sentences showing the difference between *adopt* and *adapt*

    a.

    b.

5. three sentences using different meanings of *tune*

    a.

    b.

c.

6. a sentence using a metaphor

7. a sentence using a hyperbole

8. three sentences using different meanings of *mad*

a.

b.

c.

Vocabulary List

Keep a record of words whose meanings you have looked up in the dictionary. (Be sure that each word is spelled correctly and that the meaning is accurate.) You may want to write a brief sentence in which the word is used correctly. You can use this list to build your vocabulary by reviewing it periodically.

WORD _____   MEANING _____

BRIEF SENTENCE _____

WORD _____   MEANING _____

BRIEF SENTENCE _____

WORD _____   MEANING _____

BRIEF SENTENCE _____

WORD _____   MEANING _____

BRIEF SENTENCE _____

WORD _____   MEANING _____

BRIEF SENTENCE _____

WORD _____   MEANING _____

BRIEF SENTENCE _____

Vocabulary List (continued)

WORD _____   MEANING _____

BRIEF SENTENCE _____

_____

WORD _____   MEANING _____

BRIEF SENTENCE _____

_____

WORD _____   MEANING _____

BRIEF SENTENCE _____

_____

WORD _____   MEANING _____

BRIEF SENTENCE _____

_____

WORD _____   MEANING _____

BRIEF SENTENCE _____

_____

WORD _____   MEANING _____

BRIEF SENTENCE _____

_____

WORD _____   MEANING _____

BRIEF SENTENCE _____

_____

Personal Spelling List

Keep a record of words that you have misspelled or that frequently give you trouble. You may want to underline or circle the part of each word in which the error occurs. You can use this list for a quick reference when revising your writing.

_____ _____ _____

_____ _____ _____

_____ _____ _____

_____ _____ _____

_____ _____ _____

_____ _____ _____

_____ _____ _____

_____ _____ _____

_____ _____ _____

_____ _____ _____

_____ _____ _____

_____ _____ _____

_____ _____ _____

_____ _____ _____

_____ _____ _____

Personal Spelling List (continued)